# THE DADDY DIARIES

# THE
# DADDY
# DIARIES

## THE YEAR I GREW UP

## ANDY COHEN

Andy Cohen Books
Henry Holt and Company
New York

Andy Cohen Books
Henry Holt and Company
*Publishers since 1866*
120 Broadway
New York, New York 10271
www.henryholt.com

Andy Cohen Books® and ⚑® are registered trademarks of Macmillan Publishing Group, LLC.

Photograph insert credits: Photographs on page 5 of insert 2, Courtesy of Bravo. Bottom photograph on page 8 of insert 2, Courtesy of CNN. All other photographs are courtesy of the author.

Library of Congress Cataloging-in-Publication Data is available.

ISBN: 9781250890924

Our books may be purchased in bulk for promotional, educational, or business use. Please contact your local bookseller or the Macmillan Corporate and Premium Sales Department at (800) 221-7945, extension 5442, or by e-mail at MacmillanSpecialMarkets@macmillan.com.

First Edition 2023

Designed by Meryl Sussman Levavi

Printed in the United States of America

10  9  8  7  6  5  4  3  2  1

*To Ben and Lucy*

# THE
# DADDY
# DIARIES

# INTRODUCTION

This is the continuation of *The Andy Cohen Diaries* and *Superficial.* Since I last published the *Diaries,* my mind went two places.

First, I developed an undercurrent of minor paranoia that I'd sold people out, told too many stories that weren't mine to share. (I keep hearing Howard Stern asking in an interview if I was *sure* everybody in this book was cool with me putting them on blast.) I ultimately came back to the idea that I actually *do* know the line between what to say and what not to, and that it *is* just my paranoia.

The second thing that happened is that, as a result of the book, I obviously became aware of what I did every day for two and a half years. It's jarring seeing in print (for publication!) all the trivial details of one's day-to-day existence. The wonderful side effect was that it cemented my decision to actually have a child, something I'd spoken of metaphorically but never meaningfully pursued.

As I approached fifty, it was clear I was either doing it or not. The repetition of my summers specifically (glorious as they were) made me wonder: *Is that all there is?* The way things were looking, it seemed I could continue this wonderfully free life of self-indulgence or try to anchor myself in a more meaningful situation. I never expected the ways it would energize my family, or how close Ben would become to his "Ma and Pa" through nightly dinnertime FaceTimes that began during Covid and have continued through plenty of in-person visits.

:::

A lot has happened since the last diary. The year before Ben was born, I lived what I called my final period as a totally unencumbered man. I said yes to everything: Grand Marshal at World Pride in Tel Aviv? Shalom! Hosting the *Attitude* Awards in London? Of course! Villa in Capri? Ciao! Boat in Greece? Please! It was a blast of a year, but it solidified for me that yes, there was something missing. I was ready to have a child.

My home has since been rocked by a seismic addition and a sad departure: the birth of Ben and the rehoming of Wacha. If you read the last *Diaries*, you know about my love story with Wacha. In the years following his rescue, my priorities shifted, and my heart opened. We were a duo: We slept together. We roamed the streets of the West Village at all hours of the night. As I stepped out of the shower every day, he was there to lick my legs dry. And this dog from the hills of West Virginia became a superstar, appearing on my show, hobnobbing with celebrities, flying to the Hamptons in helicopters. He had bad hips—common in his breed—and got one replaced.

Something about the surgery changed him, or sparked something in his past. He became distrustful of vets, groomers, and his dog walkers. I never shared this, but he was occasionally threatening. He bit me, my assistant, Anderson, and a couple others—but I was able to pinpoint a reason each time. In 2016, I sent him to Los Angeles for a month of extensive rehabilitation with an incredible trainer, in the hopes of stopping any aggression. He returned as sweet as ever, and going to the vet and groomer became manageable. Still, there were one or two other incidents.

When Ben was born, I felt a new kind of happiness I had not experienced, and it was obviously the biggest change in my life since I welcomed Wacha into my home. They coexisted, with Wacha showing normal signs of jealousy when I doted on his little brother. But there was eventually an incident, a month before Covid shut the world down, that spurred the heartbreaking realization that I couldn't trust that Wacha and Ben could live safely under the same roof. My heart ached; I felt like my skin was a weighted blanket. After six years, I said goodbye to my constant companion. I still miss him after I shower. I miss the sound of his paws on the floor when I come home. And I miss his weight on top of me first thing in the morning.

I am not the same person I was when I got Wacha. He opened me up to love and, ultimately, to having a family. I think of him with the peace of mind that we were meant to come into each other's lives exactly when we did. We rescued *each other*. Also, I know he's doing exactly what he was born to: he's following his nose in Vermont, living with the amazing man who took care of him when he was with me when I would travel out of town. We still see each other, but it's hard, like seeing an ex.

I thus began the Covid lockdown brokenhearted, but I look back on that year in total wonderment at the time I got to spend with Ben. We were together in the city for a few months (me doing *Watch What Happens Live* from my office), then we got to spend four months in the Hamptons (hosting the show from my executive producer's basement) before going back to the city. I know that year was so horrible for so many, but for me, life stood still in the best way. It was a year in which plane trips were replaced with tucking Ben into bed every night. We had endless, uninterrupted playtime. I hosted "Covid Saturdays"—sushi dinners with my old friends Jeanne and Jackie, where they got to bond with Ben for hours every week. It was a year of intense quality time that, as a single dad, I'm really grateful to have had.

⁙

On the topic of quality time, something I'm leaving out in this book—and this you'll thank me for—are the details of the consistent schedule I keep with Ben. I don't detail it much here because it would be monotonous and, I think, boring, but for my own fatherly pride I need you to know that I'm up with him every single morning. I either get him ready for the day or take him to school (three days a week until the fall when it became daily). Because of my schedule with Radio Andy (two mornings a week) and *WWHL* (five shows a week, mainly after bedtime), I'm in and out with him all day and night. We have had lunch together more days than not for his whole life. I tuck him in at night as much as I can be home for. I am incredibly fortunate to work with an amazing nanny—whom I call Margot in the book—who is with him during the week and when I go out of town. On weekends, we're home alone. For Lucy, Ben's baby nurse, Theresa, returned and lived with us for six months.

I started writing another *Diary* during my wild year before Ben was born, but stopped in horror at the thought of my son one day reading it. And on that note, there's certain stuff that isn't making the cut in this book. I don't share much dating stuff. If I get into a serious relationship, it's going in the *Diary*, but I'll never get another date if I share them all. I am dating. I am also messing around. I would love to share every sordid detail of nights of passion with you, because I consider us friends in my head, but I'm just . . . not writing about it. (This is why I won't go on a reality show—when I can edit myself in print and tell you exactly what I want you to know, how am I going to leave it all in the hands of an Andy Cohen type somewhere?! Dreadful!)

In the spirit of *The Andy Warhol Diaries*, some of the references and names in these *Diaries* may appear without exposition. Hopefully you'll recognize the names of many of my old friends who have appeared in my previous books. In lieu of a glossary, let me just remind you that my old friend group is: Jeanne and Jackie (friends from St. Louis since seventh grade, whom I affectionately have referred to as my own original Housewives), Straight Dave (college roommate), Grac and Amanda (college/coming out and beyond), Bruce (best pal since '94; father of Ava; together, we make Brandy!), Liza (twin of Jamie and TV super producer who I met through Bruce), and my *WWHL* team, led by Deirdre (my executive producer).

# WINTER

IN WHICH I . . .

    BLOWTORCH THE MAYOR OF NEW YORK CITY

    GET A STAR

    WAKE UP WITH A STRANGER

Considering how much I drank and how little I slept, I should've woken up with a massive hangover this morning, but I was wired and spry! Anderson and I had so much fun last night. I think it was a great show despite awkward satellite delays—which had me sputtering and interrupting (more than normal)—and the rants. *The rants!* It felt so *good*, ranting on CNN, about ridiculous things: *Diana, the Musical* (dancing AIDS patients?), Mark Zuckerberg (slowly killing all our souls)—oh, and "Fake Journey." They performed on the Seacrest stage, behind us, and I got covered in confetti and started feeling a way about them and said they're "propaganda" and not *real* Journey without Steve Perry. Sidenote: when you start calling something "propaganda," chances are that you're drunk.

The big rant was about de Blasio, who once again *ruined midnight* by torturing us with his dancing after eight (I said four) horrible years as mayor. The city has gone downhill under him. Fuck that. Anderson was pulling me back by my hood. (I lunged forward a step with each outburst.) Anyway, we also had Cheri Oteri doing a hilarious character, surprised Regina King with Jackée, Amanda Gorman, James Taylor. Between Omicron and Betty White dying yesterday, we had to turn it up, and I felt pressure to get Anderson wasted and giggling to ensure total fun on the air.

I was unsuccessful in getting Anderson to announce that his new boy is arriving in five weeks, and that's probably a good thing, since then I wouldn't have been able to keep *my* baby news quiet—which would've resulted in chaos at home, given Ben's lack of understanding of what's about to happen. As we pulled out of Times Square en route to Sarah Jessica's after the broadcast, I saw the de Blasio rant on Twitter, and my mouth was on the floor. "I said, '*Sayonara, sucker?!*'" I shouted! I turned to Anderson and said, "I said 'Sayonara, sucker?!'"

"Yep!" he said bemusedly.

I had no recollection! At SJ's, Jeff Richman said that rant was the wildest thing he'd seen on live TV in a long time. As we sat around talking, I wondered if that was a good thing or a bad thing. Then I started wondering about all my other rants. Did I actually go too far?

I got home and was so wired from the excitement of the night that I spent a few hours chilling, listening to music. Everyone seemed to really like our show online, especially the de Blasio thing. Woke up with Ben this morning around eight. Let him watch *Sesame Street*, which is our weekend thing. He grabbed the bongos Grac gave us and pounded away at the "Letter of the Day" theme song. Tweeted that I was a bit overserved last night, then posted a story on Insta showing people I was up and functioning and tagging the Mujen and De-Nada I'd been drinking.

I sat on my phone looking through a hodgepodge collage of texts about the night. Claire McCaskill ("the trashing of de Blasio was epic! Love you!"), Kristen Johnston ("HIGHLARIOUS"), Marie Osmond (hers just said "happy new year," so I don't think she watched), Harry Smith ("Love drunk Anderson").

Then Jeanne texted, "how are you holding up?" When one of your very oldest friends sends a smoke signal that everything must *not* be okay, you shudder. I said, I'm good. She said, "Any backlash?" I said no, everyone hates de Blasio. She was relieved to hear it. Our conversation gave me cause for pause as I realized there were a few key people I *hadn't* heard from (my parents, for starters), which then made me wonder whether I'd actually done badly.

I then went into a ninety-minute shame spiral, wondering if the show was actually horrible, and then realized I've done this exact spiral the day after hosting New Year's Eve for the last four years. (The first year, in fact, *was* arguably horrible.) It's just the weirdest show to host—on the one hand, it's wallpaper for other things that are happening in people's homes, and on the other, it's on for five hours and everyone sees it and has an opinion of it one way or another. After checking in with my parents, who were thumbs-up, and rehashing with Anderson ("I had a ball"), I felt better. (I always feel better after rehashing with Anderson.) The de Blasio thing is trending on TikTok, according to someone's daughter. As the day went on, I saw a headline that I'd trashed Ryan Seacrest. While I was yammering about Journey, clearly *loving* the sound of my voice powered by endorphins and tequila, apparently I called everyone on ABC "losers." I was like, "Oh damn," and a couple hours later texted Ryan apologizing. He's a good guy, and I like him. Spoke to Jeff Zucker, who said they're getting a lot of calls about the de Blasio thing and they may need to release a statement. When the network is releasing a statement about your messy rant, you're in the doghouse.

I went to bed early.

## ▦ SUNDAY, JANUARY 2, 2022

Went to Zazzy's Pizza with Ben, and on the walk there was fist-bumped by five different strangers thanking me for what I said about de Blasio, which made me feel great! Lunch dates with my boy have gotten even better lately: we can now sit and have conversations in which we actually understand each other. I mean, they're not *deep*, but we can certainly volley about Elsa and Anna, who I was CONVINCED after his inaugural viewing he would not care about. Now he doesn't shut up about them. *He needs a sister!* I keep floating the idea to him, and at first, he loved the baby idea but now he thinks we should put a cat in the new room. I need to check if I'm still allergic, because otherwise I'd get one.

Ben's imagination is wild. On the way home, he spent an hour running around the AIDS Memorial Park, fully entertained by a dry fountain, while I collected more fist bumps! Tyler Cameron texted and said, "I love you man." He shivers me timbers. One of my leftover quarantine traditions—"Covid Saturdays" (which can happen on any day) with Jackie and Jeanne—is still going strong, and they're still so fun. Ben adores them, and Hopper the dog. Ordered sushi from Sugarfish for the first time and loved it. (It's making me hungry thinking about it as I type.) I asked Jeanne why she sent concerning texts after New Year's, and she said she'd seen the de Blasio rant and had to turn it off because she thought it was going to trigger my downfall. She said she saw it all crashing down from that clip. Jackie's niece FaceTimed to say she has Covid and that the de Blasio thing was epic. I said, "*See, Jeanne?!*"

In the cab to Sirius, Twitter tells me Howard is talking about me. I turn it on to hear his Joan Rivers–like impersonation of me. Do I sound like Joan? He liked the de Blasio thing but went nuts about what I said about Journey. Also, he thinks I drink too much. And he and everyone on Twitter are ripping on me for tweeting that I was "overserved." You can't try to put something delicately on Twitter. Tone or intention doesn't read. YOU WERE DRUNK, NOT OVERSERVED! DON'T BLAME SOMEONE ELSE! ALSO, YOU SERVED YOURSELF. I would like to respond to each and say, "I know, sweetie. I know."

On Radio Andy, I apologized for the Seacrest thing, because there is now a raft of headlines that imply I personally attacked him. By apologizing to Seacrest, I actually turned it into a bigger thing, because today became a whole new round of press rehash with the new "news" that I apologized. I already texted him and should've just left it at that. By the way, I haven't heard back from him. Kelly Ripa tells me he knows what clickbait is and not to worry. Went to *WWHL* for the first time since Covid shut us down right in mid-Christmas, and the vibe went from Christmas cheer to January bleak.

The Salt Lake City reunion is on Thursday, and it looks like my hour-long New Year's Eve day pep talk with Mary M. Cosby about showing up to the reunion had no effect on her. She wants to leave the show, and I encouraged her to leave it while also having the last word and not giving that to the other women. So that didn't work. She's not coming. And now Jen Shah's team is convinced that we gave the questions to Erika Jayne in advance of the Beverly Hills reunion (we didn't), and they want the questions for Jen (we won't). Came home to a long Magna-Tile session with Ben, and we had a moment where Ben was Patty Duke to my Anne Bancroft in *The Miracle Worker*, when he kept asking me something and there was *one* word I wasn't getting. I made him repeat it eight times until finally I was on the floor, in his face, trying to understand. It was *garage. He wanted me to build him a garage!* We high-fived when I figured it out. It was a moment.

Mid-build, I picked up my phone to see my timeline full of people reacting to the news I'd been fired from CNN—instant diarrhea, even after I saw that it came from Radar Online, which just makes shit up and quotes anonymous sources. The problem is they get picked up by other outlets, and that's what was happening. I made a flurry of calls and found out I was indeed not fired and that CNN would release a statement saying I'd be back next year. Announced to my parents during their dinnertime FaceTime with Ben that they might see in the news I was fired but it's not true. My mom didn't take the fake news lightly.

"WHAT?!?!?! You need to EXPLAIN THIS AGAIN!"

I did and got an "Oh Jesus." Jeff Zucker called and said I was a dipshit for believing Radar Online (true). The headlines changed by the time I had dinner with Amanda and Grac at La Sirène on Eightieth and Amsterdam, the former space of that '80s/'90s vintage store Allan & Suzi. (It felt like sacred ground!) We were the only ones in the restaurant. Shaken by my near-firing, I was talking to the girls about my resolution to spend less time on Instagram (that had led to my rant against Zuckerberg), which I think is a complete waste of time yet is an intense addiction. I said if I can do thirty minutes a day then I'm good. Tomorrow, that starts. Since we were the only people in the restaurant, we were doing very inappropriate things at the table that I cannot put into print because I am a father now and expecting a second child. (Okay, maybe there was a little playful flashing at the table.)

## ⠿ TUESDAY, JANUARY 4, 2022

Started the day with an early tea party with Ben. He "makes" me whatever I want, every special order accepted. Didn't pick up my phone for an hour while we were chilling before breakfast. Felt great! All the news today is that I didn't get fired. So it was a fake story about getting fired that turned into stories that I wasn't fired. I called in to Stern. It was a fine appearance. I refused to apologize for being drunk on NYE and having a ball. However, he is worried about my drinking, which is based on me being drunk on NYE and having a bar on *WWHL* and him seeing me at parties in the Hamptons years ago. I pointed out his flawed receipts. I'm trying to get him to bring Robin's news back. How do you get rid of the news on that show?

Worked out with Stanny today and taped three *WWHLs*; we are back to all-virtual guests—which felt very depressing—but still a masked audience of fifteen or so. Covid shows are so efficient, but it takes more to drum up some energy. Barbuto reopened! Now they're at the end of Horatio Street, where I had dinner with Amanda for her birthday, part deux. Split the brick chicken and carbonara. Unbelievable. (I did nothing inappropriate at the table.) Colbert did a funny thing about NYE on his show. He showed the rant and said usually people get drunk and rage on television then have to explain themselves to Andy Cohen, not the other way around. Ha! Oh, my Instagram usage today was good—maybe twenty minutes total, and I feel like I missed nothing.

## WEDNESDAY, JANUARY 5, 2022— NEW YORK CITY TO LOS ANGELES

Today, all the news is that I refuse to apologize for being drunk on NYE. Anderson called and said, do you realize it is five days since we did that show and people seem to *still* be talking about it? Did radio from home. Ben helped me pack for LA. I took some THC tincture with two hours left in the flight, and it turned my world upside down—in the best way. The only drawback was when I landed, I got paranoid that TMZ was going to be waiting for me at the airport. (See: misunderstood comments about Kathy Griffin in 2017.) I armored myself with AirPods and a double mask, but thankfully there was no camcorder to be found. (And that will be the one and only use of the word "camcorder" in 2022.)

Went straight from LAX to Bruce's, where we had dinner. We are planning something fun for the night before I get my star on the Hollywood Walk of Fame next month. There was some talk of cancelling due to Omicron, but we are pushing forward given that we've been trying to get this on the books *since 2019* and my family is more excited about it than anything else I've done (besides have Ben), so I just want it to happen while we are all healthy and before Number Two comes. I go to the Sunset Tower where I get a Covid test. Texted Mary M. Cosby to see if she's coming to the reunion tomorrow, and she said she is "keeping hope alive," with a smiley emoji. So . . . what does that mean? That means she isn't coming. My Instagram use was horrible today—I caved on the plane and was hooked for *hours*. But I gave myself a pass. *I was on a plane!* The Fake Journey controversy is still RAGING on Twitter, and now Neal Schon himself is tweeting at me like a madman!

## ⣿ THURSDAY, JANUARY 6, 2022—LOS ANGELES

The woman who knocked at my door at 7:00 a.m. to give me yet another Covid test did not care to hear that I had Covid three weeks ago, thereby making the test useless. Texted with Kelly, who said Seacrest is in Italy and didn't bring up the clickbait stuff to her. Onward! Got an email from the *New York Times* who is working on a profile of Kathy Griffin and wants my comments on why my punishment for going off on the outgoing mayor was different from hers for holding an effigy of the president's head. Joy! (What else can be *said?*)

Half the production staff got Covid in the last couple days, and it's incredible the reunion happened at all. I had Lisa Shannon in my ear from home, with a headache and fever, and Nick directed the show by Zoom from home! Mary did not show up, as expected, and by the rules (which I referred to as the "Maloof Code," and I guess it really is, given she was the first to not show up at a reunion), she's off the show. Lots of reaction from the SLC women on that.

Considering her trial (for wire fraud! and money laundering!) is in three months and she is potentially facing fifty years (!!!!) in prison, Jen Shah showed up in purple velvet with a showgirl ring of features circling her head and crystal boob embellishments, as easy breezy as I've ever seen her. It was a totally different energy from Erika, who has faced no charges but was considered the villain. Jen says she's innocent (crocodile tears?) and told me it was racist to speculate about where she got her money. The set of the reunion was an ice-fishing environment, with real ice and lots of feathers. It looked like we were in Pixar's version of a reunion. Since the day was so long, and there were a bunch of delays, I gave myself another pass on Instagram usage. I left the reunion feeling like I didn't do my best. Did I go hard enough on Jen? Did we talk about any of the fun stuff? Whitney commented that she felt like we hadn't discussed everything, which got me wondering. We wrapped at eight thirty, and I had a tequila at the Tower and crashed. Oh, and more tweets from Neal Schon—all day long!

## ▦ FRIDAY, JANUARY 7, 2022—LOS ANGELES TO NEW YORK CITY

The MedMen on Robertson is out of that tincture I like. (I went on the way to the airport.) John Mayer FaceTimed me from his Covid-bed while I was killing time at LAX to report a rumor that he'd bucked his Omicron to hit the San Vicente Bungalows with me for dinner. I told him I was seen having a late one at the Tower, so that's proof. Neal Schon is still rage-tweeting, and John said to never get in a fight with an '80s rock star. Their wrath is intense. I guess he's been *through it* with Richard Marx and a few others.

Anderson and I somehow agreed to act in a radio play that Patti LuPone is producing. We're playing a gay couple, and Patti herself is coming over to direct us tomorrow morning. I can't believe it. I'm a *terrible* actor. I wonder how Anderson will be. Better than me, is how.

The greatest hugs and euphoric reunion with Ben tonight when I got home. He was in his yellow PJ set and smelled so fresh right out of the bath, hair neatly parted, with his big smile and little teeth. I could just die.

Hickey came over for a nightcap. I don't believe the nightcap culture exists outside of New York City. People don't *drive* to a friend's house for a nightcap. It's been a constant part of my life since I got here, in 1990, and having so many West Village pals especially lends itself to the habit. I will never move. I love it here.

Watched the Housewives episode of *Project Runway* before bed, and it was very fun. I look like I have lipstick on, and crazy makeup. I need to know if other people think I look as crazy as I do. I guess the internet would tell me. Before bed, John FaceTimed to see if I'd be on the return of *Current Mood* on Sunday night. I said yes. Speaking of Instagram, I once again gave myself a pass today because I was on a flight, with post-reunion brain jelly. That included a long Instagram Q and A in which I shared that my favorite porn star is Steve Hammond, on whom I do as deep a Google dive as I can probably every two years to find out what happened to him. Someday, in my heart of hearts, I'm hoping to hear from "Steve" one way or another. In my imagination, he now lives on a ranch in Montana, where he is a carpenter. He suggests I come visit and see what the quiet life is all about. But the real truth is that I think he was gay for pay and I fear he isn't alive. Porn stars burn fast and bright.

## ⦙⦙⦙⦙ SATURDAY, JANUARY 8, 2022—NEW YORK CITY

Ben was too deep into *Sesame Street* to pay the "Queen of Broadway," Ms. Patti LuPone, any mind this morning when she showed up with her (amazing) son Josh to record Anderson and me for her radio play. We set up shop in my closet, and Patti gave us the *full* backstory on our characters, our motivations, and the mise-en-scène, though Anderson and I were of the "Let's just press play—and record—and see what happens" vibe.

I was fine, and Anderson was perfect as my erudite wine connoisseur husband. I told him he is fantastic at playing pompous! Patti had two shows today, and I'll be holding my breath that she didn't catch Omi at my house.

Ben and I built many houses/garages/planes/tunnels out of Magna-Tiles, but he kept destroying what I'd built and asking for more, which was making me nuts. We played an extended game of catch with mini basketballs, and every time the ball was thrown, he said, "Good catch!" I tried to explain that he should only say it after someone *caught* the ball, but that didn't land. Liza saw the *Runway* episode and my "lipstick" didn't register to her. Phew. Watched two episodes of *And Just Like That* in advance of dinner with SJP and Amy at Barbuto (twice in one week). I was feeling good that I matched a beige mask with a camel coat, but then it made me sad that I was proud to match a mask to a coat. We had a lot of big laughs and long stories at dinner, and the girls walked me home. Danny had put Ben to bed and was watching *Rent*, the movie, and man does it pale in comparison to the stage show. I got carried away watching, though. I love *Rent*! My Instagram usage today was TOO MUCH. I need to focus. Enough with giving myself passes!

## ⠿ SUNDAY, JANUARY 9, 2022

I was so insane about Ben not being in front of a TV for the first two years of his life (with an occasional exception for *Trash Truck*) that I harbored guilt all day for the whopping 130 minutes of *Sesame Street* I let him watch this morning. It's *educational*, right? Ben and I went to Corner Bistro for burgers and fries, and it was pure joy sitting there with him—the best part of my day. A family on the other side of the restaurant was in deep negotiation about phone time for the kids, which was a preview of things to come for Ben and a reminder that I'm a runaway train with the phone. I'm hoping to channel Instagram time into diary time. He napped and I napped, deeply.

My mom is aflutter about what to wear to the Hollywood star thing. I have been on the receiving end of "What am I SUPPOSED to WEAR?!!?" calls throughout my life. Jackie came over for dinner, and I took the ornaments off the tree but can't figure out how to disconnect the lights on this fake tree. I hit a dead end in the process, and now I wonder how long I'll be tortured by the silver and gold towers. Will I have to Google the answer? I am such a Jewish man: helpless. (Although most Jewish men don't have two fake Christmas trees.)

Right after I put Ben down and was gearing up to be on *Current Mood*, I got a text from John that was like a punch in the gut: "Andy, Bob Saget died." Bob *Saget*? Bob of the sweetest out-of-the-blue emails telling you he saw you somewhere and you're doing a good job and he loves you? Bob of the tireless effort to fight scleroderma, which took his sister's life? Bob the big, huggy mensch who I really got to know on Mayer's fortieth birthday trip to Brazil?

Time stands still when someone dear vanishes from life.

## ⣿ MONDAY, JANUARY 10, 2022

It was a blue night that transferred into a blue morning. Everything was blah. Ben didn't want to go to school, I was so blue about Bob Saget, and it was freezing cold. My heartfelt remembrance of Bob on the radio this morning was accentuated by John (Hill, not Mayer) telling a story of Bob fingering his friend in a parking garage, in the early aughts, and how the act of digital pleasure might be construed as intrusive, but that his friend reported not only how adept he was but how gentle he continued to be after pleasuring her. I feel like Bob would've *loved* that memorial! He was a gentle man and a gentle lover.

And how was I supposed to know peanut-butter-and-jelly sandwiches are banned from school?! Thankfully, the little girl with the peanut allergy was out today with Covid (I'm celebrating that she was OUT, not that she was sick with Omicron), so they let Ben have some of the sandwich. We taped two shows today, and I had dinner with B. J. Novak at Morandi—our first solo date. (We've always been out with others.) Was nice sharing stories about Bob. B.J. gave us a New Year's resolution for CNN, and it was to give more compliments—ironic, given that was just Bob's specialty. Dinner was a smash. It was one of those nights where, in the warmth of the restaurant and the honesty of the death of a friend, you find safety in your companionship and both wind up spilling a parade of very personal secrets that you know will fall in an entirely safe place. On the walk home, in the cold, I was happy to see the restaurants packed inside; maybe everyone feels like they'll just get Covid and see what happens. Very Ron DeSantis.

## TUESDAY, JANUARY 11, 2022

Not sure I remember all of B.J.'s secrets, which is probably a good thing. Today was the coldest, and I convinced Stanny to come work me out at home, which was fantastic because Ben joined us and made it incredibly fun. He had a playdate with Wyatt at the house, and it felt very cozy here all day. TRITE SENTIMENT ALERT: before Ben I thought this house was a home, but he made it so. I still miss Wacha every day and can't forget his sad wail when I said goodbye to him during our last visit. It broke my heart. We've only seen each other five or six times since he's been living with Sherman full-time, but every time is great until we say goodbye. Tried to teach Ben how to play catch today, which one might characterize as the blind leading the blind. But damn it, I *do* know how to catch! He won't hold his hands out or follow the ball, is the issue, and every time I tell him so, he tells me to "slow down," meaning I'm being too hyper for him. This is going to be a long ride!

Feel good about my (minimal) Instagram usage for the last two days. Conversely, I've been very active on Word Chums, which is at least supposed to help your brain as opposed to slowly killing it in various ways.

## WEDNESDAY, JANUARY 12, 2022

Today was the day I thought I sexted Carl Bernstein. He was on the radio with us this morning. (John was bored, but I was engaged.) Anyway, Carl called me after the show, and then texted to say he has an idea for us to work together and to ask if I'd post on Instagram about his book. I was on a booking call for *WWHL* while juggling texting Bernstein back and, separately, texting Hickey. I sent Hickey an incredibly, graphically lewd text and didn't hear back and for a panicked five seconds thought I'd sent the filth to Bernstein. Thank the Lord I didn't. (Writing this down reminds me that Hickey never did respond to me, which is odd.) If I said the text had been about deep throating, would you believe me? It wasn't.

Ben somehow got into the VapoRub and put it on his face and, inexplicably, his *tongue*. The poor kid was in the tub, sticking his tongue under the faucet, calmly saying, "It burns, Daddy." It was hard to take the pain seriously given how cute it all felt.

Tonight at *WWHL* felt like the first time we were really *back* in a month—we taped a show and had one live, with all in-person guests. The first show was Heather Gay and Lukas Gage, who is a flirt machine with a deep bench of Bravo knowledge. He was with his best girlfriend, Maude Apatow, and they were texting afterward from Paul's Casablanca, trying to get me to come for a nightcap. Hung post-show with Danny, JJ, Melissa, and Nick in my office, which—given that I was housed in the greenroom during our Covid shows—is like the site of an archeological ruin that I've not visited in years. I found an envelope of old correspondence and played a game where I'd show them the stationery and handwriting and give them four choices and they had to guess who sent the note (e.g., was it Padma Lakshmi, Karlie Kloss, Amber Tamblyn, or Kristin Chenoweth?). It was surprisingly entertaining. Went to Paul's Casablanca and it was thumping—no Covid in there! (*Or* it was full of it—time will tell.) Lukas was there with Heather Gay. I left before I could get into any real trouble.

## ⁚⁚⁚⁚ THURSDAY, JANUARY 13, 2022

The last time I wrote a diary it was all late nights and travel. With Ben now dominating my life, the highlights are buried in the monotony and simplicity of my current schedule. Worked out. Went to the CBS Broadcast Center on Fifty-Seventh Street to do a guest spot on a new daytime cooking show as a favor to Gail Simmons. I faint every time I walk in and see that Gilda is still the doorperson there! I love Gilda! I spent all those early mornings while I worked for *CBS This Morning*, in the early '90s, waiting for guests to show up with her. I bet I met SJ for the first time in front of Gilda, when she arrived late (only time she's been late since I've known her!) for that guest spot promoting UNICEF. The producers of the new cooking show kept telling me to have the *best time ever*! Met Daphne Oz for the first time. Couldn't keep my eyes off her hair—lots going on there, but I can't determine what. She is blessed with a good head of hair. Ran into Drew Barrymore backstage—she brought the hosts of the show a tuna casserole in the segment before mine and was complaining to me that she smelled like tuna, and she did! She'd just been on a virtual date with Sam Talbot. I had a nice date tonight with the hot Spaniard from last summer.

## FRIDAY, JANUARY 14, 2022

There are men outside of every window of my apartment, which kind of sounds amazing at first, but in truth they're freezing their asses off in jumpsuits, making the bricks on the building hurricane-ready. They're going to be there for another year, I think. They've seen me shit, shower, shave, pick my nose, look at my phone, dress, undress, wander around, eat—everything. It's endless. I do have a running thing going on my Instagram stories where I'm madly in love with one of them and he's really dicking me around. It's daily fodder. Sat with Ben, looking at a picture of a cake, for a half hour, and it was amazing. I didn't know I had the patience. Em and Abby are in town. Went to Barbuto AGAIN. It's that good!

## SATURDAY, JANUARY 15, 2022

It's twelve degrees out, but Em and Abby are visiting from St. Louis, and we had a great day with Ben. We all took a cooking class at Dō, the cookie dough store. He loved it. Who wouldn't? Every time I ask Ben if we should put a baby in the new room, he talks about a kitty cat, so I'm thinking maybe he can nickname his sister "Kitty" so everybody wins. I'm gonna really connect the dots with Ben when Wyatt's brother comes in a few weeks. Spoke to John about his week of mourning with the Saget crew, and it crystallized that I was around John's age when Natasha Richardson died, and that her death and Ben's birth were the two biggest shape-shifters of my adult life. Seismic bolts that changed every day. Had a spontaneous dinner party over here tonight: Amanda, Jackie, and Jeanne joined Abby and Em for sushi. It was a lot of laughs! We turned it into a party.

## SUNDAY, JANUARY 16, 2022

*Below Deck* reunion today. On the *Lord's Day*, yet! Have been singing Hickey's "Buckaroo" song to Ben before bed ("Go to sleep, my little Buckaroo . . .") and tonight, as I turned out the lights, he said, "Wait, Daddy, am *I* the buckaroo?"

## MONDAY, JANUARY 17, 2022

Ben told me he loved me so many times today. I am so lucky. And the baby girl is kick-kick-kicking. Lots of texts and pictures from Lucy's surrogate, Kathleen. She is the happiest, healthiest person. I am so lucky. She loves being pregnant. She's an angel. Last summer, after a year of paying babysitters in cash and having them look at me like I was handing them a venereal disease, I can report that I finally discovered Venmo. Now it's all the rage for me, ten years late! Trained with Stan and, as I was handing him a check to pay him, was reminded what an old dolt I am. I realized I must be his only client who pays by check. Yup—I can't shake being in my fifties. Conference call with Casey Wilson and Danielle Schneider for me to pitch repackaging old *Bitch Sesh* podcasts on Radio Andy. After the pitch I told them everything I could never say on their podcast.

Got a DM from a woman who said she used to love me but she thinks having Ben has made me bitter. I took the bait and sent her back a message, saying, conversely, I've never felt more joy in my life, and perhaps *her* bitterness is what she is tuning in to. She did not care for that response one bit. It was *Summer House* premiere night, and I had a live show with Carl and Kyle, which gave me an opportunity to rag on Kyle for his shitaceous treatment of his fiancée. Not the first time I've enjoyed grilling a cad about horrible behavior on television (see: Jax, Shep, Austen, James, etc.) and hopefully not the last. Why do my endorphins start pumping at that opportunity? Am I a sadist? On the aftershow, I asked Carl about saying in Season 2 that the best blow job he ever got was from a guy, and I wondered whether that was still the case. He explained that there was trauma associated with that story and sharing it, and after his explanation I, of course, doggedly asked whether it was still the case (it isn't, he said). And I regretted the follow-up when I got home.

## TUESDAY, JANUARY 18, 2022

I think I'm in a war with Snooki, of all people. Melissa Gorga said on her podcast that I've rejected Snooki from *RHONJ* several times (even though she's never expressed interest in being on the show), and now Snooki is responding, which led to the inevitable "Snooki Breaks Her Silence on Being Banned from *Housewives*" clickbait headline. Saw Anderson at the gym, which makes me gleeful, but he never fully wants to have the level of kiki that I do, which is often the story of our relationship and why I keep coming back for more. I'm like the stalkarazzi with him because I always want to put him on my Instagram stories, which he grudgingly accepts.

Got home from the gym to Ben screaming, "Tickle me, Daddy! Tickle me!" Delightful.

Surfin greeted me in the lobby with more complaints from the downstairs neighbor about my ice maker. He is ACTIVATED. The tale of my too-loud ice maker has been months long. I replaced my last one because the cubes were—am I really going to finish this sentence? Okay, it doesn't matter about the cubes, but the new machine makes a whirring sound that is apparently deafening downstairs. Watched two episodes of *OC*, one *Miami*, and one *Jersey*. All were good. Had two shows tonight. We played Have! They! Crapped! Their Pants?! with Kristin Davis and Laura Linney, which was hilarious, and then on the live show, I had a terribly inopportune fit of giggles when I was announcing that our bartender had donated the proceeds from his hot chocolate sales to victims of the big fire in the Bronx a couple weeks ago. I don't know what triggered me, but I simply couldn't contain myself, and they had to cut away from me to mask it from the audience. Then Tom Schwartz showed me his ass tattoos, and then, just as we were coming back from the final commercial break, I found out that André Leon Talley had died. So it was a roller coaster. André was so wonderful. And too young—seventy-three. Checked my DMs before bed, and there was Trishelle, of *Real World: Las Vegas* fame, saying that "Daddy Anderson" (her words, not mine) is on her top 5 hall pass list and has been for ten years, and she loves seeing him on my stories. You never know who you'll hear from in your DMs.

## ▦ WEDNESDAY, JANUARY 19, 2022

I woke myself up laughing today, a wonderful start to the day! I know dreams are boring, but I have to share what woke me up: I walk into a restaurant to meet Khloé Kardashian for dinner. (IRL we've never had dinner or done anything where cameras were not present.) At the maître d' stand I see Bethenny and whisper inappropriate sexual things in her ear, which make us laugh. Khloé blows me off, then I move tables three times, and then they don't have chicken quesadillas anymore and I order a burger, which I hate doing at a Mexican place. So I'm already frustrated. And then I'm at a table and looking at the placemat, which is an ad for religion, and the people in the picture start talking to me through my AirPods, which are still in from a phone call. They're asking me, "Do you praise Anderson? And when you praise Anderson, do you do that with call-and-response, or how does that go?"

Then I start flipping out at them and screaming that I'm just trying to eat and I don't owe them any explanations about my faith. At that point I realize I'm standing in the restaurant screaming at a placemat and wake up in a fit of giggles, laughing out loud at the sight of myself screaming at a placemat in the middle of a restaurant! What did that dream *mean*?! We tried to analyze it on the radio, but it was terribly boring.

Bravo announced that *WWHL* is coming back for two more years. That will take us to fifteen. I wonder if that'll be it? I texted Anderson and asked if he knew who Trishelle is. He didn't. Saw him later at the gym and told him he is on Trishelle's top 5 hall passes and—ever the intrepid journalist—he followed up, wondering who were the *other* guys in the top five. I don't consider Trishelle to be in my friend circle, but I happily DMed her and asked the question. She said the other four are Paul Walker, Joel McHale, Evan Peters, and Ryan Phillippe. So she has a type! I said I don't see AC being her type, and she said he's not but she likes a challenge. Maybe that's why she has appeared on multiple seasons of *The Challenge*?! Anyway, today I have devoted a chunk of time and thought to Trishelle, which was not on my bingo card for January 19!

My timeline is full of people demanding Jennie be fired for posts she made on Facebook a couple years ago. She is blaming her social media manager . . . but why would she have had a social media manager a few years ago? This is going to be an interesting one. Housewives often are offensive on some level, but the line has moved over sixteen years. Tonight, we played a game where we pitted two Housewives against each other, and the guests had to decide who was thirstier. After the show, Jill Zarin texted with an updated headshot, asking us to use it if we show her pic again! ON. BRAND.

## ⠿ THURSDAY, JANUARY 20, 2022

This morning I was on Thirty-Seventh Street in a *white suit* in the *snow*, crankily doing on-camera visits to the Miami Housewives' trailers before the reunion. They all looked like a million bucks. I was getting ready, and Tamra texted saying, "you really think I'm thirsty." Apparently, I answered for Shannon when Tamra was one of the choices in the thirsty game last night, knowing Tamra was going to be her choice. I told Tamra, "I just knew she was gonna say your name because you guys are feuding." I asked Shannon who it was between Tamra and Kelly. Tamra said we need "better bitches."

The taping was easy breezy: a minimum of fighting, which was a pleasant change of pace, in the midst of lots of personal stories from each of them, which made it all really engaging. I came away grateful and even more invested in them personally, and excited for another season, which will be a blowout. Now they're a real, connected group.

There are two ways to feel after a reunion: buzzing or comatose. When I got the white suit off in my (for some reason freezing cold) apartment, I was comatose. I was just lying on my bed and listening to Nora En Pure DJ—I have been really appreciating the lighting in my apartment lately—feeling kinda moody about where things are going. In a Manhattan flash, Ralph texted for a nightcap, having just arrived from London, which means a few days of neighborhood fun. So I got a fire going, and the English Patient himself and I had the best reconnect. I am so *American* to him: over the course of an hour, I pushily turned a dinner between him and Liam into a dinner *party* including Hickey and me, asked about his finances, and played a random practical joke on him. He turned the night around.

## ⠿ FRIDAY, JANUARY 21, 2022

I think I found a typo in *Corduroy* this morning! How could that *be*? This book has been around since I was a kid. It says the night watchman was "going his rounds," but I think it should be "doing his rounds." I posted on Instagram about it, and people think it's a British expression.

When I dropped Ben off at school, I also dropped my Amex and a big wad of cash in the (deep!) grate in front. Margot, who is not only an incredible nanny but the best source of info for everything happening in the building and neighborhood, said my man Alex, aka the King of Cutz, gets shit out of grates. That's his *thing*! He got her AirPods out on Greenwich Avenue.

I texted him, and he was outside the building, so we went to look. He kept pushing my hands down from pointing and telling me to lower my voice, in fear that another "grate" guy was gonna see that there was gold below the surface and swoop in before he could rescue my stuff. He got his materials, which turned out to be a long pole with a yardstick taped to it and mousetrap glue at the bottom. Genius! I guess there are grate guys all over the place?! My "big wad of cash" turned out to be ten bucks, which I gave him. (I know that sounds like a cheap tip, but we scratch each other's backs all the time, so just know things are great between me and the King of Cutz. And that I'm *grate*ful. Get it?) Bruce said there should be a show called *Grate Hunters*, which sounds like a genius idea.

During Ben's dinner FaceTime with Ma and Pa, I got an earful about playing the Have! They! Crapped! Their Pants?! game with Laura Linney. My mom thought it was disgusting. (Well, it was!) Ralph came to get me for dinner, and I showed him *Corduroy*, and he said "going rounds" is *not* a British term to his knowledge, which in my mind is extensive. We went to a *packed* Morandi with Hickey and Jeff, who said it was like 1920s Berlin. I made a game of seeing what parts of American culture have penetrated Ralph's universe. He has never seen *The Golden Girls* but has seen *I Love Lucy* and *Seinfeld*. Went to the Waverly Inn on the way home to meet Jeanne and Fred, and we closed it down. The three friends-of-Judy maître d's were DJing for us—lots of Madonna and B-52s, so we were happy, and dancing.

## ⬚ SATURDAY, JANUARY 22, 2022

*Sesame Street* and pizza with the Coopers for lunch. Wyatt was wearing the cutest Ben-Me-Down sweater. I always gasp in glee when I see him in Ben's clothes. We told Ben that Wyatt is going to have a little brother in a few weeks, and he was nonplussed.

Played in the AIDS Memorial Park for an hour in the freezing cold. Ben just collects sticks and is happy. I didn't think to compare it to the time I'd spend wandering around that park with Wacha, but now that I type this . . . At home, read him *Corduroy* and *Go, Dog, Go!* As part of my continuing coexploration (with Ben of course) of the Disney oeuvre, with which I'm otherwise entirely unfamiliar, we watched *Moana* tonight. LOVED IT. The Rock was so great—loved his number! Ben couldn't take his eyes off Moana, whom he called "Banana." After I put him to bed, I spent too long (my Instagram use has gone to shit again, which is why I haven't mentioned it) looking at friends, acquaintances, and strangers in Miami and at Aspen gay ski week, trying to reconcile my FOMO about not being anywhere but here. By the time I put my phone down, I thought about the day and realized I was exactly where I wanted to be. *Moana* was that good!

## ⦙⦙⦙ SUNDAY, JANUARY 23, 2022

Today was a day of great New York City drop-bys. I got Ralph at 8:50 a.m., on the way home from the gym. Ben was too engrossed in *Sesame Street* to care. Ricky and Caroline came before Corner Bistro. Bevy Smith was in the neighborhood this afternoon, and Ben told her he loved her several times. The kid is handing out love on a platter. And tonight, I got Hickey for a nightcap. Again, who drops in on people in other cities? Beach towns, maybe? Big article in the *Times* about Kathy Griffin today in which she calls me Eve Harrington and says I wanted to *be* her. Oy to the whole thing. Anna and Elsa talk quelled today in favor of Banana (Moana), which was a nice respite. Ben and I had a Sunday-night dance party under the disco ball, a Covid favorite. Ben went to bed, and I fished around for songs for the *Kiki Lounge.* There are endless INCREDIBLE covers of "I Was Made to Love Her"—by the Beach Boys, Sister Sledge, Jerry Garcia . . . *Who knew?*

## ⦙⦙⦙ MONDAY, JANUARY 24, 2022

There is a handsome trainer at my gym who I realized today is basically getting women off while he stretches them. He is doing tantric, engaged, double-body moves. He is *pressing* against this beautiful woman. Stanny and I felt like we were watching them make love. I was agog the whole hour. Stan says he's like that with all his clients, including men to some level. Of course the conversation became that at some point I'm gonna dump Stanny for this guy. I need to experience it.

Got to work to discover that Graham Quinn, the amazing owner of

Sam's Pizza, was bartending on the show. I was so happy to see him—the first time in all these years that I've ever seen him outside of Sam's, in fact! He brought me two medium mushroom-and-onion pizzas—drove them from Long Island!—which sat cold for I don't know how many hours. I didn't care—I grabbed them after the show, brought them both home, and put them in the freezer for a rainy night. Caught up on *Euphoria* after the live show. That Jacob Elordi—I've never seen bone structure like that in my life.

## TUESDAY, JANUARY 25, 2022

I've been texting with Cher a bit since New Year's, and today she thanked me for saying something nice and ended by saying, "Love to the angel emoji [Anderson] and the kids." I responded that one day she'll figure out that *I'm* the angel emoji. Ben thinks Wyatt's brother should be named "Wheels," which I think is about the coolest name I've heard. The apartment next door (that'll soon be part of mine) is full of people working, and I had to make ten fast decisions about things that I'll either wind up regretting or being glad I did. I just want that room *done*! The baby is due in three months and change! The workmen outside the windows were pounding away all day—it's coming from all sides. And there's dust everywhere. I had to stop my Instagram rant about my love for the workman outside because I found a DM from a woman saying she's friends with the WIFE of the workman I'm putting on blast. She and the wife watch the stories together. So I felt pukey, and that was that. But I see him every day. So it's weird.

We stopped filming with Jennie today, and I had a productive call with Candiace about it and about Bravo's handling of issues of this kind. We are trying to produce a show about women who are often politically incorrect and outrageous, in 2022—which could wind up being an impossible task. We do a Q and A before *WWHL*, and someone asked what's the most surprising thing about John Mayer, and I said it's that he is the guy who always shows up. And about five minutes later, I get a text from him saying he just wanted to tell me how excited he was about all the festivities surrounding me getting my star next week. *This guy!* And JUST when I was starting to feel guilty for asking him to speak. Went to dinner at Via Carota with Deirdre, JJ, and Melissa, and I surprised them with Anthony, whom we are missing at the show. My *WWHL* team are the best *reactors!* They're the perfect audience for everything. Long, rambly talk with Bruce when I got home.

## ⦙ WEDNESDAY, JANUARY 26, 2022

Cher texted at 4:21 in the morning: "you're so NOT the angel emoji." The guy at the gym was stretching a gay guy today. So he *is* equal opportunity. He literally had his hands cupping the guy's ass while he was doing squats. Full feel-up! I want this experience!

I subscribe to a service that emails me every morning with clippings anytime my name is mentioned on a TV show. I love this service because it's so random, and this morning was full of surprises. TMZ must have a dearth of content, because they ran my Instagram story about the King of Cutz fishing my money out from the grate. And last night, some guy on Newsmax was reporting about us stopping filming with Jennie from SLC, and he called me a "pansy." I have been called a lot of shit, and nothing seems to bother me, but this brought me back to sixth grade, and I was seeing red. I wanted to beat the crap out of this guy. The guy would've *loved* for me to get into it with him publicly, but I restrained myself from tweeting at him all day (for the record, my leading contender for a clap-back: "Who was the pansy when you were blowing me last night?").

John and I did a deep dive on the Newsmax guy's social media during the radio show, and he is unfortunately fairly cute. I sat down in the control room and immediately commented on Deirdre's bright-pink sweater, and she told me that every single time she's worn that sweater over the last ten years I've made some sort of snide comment about it. (Tonight's was "So you went with the *pink?*"—not *so* snide if you ask me.) What is it about that sweater that *activates* me, I wonder?

Paris and Kathy Hilton were on the live show. We played what turned out to be the funniest game with them—well, they made it funny. It was What's! In! Kathy's! Bag! As I handed Paris the Ramona eyes, I thought to myself, *She's not gonna put those on.* Sure enough, she realized she was going to look funny in them and started pushing back at me, suggesting she play the game turned to her side, conveniently in her Paris pose. Kathy said she's so vain, and I said just close your eyes. But when I pointed out she was the first guest in twelve years to refuse the Ramona eyes, I shamed her into putting them on. And of course she looked amazing in them. Despite having been briefed on the game, Kathy had no concept that she was to pull items out of the bag and describe them to Paris, instead pulling them out and saying "I've got my hat! I've got my sunglasses!" It was a roller coaster.

It was Belle's last night working at *WWHL*, and we all stayed drinking very late, and I kept saying it was BLN (Belle's Last Night) and we weren't going home until the sun came up. I did an Irish goodbye around one thirty.

## ▦ THURSDAY, JANUARY 27, 2022

"The sun is up!" is how Ben yells for me when he wakes up. I tell him that is a technicality in relation to what time we start our day, but that's not landing with him.

Had a Zoom with Richard LaGravenese, who is writing a new movie and wanted to pick my brain about the Housewives. I fanned out over *The Bridges of Madison County*. It's underrated! I sobbed at that gas station scene. Have been in a frenzy planning for the star ceremony next week. The Hollywood star people are being very restrictive about the number of people who can be there and Covid testing. Poor Daryn is having to deal with a lot of crap I don't even know about. Everyone in the family is so excited about it, and I am too. We've been talking about this for two years. I am really going to stop talking about the horny stretcher at the gym, but he was back "stretching" a client and I was transfixed. Patti LuPone and Cynthia Nixon were on the show tonight. Mom texted after: "Very enjoyable! And Unfilthy!"

## ☷ FRIDAY, JANUARY 28, 2022

Today was Ben's third birthday party. His actual birthday will happen when we're in LA next week, so I wanted to do something before for his little friends. I felt triumphant that I went to Party City and got him plates with Anna and Elsa from *Frozen*. Ben specifically wanted BLUE CUPCAKES, so Amy Sedaris made a batch (Ben's request). Even though all I had to do was that, and buy plates and napkins and balloons, and get a pizza, I felt tremendously accomplished and dad-like. Ben would be happy chasing a balloon around the room, so the party with seven toddlers was awesome. I offered the other parents rosé and had to sidebar with Margot to see what the protocol on offering nannies wine is. She said you make the offer, and it's up to each to decide. Ben was a great host to his little friends, checking to see if they had beverages, and after the pizza, he took the words out of my mouth and suggested a dance party. We all went upstairs and turned the disco ball on and the kids ran around. THAT'S a party! I was riveted by the Janet Jackson doc tonight! Took a bubble bath before bed during the big snowstorm. Felt like Valerie Cherish. Then I watched some of *The Comeback* and crashed.

## ☷ SATURDAY, JANUARY 29, 2022

Felt cocooned in cozy during the bomb cyclone snowstorm that pounded us from last night through today. I lit a huge fire while Ben watched *Sesame Street*, then we spent ninety minutes looking at a Richard Scarry book. Would I *ever* have had the patience to spend ninety minutes looking for Goldbug hidden on pages? I motivated us out into the snowstorm, and man, what a pain in the ass it is putting gloves on a little guy. Our outdoor activity consisted of lunch at Corner Bistro. We watched *Encanto* in the early evening, and I wasn't as wild about it as everyone else. I'm a *Moana* guy! I might add that every time Moana was onscreen, Ben kept turning to me and saying, "I *love her*, Daddy." And, during *Encanto*, every time Mirabel was onscreen, he turned to me and said, "Who is that?" I kept saying,

"SHE'S the girl, Ben." She has a vain sister who is really pretty, and Ben thought SHE was the lead.

Had another date with the beautiful Spaniard after Ben went to bed. I said if this relationship gets serious, we have to have a real discussion about the elephant in the room. I was referring to my kids and all that entails, but to him the elephant in the room is that I'm famous. So that triggered a long conversation about why my being famous was an elephant to him and why I thought he should look at it like a gnat. The happy part of the conversation was that he doesn't view my having kids as an elephant in the room. After all that heavy talk, we did a lot of smooching in front of the fire.

## SUNDAY, JANUARY 30, 2022

Spent most of the day looking at the Richard Scarry book with Ben.

## MONDAY, JANUARY 31, 2022

Sent Mom the schedule for the star festivities, and she emailed back, "Well this looks great if we can get there with the SNOW!" Looked online, and a big storm is hitting St. Louis tomorrow, and it's going to last a few days. I called her and FORCED her to change their flight to tomorrow, which was exhausting. Em was involved, and we really double-teamed her. If they don't leave tomorrow, they won't make the ceremony, and then *what is the point*?!

Now I can't decide what to wear to the Hollywood star ceremony. Looked online at other people getting their stars. Discussed it on the radio and, a few hours later, got a DM from a stranger telling me to wear the teal suit. The perfect choice! It doesn't matter how many times I wear that suit—I get compliments every time. Went to the gym. Taped two shows. Amanda texted that she was watching a video of us at Grac's wedding and noticed how much lighter she seemed. I thought about that a lot today and texted later to say we were both lighter then, actually. Life has a way of making you heavy. How can a person carry the weightlessness of being twenty through other generations? We've done pretty well, though, in maintaining our spirit.

## ⊞ TUESDAY, FEBRUARY 1, 2022

My surrogate, Kathleen, says the baby wakes her up every morning at 4:30, so that's lurking! Mom and Dad made it to LA, and by the time they'd landed, all the flights for tomorrow had been cancelled. Em made it out too. I'm incredibly relieved. They ran into Bruce on Rodeo Drive. Hilarious.

Today was insane with trying to get out of town tomorrow. Pre-taped radio, took Ben to the doctor, then pre-taped two *WWHL* episodes and did one live with Teresa (and Gia at the bar—she's twenty-one now! I'm old). Ike Barinholtz was on the show for the first time and offered me a part in *History of the World: Part II*, which he's making with Mel Brooks. I couldn't say yes fast enough. John is deep in rehearsals for his Sob Rock Tour and I've had lingering guilt about his speaking at the star ceremony. Got a text from him tonight saying, "I can't wait to celebrate you Friday. I'm so excited." I love when my fears get put to ease subliminally.

## ⊞ WEDNESDAY, FEBRUARY 2, 2022— NEW YORK CITY TO LOS ANGELES

Woke Ben up extra early to give him Dramamine so he didn't puke en route to the airport. It worked. I had Meghan McCain and Kelly Dodd texting me as we were taking off. You never know who you're going to hear from in a given day. My new bestie Ike Barinholtz was on our flight, and we discussed dates for the show, and when I sat down again I realized I had just committed myself for my vacation week at the end of March, although a vacation in LA with Ben while I work part of the time doesn't sound so bad.

Zucker announced he is stepping down from CNN because he had a consensual affair but didn't report it. In a galaxy of horrible things, that doesn't seem like a reason to step down to me. I'm bummed. Ben was wired for the entire six-hour flight then fell asleep ten minutes before we finally got to Bruce's. All the Beverly Hills women are in a tizzy about discord with Kathy Hilton on their last night in Aspen. Spoke to Rinna about it. She is really upset and is planning on bringing it up on the show. We have no footage of it anywhere so I'm trying to figure out how it's going to land within the body of the show. In the meantime, someone is leaking information about her alleged meltdown to TMZ and it's making me nuts. I never understand what benefit it is to, say, a Housewife, to leak stuff like this before it can play out on the show. What's the point? Rinna insisted it wasn't her leaking. In the meantime, I hung up and then realized she'll be at the star ceremony Friday. Went to Kimmel, who, during an otherwise really fun segment, proceeded to totally take the wind out of my sails about the Hollywood star ceremony. I mean, I wasn't expecting the Oscars, but to say he lowered my expectations would be a kind way of putting it. He said you can't hear a thing, the mics are bad, the city officials are creepy and weird, there are people in Spider-Man costumes, and it's all very random. *But* the good news is you walk away with a star. Well, okay then.

On the way from Kimmel to pick up my parents and Em, I felt defeated about the star and reached out to Randy Barbato to find out if my parents would be able to hear, at least. He put me back together and got my mind right. Picked up the Cohens and took them to Bruce's to reunite with Ben, who was lit up like a Christmas tree. Dinner at the Polo Lounge, which was otherwise empty. My family are always very engaged with whether a restaurant is full or empty, or where it stands on a level of "hotness." If it's crowded, Dad will say, "This is a pretty hot place!" If it's empty, he'll some-what dejectedly report, "Pretty quiet here . . ." To make matters worse, we were all the way in the back, and the service sucked, which is karma for being gay and going to the Polo Lounge. If the Polo Lounge tells you they hate gay people, shouldn't you listen? (Call me Mr. Angelou.) Once our drinks arrived, Mom and Em pulled out presents they'd brought to give me on the occasion of the star, with lovely cards. My heart was so full, and they erased all my new pessimism about the event. (Mom and Dad got me a thick sterling silver bracelet, and Em an engraved Nambé star paperweight.) Those McCarthy salads at the Beverly Hills Hotel are forty-four dollars! On that note, Mom is getting her hair washed and blown tomorrow and she said, "GUESS how much it COSTS! GUESS!!" I guessed $120. She said it was gonna be $100. I said, "Listen, this is the big time. Beverly Hills. If you wanna be big-time, you gotta pay for it!" My dad agreed! Took a family photo on the red carpet in front of the hotel and had nightcaps with Bruce and Bryan.

## ⁝⁝⁝ THURSDAY, FEBRUARY 3, 2022—LOS ANGELES

Woke up at 4:30 a.m., jet-lagged and stressed about the speech I have to write today, the table settings I have to do for Bruce's dinner tonight, and more *BH* drama with the women, who keep leaking shit to TMZ. Again, I don't understand how. I don't understand how or why they think this HELPS anyone, to leak stuff. Tried unsuccessfully to nap. Ben went to lunch with Mom and Dad at Nate 'n Al's and wanted to stack his eggs on his bagel like Daddy does. What a tribute! Had lunch with Susan Rovner at San Vicente Bungalows. Met John Hill for tea, and we wound up having a very emotional talk about our past. We cried!

Came home and set up Ben in the movie theater with *Frozen*—his first film in a real movie theater—and banged out my speech for tomorrow. The main event was tonight's joint birthday party for Mom (turning eighty-five in ten days) and Ben. As guests were mingling, Ben was dancing, saying, "I love the music at your party, Daddy!" It was my favorite part of the night. Bruce gave a tour of the house to the Clampetts from Missouri and JJ and Lynn—a *real* Beverly Hills house.

The night brought together an amazing group of people with connections that crisscrossed my life: Straight Dave, John Hill, Liza and Jamie . . . Jeremy came from Washington, DC, and surprised everybody. Lynn, whom I interned for at CBS News in 1989, told the story of me coming out to her. Apparently, she tried to set me up with someone, and I incredulously asked her if she was fucking with me.

"I'm gay," I said.

"I'm getting divorced," she replied, realizing I'd just opened up something private to her and wanting to share something personal from her own life. We had a cake for Ben and one for my mom and one for me—three cakes! Getting my family in an Uber to the hotel was a whole thing.

## ⸬ FRIDAY, FEBRUARY 4, 2022—LOS ANGELES

Rarely does a day you've looked forward to for years match already high expectations, but today did! I'd say it was like my birthday, but it was actually Ben's third, and that kicked everything into another dimension of happiness. He was wearing the shirt Grac gave him, emblazoned with a digger and *I'm Digging Being 3*. Caroline came to do my beat. I have a few regular makeup artists in LA, but no one makes me look like Caroline. You would think over twelve years I would've paid attention enough to watch and understand her four-minute process, but no. Ben, Margot, and I rode to the event with Lynn and Dave, which felt festive, although Ben was bordering on melting down, to the point that I resigned myself to the possibility of him wanting no part of this event and losing his mind in front of a wall of press.

So my expectations of his participation or being able to get a pic with him by the star were low. And although we've said for a week or two that Daddy's getting a star today, I'm sure he was wondering where the hell we were taking him to do this, whatever it was we were doing. Got out of the car into the bright, sunshiny Hollywood morning to see my face on a marquee and crowds of cheering people, many of them calling Ben's name or saying happy birthday, which he LOVED. Soon enough, he was waving at the crowd across Hollywood Boulevard who were singing "Happy Birthday" to him and giving a thumbs-up to a California Highway Patrol guy. His wide-eyed, big-smiled euphoria lifted me and everybody else around us. I was so happy to be among my amazing mix of old friends and business friends—B. J. Novak came, and Jerry O'Connell. A lady in a bright-pink pantsuit and square sunglasses (who I think was from the Hollywood Chamber of Commerce?) assured me quickly that they'd tested the mics and *contrary to what Jimmy Kimmel said*, the sound was *pristine*.

I thought, *Jimmy wound up saving the day*. He put everyone on notice! We were sitting down, ready to start, and Mayer was two minutes out, and Dad was making rumblings that maybe Mayer wasn't going to show. I said rock stars roll in, and then it starts—that's why they're rock stars. And with that, he rolled in. Sat between John and Frances. What I didn't know is that they call you up on the little stage and make all their remarks with you standing there, in front of the photographers and crews, with your people on your right. Rinna and Garcelle Beauvais spoke on behalf of the 139 Real Housewives. At the end of their remarks, Rinna said for everyone to get on my star and dance for me. Classic.

My crew in the audience thought the pink-pantsuit lady was auditioning to be a Housewife. When she introduced John to speak, in giving his bio, she said he's one of the world's most influential watch collectors, to which he screamed, "Thanks a lot for putting me on blast!" John's speech had me floating on air. He wrote a beautiful tribute full of deep, nice thoughts about me; it felt like I got to hear him deliver my eulogy. (Or my professional eulogy.) One line that I loved was: "He's an A-lister who parties like a B-lister with the spirit of a C-lister." During my speech, a TMZ bus went by, and I waved and called them out. Then the bus announcer guy was trying to get me to do something else, but I couldn't really hear what, and I said, "Listen, I'm getting a *star* over here—do I need to do Harvey Levin's business right now???" Oh, and at one point Pink Pantsuit Lady tripped on the stairs of the little stage—fell and ripped her pant leg, possibly securing an RH friend slot. Took every variation of photo after the unveiling, including with Ben, who did a little dance on the star and was so joyful.

Bravo threw me a great lunch outside at Craig's that felt like the reception after the bar mitzvah, including everyone I would've had at the star if it wasn't Covid. (By the way, with all the Covid precautions about getting tested before the star ceremony and a long list of rules, no one at the ceremony actually checked anyone's test results. Whatever.) Bruce facilitated Jason Blum and me hashing out his feelings about not making the cut of the star ceremony. We worked it out when he admitted he was actually relieved he didn't have to go (which was what I THOUGHT his reaction would be), but then he was annoyed when he saw who did. Ricki Lake and her amazing new husband, Ross, schlepped all the way from Malibu. Straight guys' table was B.J., Mayer, Jerry O, Jason, and Michael Davies. My mom sat with Ben, Garcelle, Rinna, and Lynn. Garcelle and my mom totally bonded. Rinna had to go shoot a lunch with Crystal. We had two more cakes for Ben and Mom! The kid has gotten like six cakes in the last week—I'm Joan Crawford, but the *good* version. B.J. said the scene at the star ceremony with TMZ going by and Ben waving was like a page from Richard Scarry's Busytown books. No analogy can I identify with more closely at this moment than one involving Busytown!

On the way out of the restaurant, a TMZ guy asked what I'm thinking about Whoopi's suspension from *The View*. I said, "I'm not thinking about it at all!" He said, "How are you gonna celebrate the star?" and I grabbed Ricki and said, "I'm gonna take this lady home and make love to Ricki Lake!" Then, twenty seconds later, I was about to get in the car when a *new* person from TMZ showed up, a woman who wanted to do the whole thing over again, and I said, you're late and I'm not doing this again. So it was also a day of TMZ trying to make content everywhere you turned. That night we watched *Spider-Man* in the screening room. I cried twice. Mom didn't get it. Ben watched a bunch of it, and I wondered whether I was a bad parent for letting him see it. We had nightcaps and more talk after dinner. I was the best kind of exhausted after feeling the exhilaration of a Hollywood Star! Listen, I know it's cheesy, but I felt like a star.

## ⁛ SATURDAY, FEBRUARY 5, 2022—LOS ANGELES

Woke up and thought of five people who should've been invited to the lunch at Craig's yesterday. UGH! Also to a text from the East Coast—Jose saying the downstairs neighbor is fuming about my ice maker some more. I saw him last week and kept my head down. Brunch at Nate 'n Al's with Mom, Dad, and Ben, then we drove to look at the star without all the people around. It was already dirty! It was very Hollywood, seeing it in the sparkle of yesterday and then the bleak grime of Saturday morning. One day you're a star, the next you're filthy. Brought Ben for a long playdate at Jason and Lauren

Blum's; Jason taught me how to clean a baby's vagina. (Wipe front to bottom—it's a whole new world for me!) Someone said Pink Pantsuit Lady got the outfit yesterday from Rent the Runway—does that mean she's gonna have to pay for the ripped leg? I feel bad. Dinner at the Sunset Tower with John, Bruce, Bryan, and Kevin. Kevin and I went to the opening of the club formerly known as Rage, but now called Heart. The LA gays were OUT in force! Saw Lance Bass and talked babies (I forgot all my Britney and Justin questions, damn it!); Sam Smith; Lisa Rinna's cute hair guy, Scott; and Ivan and Yeison from San Diego. Ran into Felipe, whom I met in New Orleans maybe five years ago when touring with Anderson and flirted with through 2017. The look of sheer disgust on his face after I asked him if he still had the same number and suggested we hang out again stopped me in my tracks. Like, I had to laugh out loud! Before bed, I watched Mayer's tribute to me from yesterday on YouTube. It made me feel a lot better.

## SUNDAY, FEBRUARY 6, 2022—
## LOS ANGELES TO NEW YORK CITY

Sad flight back to New York. After all that hype, it was over! Hickey came by for a nightcap after I put the boy to sleep, and we downloaded about the weekend. He said goodnight, and we put it all to bed. As I was turning all the lights out downstairs, Loic, Antoine, and two friends came by from the DL and turned my apartment into a mini-version of the club until about twelve thirty. In Manhattan, you never know where a night is going to go . . .

## MONDAY, FEBRUARY 7, 2022—NEW YORK CITY

All day was waiting for Anderson's son to be born. Early morning was with Ben, getting him ready for school. He had cupcakes at school for his birthday, and it's safe to say even he is over it at this point. Kimmel was on the radio with me this morning, and we agreed that his warning wound up making the whole thing better. Visited a potential nursery school for

Ben. I'm the parent who walks in, sees the room and toys, and says "Cute! Where do I send the check?" I mean, how long do I really need to spend on a nursery school tour? SJ is on *WWHL* tomorrow, so I watched the last three *And Just Like That* . . . episodes *and* the documentary about the show's production. King of Cutz closed. So sad.

Sebastian Cooper was born around five thirty. Ben seemed disinterested ("*I don't like him*" might've been his first response) but when he saw the picture he really engaged ("*I like him!*"). Read *The Three Little Pigs* and was very impressed with my own wolf voice.

## ⸬ TUESDAY, FEBRUARY 8, 2022

Upon further reflection as I read *The Three Little Pigs* at seven thirty this morning, I actually think my wolf voice sounds like Harvey Fierstein. Ben is literally cooing at all the pictures of baby Sebastian. I hope he feels the same way about his sister. Kathleen sent new pictures of the bump today. We're in the third trimester! Final stretch! Dr. R. suggested to us this morning that we move Ben to a big-boy bed, and the suggestion did not go over well with him.

Have a twenty-four-hour trip to LA tomorrow to host the John Mayer Sirius concert, so I pre-taped tomorrow's radio show before the gym, where I had a VEXING encounter with an incredibly handsome man who came up to me while I was on the phone with Lance Kash about money matters to congratulate me on the star. I was so discombobulated by his looks (he was an all-American *specimen*, is the best way to put it) that I was scattered with Lance and—worse—scattered with *him*. He apologized for disturbing me and walked into the locker room but turned around to give me another look (pro tip: that's called *cruising*), which I matched. I texted Stan when I got home, telling him to look for this guy and find out who he is. No luck. *How am I going to find him?* HE IS MY HUSBAND AND HE DOESN'T KNOW IT. Had two *WWHL* tapings and one live show this evening. The SJP show was a lot of fun.

## :::: WEDNESDAY, FEBRUARY 9, 2022—
## NEW YORK CITY TO LOS ANGELES

My 7:00 a.m. flight was a killer. Slept for an hour, watched two episodes of *Jersey*, wrote questions to interview John, landed, and had a listless call about the future of *RHONY*. We need to figure out a way to revive it without losing our audience who loves it. I had time to kill, so I went to three dispensaries looking for that sativa THC tincture. Found it! The interview with John was good. Spoke to a lot of press after, and called Imani on my way out to have her find out if I said anything bad to *Entertainment Tonight*. They asked about Jennie and Ramona and a bunch of stuff that I'm not sure I nailed. Imani said it was all fine. Bruce picked me up and we went to the Mayer concert together. Was fun being backstage with him and his crew again—all great people whom I only see at happy occasions (John concerts). The show was fantastic and a great preview to his tour, which starts in a week.

Toward the end, Bruce and I were trying to get to Liza and Jamie and were stopped by an overzealous badge-cop lady going down the flight of stairs we'd come up. I didn't have the right badge to get back there, even though I'd come from there and was on the stage introducing John an hour before. I don't know if it was the tequila or the fact that it's been years since I fought with a mall cop, but I went nuts. Nuts!

"I'm HOSTING this show!" I pleaded. (Bruce literally stepped to the side and checked his phone, waiting for it to pass.) I was ACTIVATED and PISSED. Finally, someone from Sirius came up and gave me the right badge. Bruce dropped me off at the San Vicente Bungalows, where I met John and a group of his friends. It was a pileup of stars. Lukas Gage apologized to me for saying something about swaddling to me the night I met him at Paul's Casablanca. I said not to give it another thought, because I'd totally forgotten. Kiernan Shipka was at the table, then Jon Hamm showed up, and they had a big father-daughter reunion. I love *Mad Men*. Allison Janney was there too. She and I made out. Not our first time!

## THURSDAY, FEBRUARY 10, 2022— LOS ANGELES TO NEW YORK CITY

I have shame about fighting with that mall cop lady at the concert. What got into me? So stupid! Got about four hours' sleep and worked the whole flight home. The flight attendant gave me his card, and I clumsily dropped it as he was trying to discreetly palm it to me. This reminds me, where is my mystery gym lover?! On the plane home, I think I came up with a plan to save *RHONY*—split it into two shows, one with all new women and one featuring legacy cast members. That way we can reflect a more modern version of New York, tell new stories, while still following some of the vets, who are legitimately friends. I'm gonna pitch it to Bravo. Work calls in the car home, then a concentrated forty minutes of play with Ben before changing. Spoke to Jose at the door about the mask mandate, which the governor lifted today. Yay!

Took the subway to *The Music Man* opening night starring Hugh Jackman and Sutton Foster. Walking in, I bumped right into the governor, of all people, who I thanked for the mask thing. I was a disaster walking to my seat, running into all these people who were saying hi but whom I couldn't recognize because of their masks. (Mandate NOT lifted for inside the theater.) Then Maureen Dowd was sitting in front of me, and I recognized her voice but couldn't for the life of me figure out who she was. (I should mention I was high on the THC tincture.) During the show I second-guessed what I said to this reporter on the red carpet who asked me if Bravo needs to do a better job vetting. I said it's a work in progress. It is, isn't it? The show was great.

After it was over, Cynthia Nixon came over to say hi, and Maureen Dowd introduced herself, and I was so embarrassed to have not placed her. Her voice should've given it away! I'm an idiot. The masks cover everything! There was a beautiful dinner after at Jazz at Lincoln Center, overlooking the park. We were sitting with Hamilton and Fran Lebowitz, who—surprise—didn't seem to love the show. The table next to us was all the big politicians—the governor, Mayor Bloomberg, Nancy Pelosi . . . I met Mayor Adams, who was in a snazzy suit. It made me wonder if he wondered whether I'll be going off on *him* next New Year's Eve. At the rate he's going, I might.

## ⠿ FRIDAY, FEBRUARY 11, 2022

Looked for the hot guy, but he was not to be found at the gym. Danny Neeson came over with a De-Nada shotski that he wanted to give me and I sent him home with it. I can't handle another shotski! He can use it! I did keep the tequila he brought. Pitched my plan for splitting *RHONY* into two and I think it went well.

Watched *The Little Mermaid* with Ben tonight. He liked it. He LOVES a princess—falls in love with each and every one. In the middle of the movie he said, "I love her, Daddy." I liked but didn't love it. I'm watching all these Disney movies that were so huge in their day, and some of the '90s ones we spent a tremendous amount of time promoting when I was at *CBS This Morning*. This one wasn't worth the hype. Put Ben to bed and took an edible and watched *Celebrity Big Brother*, where I witnessed a fight between Cynthia Bailey and Todd "Willis" Bridges from which I will NEVER RECOVER. Hickey came for a nightcap!

## ⠿ SATURDAY, FEBRUARY 12, 2022— NEW YORK CITY TO NEW ORLEANS

"DADDY—THE SUN IS UP! THE SUN IS UP!" I woke up to that at 6:45 a.m. and simply could not stop the train. So by the time we got to Anderson's to meet Sebastian, I was bleary-eyed. Ben was very sweet with him, then he hit Wyatt in the face and had a time-out. Went with Anderson, Benjamin, and our sons to the playground, then to Zazzy's for pizza. Jose texted that the neighbor downstairs said my ice maker was "especially loud" last night. I feel terrible—the guy is SPINNING OUT down there. But there are no levels to the amount of whirring it's doing. It's the same every day! I finally have a solution to the problem, though: this one, with the superior cubes, will be moved to the new bar very soon, and I'll replace it with one he won't have to worry about. Was on a two thirty flight to New Orleans for Chris Williamson's fortieth birthday. Landed and grabbed some food in the Quarter—French onion soup and salmon tartare—which wrecked my stomach. Took a gorgeous two-hour nap, then to the party, which was epic. He had rotating DJs from Sammy Jo to Jake Shears and Amber Martin, then Jake and Amber did a surprise song, Jake's newest ("Too Much Music"), which is on par with how I think the halftime show will be tomorrow night (great!). The night was wild.

## ⠿ SUNDAY, FEBRUARY 13, 2022—
## NEW ORLEANS TO NEW YORK CITY

*Is it possible he's sleeping with his eyes open?* I wondered, waking up at ten thirty with a THUMPING hangover, after four hours of sleep. I turned and saw my new friend from last night, sound asleep on his back. I looked closely and realized he had glitter on both his eyelids. It was so trippy. My contacts weren't in, and I had my face up to his, wondering if I was looking at clear blue *open* eyes. Spent a half hour deliberating going to the lobby to find aspirin before doing so and falling back asleep for an hour. Raced to the airport and ran into Shady Bill at the bar of the Chili's. We looked frightful as we tried putting the pieces of the night together. Got home and watched part of the Super Bowl with Ben, who was all cozy in his pajamas. Kept him up for the halftime show. He grabbed his bongos and was banging away with all the rap legends. Took a steam at ten thirty and went to bed.

## ⠿ MONDAY, FEBRUARY 14, 2022

Got Ben ready and bundled up for school, and in front of the elevator he turns to me and says, "Are you going to give me shoes today?" Whoops. Jackie came over for sushi tonight, and we asked Ben what was going to go in the new room, and he said a baby and then a cat. So he seems to already know what's happening. She and I made decisions for tile in all the bathrooms of the beach house, so it felt like a productive night! Tamra was on the show, and it was the first time we'd seen each other in several years—"Not since you fired me!" She *loves* to say I fired her. Well, I did. She brought me her latest set of implants she'd had removed. Put them on the shelf with her other implants.

## TUESDAY, FEBRUARY 15, 2022

Mom is eighty-five today! Ben sang her all of "Happy Birthday" on their nightly FaceTime and pretended to make her a cake. Been texting sweetly with my glitter-eyed beau from New Orleans. He's coming to New York City soon, and we'll have a proper date. Saw Sandra Bernhard at the gym. Read about how all the coasts will be completely flooded in less than thirty years and wondered what kind of fool I am to be building my dream house on the ocean in Amagansett. There was a new TMZ lady in front of *WWHL*. She was just horrible. The question she yelled was: "Tell me what's going on with the Housewives?!" I said, "*That's* your question? What *about* them?" She didn't know. Then she spent ten seconds trying to remember Erika Jayne's name and, when she did, asked me what I thought of her. I said, I'm sorry but I can't do this. I couldn't pretend! I just couldn't do it. Tonight's *WWHL* was me watching Jennifer Aydin get absolutely blitzed live on TV in the course of thirty minutes.

## WEDNESDAY, FEBRUARY 16, 2022

We played Bravo Phone-a-Friend on the radio this morning. People called in and named a Bravo person they wanted to say hi to, and then I'd text them and see if they'd get on the phone. The people who responded were Dorinda, Kim Zolciak-Biermann, Margaret, and Kyle. Porsha texted later, saying she's in Anguilla. Taped an *And Just Like That . . .* town hall for Sirius. Bruce sent out an invite for a shower in which he revealed

Lucy's name to all on the list (many already knew). Julie Chen is texting, trying to get me to come on *Celebrity Big Brother* via Skype Friday night because she knows I watched the show and have opinions, but I don't want to go on and make Carson or Cynthia feel bad by calling out their boneheaded gameplay. Dinner for Jeff's birthday with Hickey, Victor Garber and Rainer, and Gary Janetti (whom I drunkenly called Brad at one point) at that Spanish place on Sixteenth Street where apparently—like being in Spain—time is but a concept. The meal took three hours but was a lot of fun! Hickey told me I need to stop referring to *Plaza Suite* as a great episode of *The Carol Burnett Show*, because it's actually a Neil Simon play and not a sketch-comedy TV show. We debated it for a long time, because I think my characterizing it that way would sell a lot of tickets. Who *wouldn't* want to see SJP and Matthew in a great episode of *The Carol Burnett Show*? Victor agreed with me, but I will stop because Hickey said so.

## ⊞ THURSDAY, FEBRUARY 17, 2022

I can't believe I called Gary "Brad" at dinner last night. Rookie move! Lunch with Jeff Shell at 30 Rock. He is the big boss. Long FaceTime with Mayer while I hung in a massive executive conference room right out of *Dynasty*, waiting for a conference call about *RHONY*. A normal person in 2022 would say it was from *Succession*. You can take the boy out of the '80s, but you can't take the '80s out of the boy.

Anyway, I was killing time in there. John starts his Sob Rock Tour tonight in Albany. He was in a weird Airbnb. I love when he's on tour because he's pretty available. Saw *Just For Us* (on a date with the beautiful Spaniard), which we loved. Met Alex Edelman after. He had the best line in the show: "I'm from a racist part of Boston, called *Boston*." Apparently SJ posted about being there the other night, and tickets went through the roof. He is so sweet—told me his girlfriend is Hannah, the young lead of *Hacks*. The date continued at the Commerce Inn, which is a new Shaker restaurant from the owners of Via Carota. It's a lot of meats and beans! Romantic time on Commerce Street in the rain, sharing one of his freshly rolled tobacco (with a teeny bit of pot) cigarettes. The Spaniard and I have been on eight or so dates, and when I'm with him I wonder if we should be boyfriends. Then . . . I don't know what happens. Tonight, he told me he's most likely quitting his job and moving to Spain, so there goes that. I got us a car, dropped myself off, and sent him uptown, for a grand total surge price of seventy-nine dollars. That is some fucked-up surge pricing, Lyft. And I'm the FOOL who paid for it.

## ⦙⦙⦙⦙ FRIDAY, FEBRUARY 18, 2022

"Tell me about your day, Daddy!"

I know there's gonna be an expiration date on this boy being so adorable, but when he earnestly asks a question like that, it's really hard to have a bad day. Talked to Jerry O'Connell for most of my workout today. Stanny loves when I talk on the phone; it takes my mind off what he's telling me to do, and I just do it. I'm submissive, a rarity. Saw Amy Sedaris at the gym and tried, unsuccessfully, to convince her to come for a nightcap at ten with Hickey. Liza came by and played with Ben. Took a hard-core nap while Ben did. In construction news, the first floor seems to have been put into the Amagansett house, and I realized I stupidly hadn't planned any overhead lighting in the baby's room in NYC, which I set in motion today, at the ninth hour. Watched the first episode of *The Andy Warhol Diaries* and loved it. (BREAKING THE FOURTH WALL WITH YOU READERS: this series of books is inspired by Warhol's diaries.) Friday movie night was *Cinderella*—the original. Ben LOVED IT. There was a lot of cat action in the movie! It's like 50 percent cat frolicking and cat drama. I convinced myself the evil stepmother was Phoebe from *All My Children*—Google says no. I like the slow pace of an old Disney movie. Wrote for a few hours, watched *Celebrity Big Brother* (and found myself very activated by Todrick Hall and feeling horrible for Carson Kressley), and Hickey came for a nightcap at eleven forty-five. They are knee-deep working on *Plaza Suite*. Another sweet Friday night at home!

## SATURDAY, FEBRUARY 19, 2022

The greatest day with Ben. Saw Sebastian, ate pizza at Zazzy's, made an airport out of Magna-Tiles, drew together, and went to Deirdre's in Brooklyn, where he played with little Isla so well. Then, after twelve hours together, Ben completely melted down when I left for dinner at his bedtime. Met Mayer at Carbone for a celebratory dinner in honor of his selling out Madison Square Garden Sunday and Monday nights. That's gotta be commemorated! I ate like a pig, and we talked and talked. If I was reviewing the dinner, I'd say, "An energizing night of edge-of-my-seat wordplay!"

## SUNDAY, FEBRUARY 20, 2022

Kelly came to play with Ben today. The Spaniard joined us for lunch at the Corner Bistro. Ben and I both took long naps after (mine was delicious, thanks for wondering!). He's been asking for a night-light, and I keep forgetting to buy it. The only Snoopy night-lights I can find online (everything has to be Snoopy or else really, what's the point?) are Christmas ones on Amazon. I bit the bullet. Had a very early dinner at Morandi with Casey Wilson, Danielle Schneider, and Matt McConkey. Was lovely. Was leaving to see John at MSG and explained to Ben that he was going to be playing music for a lot of people, and Ben wondered if he'd be playing "Twinkle, Twinkle, Little Star." Fair question! The show was spectacular. The Spaniard was my date—it was fun being at a concert with a date for once. I'm always intrigued by the amount of straight men who look at John with love in their eyes. He drenches *their* panties too. The guy behind me touched my shoulder and said, "Man, I just want you to know that I feel closer to John because I'm watching the show next to you." I said, "Well, you realize I wrote most of the material tonight, right?" He was confused.

## MONDAY, FEBRUARY 21, 2022

It actually felt like Presidents' Day today, except I wasn't on a plane home from Miami, which would seem like the obvious Presidents' Day activity for me. Instead, I taped a show, worked out, and was back to MSG with Hickey for night two of John, which was pure magic. He does a different show every night, and for this one, John's drummer and one of his backup singers got Covid, so they had to totally reimagine the show, which became mostly acoustic until Questlove surprised everybody and drummed for the last half hour. If last night was all show, this was all heart. We were sitting with John's brother Carl and his wife, Shera, whom I love, and their daughter, who spent most of her first time at MSG fast asleep. I guess that means when Ben is five, I can bring him to see John at the Garden. This just keeps getting more fun!

## TUESDAY, FEBRUARY 22, 2022

Ben kept asking to see videos of John singing. He had a sweet reaction watching it. Wendy Williams is being replaced on her own show. I feel so sad about it—it doesn't feel right. Francesca was here babysitting and sang the entire score from *Frozen* to Ben. The Snoopy Christmas nightlight arrived—it's Snoopy and Woodstock sitting around a campfire with a Christmas tree. The flickering light is cute, but it doesn't emit much *light*. That's my Yelp review.

## WEDNESDAY, FEBRUARY 23, 2022

People are coming back to Sirius. I actually saw Megyn Kelly in the hallway. My girl! I had Lucie Arnaz on the radio and told her I thought her mom was a terrible talk show guest. Good discussion about that and other Lucy stuff. Had a really emotional workout with Stanny, whose whole family is in Ukraine, and Putin has begun attacking them. I was all welled up with emotion, and poor Stan, I can see, is so worried and red-faced and just upset. Of course he is. So many emotions. Trump is supporting Putin. The world is upside down.

I was walking into the building this afternoon and came face-to-face with the ice maker neighbor. I'd been keeping my head down around him, but today I bounded over to him. I had *news!* The noisy ice maker is going into the bar in a few weeks, and the new, quiet ice maker (with the inferior cubes) is going into my kitchen. *When?* He asked as though wondering when the water bottles were arriving in the Sahara. SOON! I said. SOON! And, I said, here's the best part: because of a random series of events, I happen to have an *extra ice maker*, one that is *quiet*. And since I've put you through so much, I'd like to offer it to you. I think he kind of almost smiled, but then he shook his head vigorously. I said, wouldn't that be such a fun way to end this whole thing, on a positive note? He kind of scurried away after that. Got back upstairs and Jose texted me an applause GIF and said, "I give you an A++." That meant a lot—he'd witnessed the entire thing, after logging many complaints over the last couple years. I wish the neighbor would've taken the ice maker. How fun would that be?

Had dinner with Grac and Amanda at Pastis and almost ordered my all-time fantasy order there: double French onion soup, appetizer, *and* entrée. I didn't. Grac got pommes frites. She says if you go to a bistro you have to get it, and that's that. Talked for a while about the prank Grac played on my mom (thirty-plus years ago!) and how that ultimately tainted their relationship since. Here I was, sexless and closeted, and my parents came to visit me during my semester in London. At the Victoria and Albert Museum, Grac told my mom I was in love with a girl in the program who was fairly gawky and unassuming. My mom was in disbelief that after all these years, *that* was the first girl I was in love with. She was so confused, but even more so when she found out Grac was fucking with her. Saw Julianne Moore with her son on the way out. They are lovely.

## THURSDAY, FEBRUARY 24, 2022

It was all bad news today. We seem to be on the brink of World War Three. Cancer everywhere: Jim's sweet sister passed away last night, George has a brain tumor, Larry's husband has stage 4. Then Mayer got Covid again. And Anderson is going to Ukraine this weekend.

Bedtime with Ben almost restored my faith in humanity; he was all snuggles and optimism and coziness. Lit a big fire and talked to Dave on the phone for hours, which brought me back to earth. I posted a fake Wordle page with the word "peace" on it this morning and before bed saw a miles-long thread on Twitter about what a douchebag I am for posting that, and I chose not to read a word of it! It felt great.

## FRIDAY, FEBRUARY 25, 2022

I navigated the tantrum of tantrums before school on the rainiest day. I can't believe I successfully got Ben out the door. *Treacherous.* By the way, the Snoopy night-light that emits dim light BROKE. I paid twenty-four bucks for that hunk of plastic! I blame Amazon. This lady at the gym has been terrorizing me with stories about her beagle, because she knows I love them. She keeps talking to me about Wacha, and I guess she doesn't know I had to rehome him and I don't really want to go through it with her because I know it will be a lot of questions and emotion. Anyway, *enough with your beagle!* Benny's Burritos is closing, so there have been lines around the corner the last few days.

Tonight was Surfin's fiftieth at the Chelsea Italian on Eighth and Sixteenth. Since Surf is the super he invited all the building staff, whom I sat with. Had a lot of fun shooting the shit with Mike, Pablo, and Johnny. I asked them if I'm the biggest drunk in the building. They said not by a mile and that I don't want that title because the titleholders are not in great places. Then Pablo said I'm the "good-time drunk of the building." I embrace that! I can't get over all they see. People dying, coming home with babies, all the secrets people have—these guys see *life.* They are so discreet, by the way, about not saying a word about other residents, and as the only resident at this dinner I was trying! And they love my neighbor Sally Field.

Saw the Atlanta premiere, and it's so good—feels kinda like old times having Shereé back.

## SATURDAY, FEBRUARY 26, 2022

Another great day with Ben. Read him the same two stories three times (*The Gruffalo* and the one about the bulldozer and the flower). Went to say goodbye to Anderson, who is leaving for Warsaw tonight and driving across the border to Ukraine. He is so stoic. It feels different saying goodbye to him when there are two kids in the picture. Mayer said he was on Instagram and weirdly got sucked into a hole of people saying Lucy was rude, which is crazy given my Lucie Arnaz convo about her being brusque.

Texted Marysol Patton to tell her I was coming to Miami at the end of next month and need help with any hotels on Miami Beach. Everything is either sold out or like triple the normal price. She is so connected and so nice. A major hub for the Housewives in Miami.

On the way to dinner I stopped by Benny's—which was mobbed—and did a final shot with the owner, Ken. He said it was just time, after thirty-three years. Then met Chris and Shady Bill at Barbuto. Chris set up my Oculus. I'll never watch porn the same again.

## SUNDAY, FEBRUARY 27, 2022

As Putin is threatening to use his nukes, I'm focusing all my attention on Ben. We went to Padma's for brunch, and in the face of a gorgeous spread of fresh fruits and cheeses and eggs and toast, he refused to eat. The irony of Padma cooking a meal for us—something people would bid good money for at a charity auction—and the boy not wanting to eat a thing made me crazy. After a time-out, he was back at the table, happy as

Tom Colicchio on finale night. Jackie came over for a Sunday-night play and hang. After dinner (and Ben's bedtime), I showed her virtual-reality gay porn, and it was, I think, the funniest ten minutes of my year so far. When you put the headgear on, you're literally in a room with two guys, and when you look down you see that you have legs and are a dude. She couldn't believe she had a dick, which of course came out. I was HOWL-ING at her commentary.

## ▦ MONDAY, FEBRUARY 28, 2022

Ben woke me up at seven, raring to go. I didn't even mind. I marvel at the person I've become: walking around with yogurt stains on my robe, making him breakfast and packing his lunch, having the same conversations over and over. Who am I?! Texted a lot with Anderson, who is in Lviv, Ukraine; he said it's pretty quiet there and he wants to go to Kyiv. If he goes to Kyiv I will not sleep. (Obviously, neither will HE, but that's another story.) Speaking of sleep, last night I dreamed (yes, I'm going to tell you about my dream, I know that's torturous) I was executive producer of *The View*. It was such a lifelike dream—I was having meetings, and we were doing actual shows. I don't want to brag about my talent in totally hypothetical situations, but I was a *great* EP of *The View*. To make this detour even more annoying, I'll report that in the light of day, I agree with my dreamscape self that I would kill it. *Anyway*, as hypothetical EP of *The View* I came up with what I thought was a great idea for a talent/producer hire and called Mary Noonan, who now is in the talent department at ABC, on my walk into Sirius. I pitched her my candidate from the dream and I think she agreed. So maybe she'll do it!

Wound up booking the last great room at the Standard in Miami, and writing this makes me realize I gotta tell Marysol I'm okay. Saw Amy Sedaris at the gym, and we made a plan for Saturday night. She said, "Let's do it up!" So I feel challenged, because we're on a streak of real humdinger dates. Had Lindsay and Carl on *WWHL*, and they really are the Bravo couple everybody's rooting for. Given that they're the current First Couple of Bravo, I offered my (unsolicited) services to officiate their wedding (they're not even engaged yet), and then they told me of Carl's connection to Captain Lee and I said forget it, he should do it! Then I felt stupid for offering. These people have *families* and *lives*.

# SPRING

IN WHICH I . . .

HITCHHIKE IN MANHATTAN

FIGHT WITH A TODDLER BED

BECOME A GIRL DAD

Ben's new thing when I wake him is to ask if it's the weekend, which on the one hand is cute, but on the other, it's metaphorically bumming me out that he's becoming aware of days and schedules and the idea that one day could be more fun than another.

When I don't drink, I dream a lot, and *yes*, I have to make a record of my second whopper dream in a row: John was rehearsing for *SNL* and I was backstage somewhere playing with his crossbow (*I mean*), when Sarah Palin came out with a bunch of toddlers and was trying to teach me how to use it. I was seeking her advice, but her gang of kids were running all over and into my shot. Then I brought my mom in to see John sing "Gravity" and I had to carry her because there were so many people. (Just spitballing here, but does this mean I was playing with John's dick, and Sarah Palin came in and tried to get me to kill my kid, and my mom walked me down the aisle to get John?)

Saw Sandra Bernhard at the gym, and we commiserated over the bleak state of affairs in the world. She walked me to the Associated Supermarket on Seventh Avenue and Fourteenth (Hickey hates it there, but I think he's just being snobby) and explained what the perfect avocado feels like. I think she said a little soft? I forgot. Hit the jackpot when I went inside: a whole fire station full of FDNY was food shopping, which is at the top of my list of events I love to join in progress at the supermarket. Why is a group of dudes in uniform debating cuts of beef SO DELIGHTFUL?! Took a lot of pictures with them for their girlfriends. The Adonis of the group was carrying on about how much his girlfriend was gonna love the picture, and I said, "You should bring her to the show!" but he didn't hear me. So that was bungled.

Ben asked if John serves snacks when he sings. When I said yes, you can get snacks at a John Mayer concert, he said, "I wanna go there!"

## WEDNESDAY, MARCH 2, 2022

Listened to "Gypsy" by Lady Gaga maybe twenty times today. I just rediscovered that song and I'm having a deep moment with it. Tried (unsuccessfully) to teach Ben how to pedal on his tricycle. Midtown is back. People in the lobby of Sirius seemed to have forgotten how the elevators work.

Last week I sent Mom this diary (fourth wall!) because she was concerned about what I might be writing about Ben and whether I was completely invading his privacy or just sharing some cute stuff. The verdict tonight was . . . unclear:

"The BRACELET we got you for your STAR was NOT STAINLESS STEEL! IT'S STERLING SILVER!"

"Okay, I'll change it. What about the Ben stuff?" I asked, hungry for her insight.

"You don't need to have me CARRYING ON about how expensive it was to get my HAIR BLOWN OUT!"

When we finally got to it, after a few more notes, she said the Ben stuff seemed *fine*. All right then!

Dinner at Barbuto with Hickey and Jeff between shows. Sam Heughan was on with Brooke Shields. He is so beautiful, and she comes in looking like vintage Brooke. That nervous, unprepared new TMZ lady was back, waiting for me. She once again couldn't get her question together. She said I make her nervous. I felt bad and stood there as she tried to piece together a question about whether Erika should keep the earrings, but it never really formulated, so I just gave her a nonanswer and walked away. I guess people buy camcorders (I can't believe I used that word again in this book), stick a TMZ sticker on them, and hound celebrities, and if they get anything interesting TMZ will buy it. I think that's how it works. This lady ain't gonna sell anything to TMZ.

## THURSDAY, MARCH 3, 2022

The whole evening was the juxtaposition of me making Ben feel safe and secure while I was reading online that a nuclear power plant caught on fire in Ukraine. After I put him to bed, I watched CNN until the fire was contained. I keep forgetting to buy Ben a new night-light, and I'm kind of frozen because the crooks at Amazon only have like two other Snoopy ones and I don't want to give them my business. This will play out like my Instagram break that lasted a week. And, no, I haven't forgotten my resolution, but I was hoping you had. (I BROKE THE FOURTH WALL AGAIN! I'M TALKING RIGHT TO YOU! ARE YOU FREAKED OUT? I KIND OF AM!) Cher called Anderson during a commercial break tonight to tell him he was doing a great job. Life is a ride.

## FRIDAY, MARCH 4, 2022

Got a new phone today, which means Apple will be announcing a new model in the next forty-eight hours. While it was syncing, I visited George in the hospital. Last night he found out he has a rare form of brain cancer. Time and space felt suspended, sitting in the random hospital room on Second Avenue, looking at my friend of many years and his husband (theirs was the first gay wedding I ever attended, twelve years ago). George is clearheaded and has a line to G-d, and those two are *so* in love. The whole afternoon outside my apartment felt heartbreaking and just *still*, and made more so without the nasty phone, which I'd left home to sync.

My evening was obviously completely reframed after being with the boys. It's trite, but man, did I hug Ben tighter. After a sweet night-night, Amanda and I settled into a long, deep, connected dinner at Don Angie. I needed that companionship.

## SATURDAY, MARCH 5, 2022

All day with Ben. We went to see Wyatt and Sebastian. Unclear how much longer Anderson will be in Lviv. I don't ask him questions I don't think he wants to hear, but I could be overthinking it. Wyatt calls a vacuum cleaner a "cacalo," which sounds like a garbled version of "vacuum cleaner" if you think about it. (And I have.) Bit the bullet and bought another Snoopy Christmas night-light. Ben picked it out (there was only one other choice).

Grac came for a couple hours and told me my movie choice for the night—*Snow White and the Seven Dwarfs*—was potentially problematic. She said there's a very scary forest scene and a knife and I don't know what else, but I went on some parents' movie-review site, and they were rating stuff he'd already seen as too scary for him, so I totally blew off the warnings. The result was that his eyes were POOLS of water during that fucking forest sequence. I was pleading, "It's fine, it's fine, it's her imagination!" But he was SHOOK. The dwarfs you just want to view as cute and not as actual people, and the entire threat to Snow White is because she is more *beautiful* than the (objectively GORGEOUS) queen. Essentially, it's a bit of a twisted mess, but the animation is beautiful, and it's good to link into 1937 every once in a while, right? 1937!!!

Amy Sedaris came over for our Saturday "Do it up!" night and had Ben in hysterics while he was in the tub. Put him to bed, and she and I did up some edibles and had a long hang at the Polo Bar. Our waiter, Caleb, was on to us the minute we ordered: our first course was all raw fish (shrimp, tuna, salmon), and the second course was all fried stuff—zucchini, calamari, French fries. Amy said it was *leather and lace, country and rock 'n' roll.* I want to usher in a raw/fried movement! Later, we met SJ, Matthew, and Hickey after *Plaza Suite* for their dinner at Café Un Deux Trois. It was delicious. Matthew is listening to the same Lucy podcast as I am and did a hilarious imitation of it. Their play just started previews and is already a huge hit.

## ⸬ SUNDAY, MARCH 6, 2022

It was pouring outside and it was the first morning Ben got bored with *Sesame Street.* Had lunch at Corner Bistro and attempted to go to the playground in the mist, but being outside felt crazy to me, and he had a fit when I said we were leaving. I let him play in that random chess park on Bleecker, but then he crouched behind a tree and pooped (in his diaper, not on the ground) and I carried him home to change him. (I could write a lot about potty training, but I'm trying to keep people reading this book, and I know you're occasionally teetering as it is.) After his nap, it was sunny, so we went back to the playground, which was PACKED. Felt like spring almost, and we stayed till dark. Jackie, Jeanne, and Fred came over, and we had such a nice night. Great time with Ben, who adores those women, and a long talk over sushi. I showed them all virtual-reality porn. Minds were blown. (But nothing else.)

## ▦ MONDAY, MARCH 7, 2022

When I say the elevator repair guy in the lobby of Sirius stopped me in my tracks—*holy moly*. On the way out, he was still there, and I threw caution to the wind and traversed back to some '70s-style cruising. His look back said he was gonna throw me some '70s-style punches. Whoops. Still, though, he looked like Henry Cavill meets Brad Pitt.

Dave came to hang with me and Ben. (Ben calls him "my Dave.") He joined me for the first of three *WWHL* tapings (Dionne Warwick and Chris Redd), and it was so good having him. When a friend is there, it kinda perks me up, like when your parents would show up at school. We played a long, drawn-out prank on Melissa, in the control room, where we told her we were going to have her mother ask a question on the show (us putting her relatives on the show is her worst nightmare). It went on and on until I finally told her it was a joke. She was pissed. It was exciting!

The live show was Colton Underwood and Danielle from *Summer House.* I was exhausted and started chugging Mujen the minute we went live. Five minutes later, I'm asking Colton if he's a top or bottom. "Just kidding!" I quickly saved myself. (I'd asked JJ before the show if I had permission to ask but realized as the words came out that it was very 2013. I used to do it a lot—and it was okay back then!) During the commercial break, he said he'd had an answer prepared for the question. JJ was in my ear, and I said I was gonna ask him what his answer was. He said to just make sure I made it clear I was asking because Colton brought it up again and not because I'm a perv. (Along with my often-faulty intuition that gets worse as lines are drawn and redrawn, I have a team of people I rely on to save me from myself.) Anyway, his big answer was essentially that he's vers, so alert the media on that. The media actually *was* alerted when he said he wasn't signing a prenup. His fiancé was in the Oprah chair and looked mortified as I fished around their lives.

The wilder part of the night was that JJ yelled at me in my ear. Like, *yelled*, which you need to know he never does. I am TERRIBLE with the pronunciation of names that I trick myself into mispronouncing. Take, for example, Tan France. I will look at his name and think it's gotta be "Taaaan" with a soft *a*. It's not. It's just "Tan," like a tan from Miami. I could go on and on. Anyway, the *Love Is Blind* couple (that actually got married) were behind the bar, and I got Iyanna's name right the first time I read it. Then they put a phonetical pronouncer in the teleprompter, and it was all wrong from me after that. JJ yelled in my ear every time I got it wrong, which during the third act was somehow twice in a row! It was a war in my ear!

## ⠿ TUESDAY, MARCH 8, 2022

Didn't I say Apple would announce a new phone right after I got one?! Do people *know* when these announcements are scheduled? Is this preventable, or is it a way for me and my phone to meet cute? Brought in the Snoopy night-light when I woke Ben up and plugged it in while it was still dark in there. He felt it was not Christmas-y enough. . . . In Christmas's defense, there was a wreath on Snoopy's house, but Ben would have preferred a tree. This led to a wide-ranging conversation about our Judaism, Amazon, plastic, wreaths. . . . I drove to the beach for a walk-through of the construction site and also stopped at the house I'm renting next to SJP this summer. My place is going to be magnificent—I was preparing for the space to feel small, but walking around felt just right. They built a temporary staircase so I could see the view from my room, and that alone was worth the five hours in the car. I had three shows tonight and I was so exhausted. I ranted about the "Don't Say Gay" bill in Florida during the live show. I'm pretty activated about it. I always feel so positive talking about gay issues at the end of the show when I can. I feel like it's making good use of my platform.

## ⠿ WEDNESDAY, MARCH 9, 2022— NEW YORK CITY TO LOS ANGELES

It was Crazy Hair Day at Ben's school today, but he didn't care to participate, and I was relieved. What would I do to his hair to make it look "crazy"? I'm very much looking forward to styling Lucy's hair when she comes. Instead of doing his hair, we looked for Goldbug in the Busytown book for a half hour this morning, and it was the highlight of my day. Ben "helped" me pack and had his first all-out meltdown about me leaving town. It's five sleeps, which is a long one, so I don't blame him. And I'm grateful it took three years for him to have a minute of separation anxiety about my absence. And (okay, I'll admit it) it kinda felt good to have someone weeping because I was leaving town—an absolute first in my life. Then leaving just felt bad.

Lucy can't come fast enough! Spent an inordinate amount of time on my phone on the plane to LA for the OC reunion, and my timeline is full of Florida lunatics who think I'm a "pedo" and a "groomer" because of my rant about the "Don't Say Gay" bill. Ron DeSantis's idiot press secretary liked a tweet telling me to fuck off. I'm gonna have to confront her at the reunion about it, and she'll blame her social media manager. (*I kid . . .* ) Bruce landed in Mexico for Billie and Austen's wedding, and there are all these B/A logos for the wedding, which I immediately equated to Bruce and Andy. So we can pretend we're getting married all weekend! Dinner with John at the Sunset Tower—we ate inside, almost two years to the day from the last time we were both in the dining room, on the eve of Covid. Told him the Sarah Palin/crossbow/mother dream, and he said sometimes a dream is just a dream. We had caviar (not to celebrate our two-year Covid anniversary) and full-throttle banter. I need to find a gay guy that I connect with as well as John. (Or drag John to join our team.)

## ⸿ THURSDAY, MARCH 10, 2022—LOS ANGELES

For the first time in a year, I got a full night's sleep in Los Angeles, which is a measure of how exhausted I was. The *OC* reunion was delayed a few hours because Shannon had a wardrobe issue, which would make me absolutely nuts if the root of the issue hadn't been that she'd flown out the *Project Runway* designer she'd worked with on the Housewives challenge last year to do her dress, and apparently it was an unsuccessful collaboration. I give it up to them for trying. I had something of a wardrobe malfunction myself; the green corduroy suit I brought had slopy shoulders and looked bad on camera. Oh well.

Noella and Heather were on each other like orchestras playing two different symphonies in different keys—not harmonious! Heather said my weekend destination, the Four Seasons in Cabo San Lucas, is very windy, so that was blowing around my brain. The script for the reunion was unusually tight, and we were wrapped by seven thirty. Met John, B. J. Novak, and Kiernan Shipka at the Tower, which had bad service for the first time in the many years we've been going. It was my second time hanging out with Kiernan, and she's interesting and impressive—so young, but has been working since she was six and so is a simulation of a complete adult in a twenty-two-year-old's body. I was so tired that I considered bolting the table for bed around eleven, but I was too happy to be with that gang so I stayed.

## ⸿ FRIDAY, MARCH 11, 2022, TO MONDAY, MARCH 14, 2022—CABO SAN LUCAS

Got a ride to Cabo, which was divine. Heather was right—very windy! But that didn't detract from the paradise that was Billie Lourd's wedding. It was all warmth and the most brilliant group that only could've been assembled by her. You had representatives of the Louisiana bayous, the Carrie Fisher cabal, Beverly Hills kids, Hollywood, and California hippies—all converging because they loved Billie and Austen. The group also featured many sexually confused, or ambiguous, or just plain cocktease-y guys. Whatever they were, they made for evenings full of possibility that ended with a great night's sleep solo in those great Four Seasons beds. The vows were so beautiful it made me realize I was missing out on true love in my life. A hippie stepgrandma tried teaching me the jitterbug for ten minutes on the dance floor, even though I kept telling her nothing was sinking in.

## ⸬ TUESDAY, MARCH 15, 2022—NEW YORK CITY

If I was searching for True Love, capital T, at the wedding, I found it when I got home last night. What a reunion! Five sleeps were over, and Ben and I were back in each other's grooves. This morning, the workmen were pounding away, and he asked what the new room is for. I told him it was a bedroom. No further questions. (Bruce gave me great advice last year: only answer what's asked, don't give extra details.) I need to tell him about his sister ASAP, but the time is never right! I'm scared of his reaction; I don't want him to feel like his world is going to be rocked in a bad way. The truth is, he's only ever greeted everyone positively, so I know he will greet her with the most love. He visited me at work this afternoon with Wyatt, and I just stared and stared at the photos of the two of them on the *WWHL* set. They're surreal—little mini versions of AC2. Anderson and I texted a lot about them. He's finally coming home from Ukraine this weekend. I'm giving him the biggest hug.

I joined Cameo for two weeks today to raise money for Ukrainian refugees. I raised $120,000 for Biden over two weeks during the election and am hoping to beat it. I don't think I will, though, for a bunch of reasons that I started to type but bored me. Hickey came for a nightcap after *Plaza Suite*, he left, I went upstairs to bed, and then Dave showed up after I'd turned off all the lights. If you turn up at my house for a nightcap, you can guarantee I'm turning all the lights on and putting on the music, and the bar is open.

## WEDNESDAY, MARCH 16, 2022

This morning at breakfast, Ben asked again what the new room was for. I said it's a bedroom. "For *me?*" he asked. Nope. End of conversation. I would've told him then but I had to get him to school in twenty minutes. I'm like a Housewife! *Ben, this isn't the time or the place for this conversation.* Seth Meyers was on the show tonight, and I had dinner with my hot bearded pals Martin and John after at Via Carota. I have fifty Cameos to record.

## THURSDAY, MARCH 17, 2022

Ben got a big-boy (kind of) bed today! One side of his crib got replaced by a smaller rail. He LOVES IT. Have raised thirty thousand dollars on Cameo so far. They're all piled up now, and I do three and stop. Had dinner with Amanda and Jim at the Polo Bar. It always feels festive in there. When we left, there were some wannabe Housewives in there who were on the attack.

## FRIDAY, MARCH 18, 2022

Got shamed twice before nine o'clock this morning. We were walking down the street with what looked like a gal who hadn't left the island of Manhattan maybe ever. There were shoes on her dog's paws, and for some reason she was butt-hurt at me pointing out to Ben that the dog had shoes on, and wasn't it fun to see a dog with shoes. We had a banter going about it, and she turned to me and said, "His paws are *cut*, if you care to know." "Okay," I said. "Okay!!!" Was I that way with Wacha? I feel like I wouldn't *want* to explain, but I don't know.

Shame number two came while dropping Ben off at school. I guess a bunch of the moms were meeting the kids at the playground, and they asked if I was going, and I was going to the Bronx and couldn't. (I'm glad the Bronx is finally making an appearance in the diary. Took long enough.) After eight or so years of storing stuff all the way uptown, Daryn and I were journeying to the past to see what the fuck I have stored and what I can use in Lucy's room or need to get rid of. I got asked twice about the playground and felt ashamed and like a bad dad. But it was a *me* thing and nothing they were throwing at me.

I'm racing trying to finish Lucy's room, order furniture, move out of the Sag Harbor house, and finish the beach house. This is one of the reasons I've been waking up breathless and stressed at four thirty for the last few weeks. I found some potential furniture in the storage unit and walked out with two cool glass orb-y light things.

I keep getting in Ben's toddler bed and having him pretend I'm Baby Ben and he needs to take care of me, like I do him. It's fun, and I get to lie there the whole time. I like games with him where I just lie down. There's a "falling asleep game" where I pretend to be asleep and he tries to wake me up—it's very fun for me! Did about fifteen Cameos today and felt kind of good about that progress. Taping Cameos is like verbal prostitution, but in a positive way. You're saying what people tell you to say.

Ben and I had Friday movie night. I gave him a choice of titles, and he chose *The Aristocats*, continuing his love affair with cats. There was a stereotype warning due to a bad Asian trope and someone calling someone a sissy. Besides those things, we loved it. Ben sat agape the whole time. Eva Gabor was amazing, and we both loved the Scat Cats! Put Ben in his new toddler bed tonight, and he got out of it twice and turned the light on. I told him I was watching, and if he did it again I was taking away *Sesame Street* in the morning.

"I'll try to be good, Daddy," he pleaded cutely.

I then sat watching the monitor for fifteen minutes, terrified I was going to have to follow through with the punishment and thus ruin *my* Saturday morning. John Hill showed up, and we toyed around with ordering some food while watching Ben trying *so hard* not to get out of the bed. Wound up bringing out the best of my Sonja Morgan toaster-oven heating/cooking: a quiche (the spinach-and-mushroom from Associated Supermarket that I love) and some "healthy" pizza (though this is statistically impossible). Checked on Ben at about nine thirty: lights *on*, and him in bed playing with an assortment of random toys from around his room. He had a Cheshire Cat grin on his face when I came in, and it was really hard keeping a stern face while I cleaned up his toys, during which he handed me a plastic bag to put his blocks in (adorable!), but I did. He was not happy to hear that I was following through with his no *Sesame Street* punishment. You gotta follow through on threats you make. And this one makes me more unhappy than him—his *Sesame Street* time is my Wordle/Word Chums/FaceTime Em/Marco Polo Grac time! I'm dropping the bomb tomorrow morning about his sister, though, so now we have more time for that.

## ⊞ SATURDAY, MARCH 19, 2022

The toddler bed is ruining my life. Ben was up at seven this morning, going through everything in his room: the shade was up, he found some scissors in a drawer(!), he went through his closet—just a disaster. And then I broke the news.

### The Conversation

DADDY: Hey, I have something fun to tell you. Wanna hear?
BEN: Uh-huh.
DADDY: You know how there's that room right there, and we've been talking about what's gonna go in there?
BEN: A cat. A doggie!
DADDY: No, not a doggie.
BEN: Yeah, I want a doggie to go in there.
DADDY: No, you know what's gonna go in there?
BEN: Yeah?
DADDY: A little *baby*. You're gonna have a *baby sister*!
BEN: No, no—a doggie!
DADDY: No, you're gonna have a baby sister.
BEN (kind of pleading): No, a doggie! Just a doggie.

DADDY: And you're gonna be a good big brother.

BEN: No, just a doggie.

DADDY: You want a doggie?

BEN: Yeah.

DADDY: Okay. We're not getting a doggie, but we're getting a baby sister.

BEN: Okay.

DADDY: Okay?

BEN: But I want to get a cat in there.

DADDY: You want to get a cat in there?

BEN: Yeah.

DADDY: Here's the thing—I'm allergic to cats. Okay?

BEN: Okay.

DADDY: I'm allergic to cats.

BEN: (sneezes)

DADDY: Bless you! See, you might be too. I'm allergic to cats, but I'll go to the doctor to see if I'm still allergic. If I'm not allergic, we'll have a conversation. But I don't think we can get a cat. But you know what we can get?

BEN: Huh?

DADDY: *A little baby girl!*

BEN: I want a little *doggie.*

DADDY: No, a little baby girl!

BEN: No, a little doggie.

DADDY: Ben, you're gonna be a big brother.

BEN: No, I wanna be a little brother.

DADDY: You wanna be a little brother?

BEN: Yeah.

DADDY: Well, we'll talk about it more later.

BEN: Okay. Read this. (hands me the Busytown book)

A couple hours later, he admitted that babies were cute and that he is "a little excited" to be a big brother. I left it at that. Jeremy came and spent the night. I had an early dinner with Brazilian Andy Samberg (see: *Superficial*) and was in bed by ten thirty, watching *The Andy Warhol Diaries*.

## SUNDAY, MARCH 20, 2022

I hate that fucking toddler bed. Ben was up at seven again, *but* he didn't go in the closet or the drawers or mess with the shade, so I guess I somehow got through to him. We spent three hours at the playground that's full of hot dads in sweatpants and no underwear. (It's too obvious not to comment on.) Anderson is back and met us. I ordered food from Bus Stop Café, and we all ate it in the playground. Jackie and Jeanne came for dinner, and we were all tired but had a ball.

## MONDAY, MARCH 21, 2022

Asked Ben what we should call his sister. He suggested Otto, which is the name of the fish in a book called *A Fish Out of Water*. I said what else, and he went back to wanting a kitty. I suggested he call his sister "Kitty," which he liked. Found a crib and everything I need for Lucy's room, which should be (better be!) done in exactly a month. I am *so over* construction. That being said, I ran into Realtor Debbie at the gym and said we need to find a penthouse with wraparound terraces in the West Village sometime in the next ten years. Outdoor space: I need it.

Did an interview with *Variety* about our *RHONY* plan. It will come out on Wednesday. We have to time when we tell the women about the article coming out—if we don't get it right they'll all leak it, so we have to do it the minute it comes out. Or ten minutes before. Or ten minutes *after*. I feel good about their likely response. Dinner with Hickey. Told him my plan for Miami this weekend is to just relax and work on this diary (FOURTH WALL ALERT!) and then figure out if I want to publish it. (If you're reading this, I decided to publish it.) The big question was whether there had been conversations behind my back among our friend group about me going too far in these books, revealing shit people don't want in a book. He said there hadn't. Craig and Paige were on *WWHL*, and it was a lot of fun. John Hill was behind the bar and was giving me shit on TV in a way no one else can get away with, and it was making me chuckle all night. Said adios to the beautiful Spaniard. It felt very unrequited and romantic. I think I enjoyed leaning into the fantasy of that situation without really getting close to the reality.

## ⣿ TUESDAY, MARCH 22, 2022

I must've really gotten in Ben's head about getting off that fucking toddler bed, because this morning he patiently sat on his bed from 7:00 till 7:20 waiting for me to come get him. I, of course, was awake and watching him, but it was the sweetest thing watching him being a good boy, obeying the rules. We hung for three hours until Margot came. I watched a tour of Kylie Jenner's new nursery, and she has the chicest crib for her baby, formerly known as Wolf. I DMed Khloé to find out where she got it. She's checking for me. I banged out ten Cameos today but have fifty more to do. Fernando Garcia got one for Kathy Hilton.

The *RHONY* story is breaking in *Variety* tomorrow at 2:00. Had a meeting to determine how to tell the ladies what's happening, and we're going to speak to them all after it breaks because we don't trust that they won't leak it. They're the leakiest cast on Bravo—all of them! Ben referred to his sister as "Kitty" today, and it made me really happy. Had Countess Luann on *WWHL* tonight, and during a commercial break she asked what was happening with the show. I said we should talk about it, and she said to come in her room after the show. I said, let's talk late tomorrow afternoon. So little does she know there actually will be real news, finally.

## ⣿ WEDNESDAY, MARCH 23, 2022

*RHONY* D-Day. The story was breaking at 2:00, but Bravo PR got a call from *People* at noon saying they heard there's major news breaking today.

I got off the radio and was in Jenn Geisser's office, trying to figure out the leak, when I realized I said on the radio today that major Housewives news was breaking! *The call was coming from inside the house.* Duh. I'm such a bigmouth. To encourage employees to come back into the office, I hosted a Q and A with Kandi in a large conference room with free lunch. If that doesn't encourage people to come back to work, what will, I ask?

News broke. I said in the article that Jill Zarin would be the first to text me, but actually I texted her a heart. Then Dorinda texted that she thought it was a brilliant idea. Leah texted and said she wanted to be on with the old-school bitches. Heard from former *RHONY* showrunners who were excited. I texted Bethenny, saying, "I think you've moved on with your life, but if there's a conversation to be had, I'd love to have it." Sent her the article, but she kept texting back that she didn't understand it. Then she was texting during the live show that we should make her our best offer and to "hit me with your best shot."

## THURSDAY, MARCH 24, 2022, TO SUNDAY, MARCH 27, 2022—MIAMI

Ben spent the weekend with Ma and Pa. He told Ma, "I'm having a little sister! I'm gonna call her Kitty!" When I told Kelly I was in Miami, she said, "Oh, you're on your babymoon." And I realized that's exactly what this is! Staying at the Standard was the right call—it's the Ultra Music Festival, and all the hotels on the beach are full of thumping music, plus the Delano (my spot since it opened in the '90s!) is closed for renovations. There's a curfew in South Beach due to wild spring breakers, so there was no reason to leave campus. (Although one night we went to Fort Lauderdale.)

The vibe here is delicious. For someone who *passionately* loved the pool scene of the Delano, I can say the Standard puts on a really good show. The Delano crowd stopped being super sexy by the early 2000s, but this place has an evolving sideshow of fun and possibility from sunup to sunset. The pool is huge, overlooking the bay, and is full of (but not crowded with) cocktailing pockets of *Vanderpump Rules* types. My daily MO was: take a little tincture, throw on my hat and shades, and slowly drink a rosé as I snaked around the pool making up stories in my head about the people around me, and sometimes having them rewritten by what I overheard. When you sit day in and day out at a pool, you really open yourself up for any lovely person or complete lunatic to come up to you. Here's a sampler: a lady came up to me daily because she thinks I should do a show about handicapped kids of celebrities, a lady who works at the US Department of Transportation and gave me her card in case I need an "in" with Pete Buttigieg, a libertarian who appreciated my DeBlasio rant, and an Italian muscleguy who started telling me what women at the pool he was banging. (I successfully fanned the flames between him and a sexy tattooed girl, who wound up together later that night.) But mainly I was on a real mellow cloud the whole stay and got little bits of stuff done. Did a bunch of Cameos. Read and loved Molly Shannon's new book. Worked on *this* book and decided to publish it. Oh, I also met a woman poolside who was carrying an old copy of *The Andy Cohen Diaries*, which she was reading for the fourth time, so that pepped me up about writing a new one.

On the last day, I was in the pool with bucket hat, shades, rosé, etc., eavesdropping on a group of guys and trying to nail down their sexuality, which was indeterminate until someone brought up Horse Meat Disco. I was really entertained by the tallest one and had to butt in when he was saying that when he is invited as a plus-one to an event, if he commits, he is also committing to *bringing it*. Whether it be a dinner party or a show or whatever, he gives it 100 percent, because he believes that's the role of a guest-of. I so appreciated the positivity of that sentiment that I had to meet him. Turns out it was Daniel Morgan, who was the guy with the Stealie T-shirt at Chris Williamson's fortieth in New Orleans. He also got into the Dead just from watching the Amazon doc, which I loved to hear. Hung out with him and his friends through the sunset and was so entertained. After many hours of it, we were all transitioning into a dinner situation when I spontaneously went back to the room, suddenly feeling beat.

Cannot believe I ordered room service last night and stayed in to watch the Oscars. I haven't made it through the Oscars in *years*. This year, I was buzzed and tired enough to just stick with it until *it* happened. I was absolutely *shook* watching Will Smith punch Chris Rock. It was disgusting. Took a long bath and had texts going with the *WWHL* kids, Fallon, John Hill, Hickey, Bruce, Liza, Lynn, and Troy. I was up until about two. I couldn't wind down. It was upsetting for so many reasons: my love of those two guys, a physical assault at the Oscars. It was just gross.

Flew back today still in a little vacation bubble that was popped when I was welcomed at Newark with a blast of 27-degree air. It was spring when I left Manhattan. Had a really sweet reunion with Ben, who had a ball with Ma and Pa. We played trains for an hour, and then he "helped me" hurriedly dress for the *Plaza Suite* opening. We all waited *two years* for this opening night! I went with Benjamin (Maisani, not Cohen). It was Laura Linney, Victor Garber, Bernadette Peters, Patti LuPone, Cynthia Nixon, Martin Short, John Slattery, Anna Wintour, and a whole lot more. Of course the Slap was what everyone was talking about on the red carpet. I said I was sad about it and admired Chris Rock's composure—that was my very lukewarm take. Also got a lot of questions about who will be on *RHONY: Legacy*. Last I heard from Bethenny was to make her our best offer, then the next day she posts a TikTok response to the *RHONY* news saying it's "boring." Okay . . .

Sarah and Matthew were so brilliant and FUNNY and PHYSICAL. They were all over the stage like spinning tops for two hours. Matthew's wigs were hysterical—some were new since I saw it in Boston right before it was shut down. Hickey did a brilliant job directing, and audiences are going wild for the two of them. During intermission, I got a glimpse of myself and realized the black-on-black shirt/tie combo I thought I was wearing was actually a black tie on a blue shirt and, instead of looking Prada-esque, looked more Men's Wearhouse. We went over to Scott Wittman's for pizza after the show. Was so fun to watch the play with the

Broderick kids and hang with them after. The girls are old enough now! I stuffed my face on pizza, and there was so much that I was ripping off random geometrics from slices and snacking on them. Was so exhausted from Miami that I left at midnight, went home, and lit a big fire to fall asleep to.

## ⊞ TUESDAY, MARCH 29, 2022

The *New York Times* has a bug up its ass about *Plaza Suite* being written before Me Too, and so the whole review is about that. I'll never understand their nonreview reviews. They do it half the time. It's like you're reading a feature side piece about the actual play instead of a review. Like, they only talked about the problems they have with the play and said nothing about the actors. I'm off from *WWHL* this week but spent the day watching cuts of shows: a cutdown of the *Summer House* season, plus *RH: Ultimate Girls Trip* and the first episode of the Dubai *Housewives*, both of which are going to be great but which I had a bunch of notes on. It's so hard launching a new Housewives show. We go through a lot of cuts getting it all right, figuring out the relationships and making each woman stand out.

I have thirty-nine more Cameos to do and then it's over. We raised a hundred thousand dollars, so that was less than the first time. It was a constant stream of two hundred video messages at optimal pep, so I won't miss doing them. Was supposed to pick up my new car on Long Island, but it's not ready. It's still freezing here, and I lit a big fire in my room and took an hour nap. In my dream, I ran into Eric Freeman on a walk in the woods with his dog. It was so picturesque, and he looked so beautiful. I asked him if he was still gone. He didn't answer, and I woke up in a fog, very teary. Then I fell back asleep and woke up laughing about something! It was an intense hour, and I credit the sound of the fire. Ben insisted we wear matching yellow PJs tonight, which was fun for the twenty minutes we did it. I read him so many books. I'm bossy about what I want and don't want to read to him.

## WEDNESDAY, MARCH 30, 2022

The Seth Meyers producer on the pre-interview this morning said, "You're one of our favorite people!" and I said, "Yeah, that's why you book me at the last minute when your guest cancels." How do you even respond to that? Had a Zoom with the whole surrogacy team, and the vibe is that it'll happen the last week of April, if not before. I'm *thrown*.

## THURSDAY, MARCH 31, 2022

Starting a reunion day at five thirty is never good. Today, a loud alarm was sounding inside my "brain" closet (where all the electronics are), which wouldn't go off. Thankfully it didn't wake up Ben, but I tossed and turned, and in order to turn it off, they wound up having to send someone to replace the equipment (I don't know what the hell it was). So that'll be stupid money for nothing.

I ended the day more drained from a reunion than I have been in a long time. It was old-school *Jersey*. It felt like we were at the Borgata, that's how intense it was. Teresa had just had her appendix out and wasn't supposed to scream, and I guess I don't have to say how that ended. More like, how long did it take? And after I made a huge deal of her being sick at the top of the show, of course she'd been screaming for more than an hour when I even remembered she wasn't supposed to be. So we both forgot. Screamers gonna scream! But the thing went on and on, and Teresa was a brick wall when it came to Margaret. I brought up Melissa not being a bridesmaid at Teresa's wedding, and that was an hour-long sidetrack ending with Joe Gorga quitting the show and leaving. He was back a half hour later, but it was a lot of adrenaline! Speaking of, I almost short-circuited in a way I haven't before. My head almost BLEW OFF! Sometimes people don't *listen*.

Margot texted around five, wanting to know whether I wanted her to take Ben to gymnastics given all the drama with the power and the kitchen. I was like, what drama with the power and the kitchen?! Apparently they were installing the new ice maker and tripped out the power on my lower level. Was texting about it during a massive fight around me between Jennifer and Dolores about something Frank may or may not have said. I told her to call Surfin and go to gymnastics. She said they figured it out.

The show kept going and going and going. There were quick pit stops for dead-end fights, followed by volcanic cacophonies erupting randomly, completely beyond my control. Teresa and I were walking back from her side spat with her brother in the dressing room, and we had a frank moment about how much longer she can stay on this show and feel like it's healthy for her. She seems over it now, and has for a while. She looked a little misty-eyed having the conversation. I said she might decide to leave and come back in a few years. Hard to get off a train, whether or not you really wanna be on.

Got home to find that the new ice maker doesn't particularly *fit* in the space. Hate the cubes too. It's quiet, so tonight will be the best night of my downstairs neighbor's life, but it's not working out so well up here. Was just tired and numb when I got home. Had an edible, put on the Dead, and guzzled a Fresquila. Texted Lauren Eskelin asking for a later pickup time tomorrow morning; back-to-back reunions are not a good idea. Stayed up until one trying to unwind and anesthetize myself from the cloud of questionable juju around me.

## ▦ FRIDAY, APRIL 1, 2022

Ben woke up at seven, cheerful as ever—he like a rushing Colorado River, and I like a dead creek. Got him to school and had an hour to myself, and the fallout from yesterday and questions about where to go with *RHONJ* were very much on my mind.

Melissa Gorga texted me a long stream of consciousness that started with "Wakin' up in the morning, thinking so many things . . ." So she was thinking about it too. I called her, and then Dolores, for some clarifications about some things that were said yesterday. While I was on the phone with Dolores, Theresa, the baby nurse, texted that she had bad news: she was moving back home. "To Trinidad???" I responded. Yes, she said, next month. The blood drained from my face, and Dolores became an adult in a *Charlie Brown* cartoon as I sat awash in the realization that I was severely screwed. This seemed so out of character for Theresa—and JUST as a text from Anderson came in asking if I'd gotten her bad news, I realized it's April Fool's Day. I hung up with Dolores and called Theresa immediately.

"I'm sorry to curse, Theresa, but *what the fuck?!?!?!*" She said she'd been watching *Live with Kelly and Ryan*, and Kelly said that no one loves an April Fool's prank more than I do. I told her I love *playing* pranks, not being on the receiving end of them. Honestly, I was so happy I don't have to find a new baby nurse in a month that I didn't care about the prank. I also realized I had a prank for my family ready to go, thanks to Theresa. I texted my family text chain: "Theresa is going back to Trinidad in a month! I'm totally screwed!"

"Shit," my dad replied.

Mom: "OMG."

Em: "What!!! Why???? For good???"

I said she hates Trump and got in a fight with her daughter. Three minutes later, I sent the "April Fools!" text. They weren't thrilled. "NOT FUNNY!" they all said.

Put on a summer suit for the *Summer House* reunion and settled in for another day poking bears. These bears all stayed asleep; despite a really dramatic season, it was a fairly lackluster reunion. They all looked fantastic, though, and I spent a fair amount of the taping playing "Shag, Marry, Kill" with the guys in my sight line. (I typed and deleted the list here twice—I can't print it because it's awkward to rank a bunch of straight guys who frankly don't want to be ranked by some old man who they probably already are annoyed by. It's for the best!) During the lunch break, I had a mind-numbingly boring conference call with my lawyers; a paparazzo is coming after me for posting a pic in 2018 that he took, so we're going to have to settle. Margot sent me a picture of this solar-system machine she installed in Ben's room so he can lie in bed and look at the stars. I had a pang of feeling like I missed something important because I was at work and missed the stars going up, and I hated that. We wrapped at seven, and

I went straight to Mark Consuelos's birthday dinner in the private room of Emilio's Ballato on Houston Street.

It was so good to see everybody. A friend of Kelly's family said, "Wow—all the channels are here!" And they were. Ryan Seacrest was there, and I guess he really wasn't annoyed by that New Year's Eve stuff because neither of us mentioned it. I told Kelly that her comment this morning led to me being punked by Theresa, and Anderson reminded me of an incredible prank he and I pulled on my mom a few years ago involving a fake story about me receiving a dick pic from a politician. Ryan said, "You say 'dick pic' to your mom, and she knows what you're talking about?"

"She's a very cool eighty-five-year-old!" I said. "And she knows what they are, but I don't, like, *send them* to her."

"Yes, of course," he said.

At dinner Ryan asked me what I've been watching on TV, and I said *The Andy Warhol Diaries*. He asked if there was anything else, and I confessed that I'd just discovered virtual-reality porn, which led to a very funny conversation in which I was trying to explain it all while also keeping it classy. I really liked his girlfriend.

## SATURDAY, APRIL 2, 2022, TO SUNDAY, APRIL 3, 2022—SAG HARBOR

Slept like a *log* last night. On the way to pack up the Sag Harbor house I stopped to pick up my new Audi in the middle of Long Island. Sweet Andrew had done it all for me: transferred my insurance, license plates, set up my Sirius—you name it. Unfortunately for him, on the way back from the bathroom inside the showroom, I fell in love with a different, bigger model. Andrew, knowing I had another baby on the way, had pitched me this one months ago, and I said I didn't want a bigger car. Margot told me a while ago that I needed one too. Well, they were right. Poor Andrew had to reverse everything he did and is looking for the bigger model. So I gotta go back in a month or so and deal with that.

I tried packing things up in Sag Harbor, but it all seemed so overwhelming. I'm under the gun—have to be out of here in a month, after *thirty years* of renting it. I've been in this wonderful love shack longer than anywhere in my life. I'm so sad about it. Went to see my new construction, and that cheered me up.

Had dinner at Sen with Jimmy and Nancy. Jimmy just hosted Kimmel's show for April Fool's, and Kimmel hosted his—was so fun hearing about that. Then a kooky older gal came and sat with us and was blithering on about roller skating for a long time. She and Nan seemed like they knew each other, so Jimmy and I got on some side conversation, and finally he said he actually thought she *didn't* know this lady and that we needed to help her out. I turned around and said "Nice to meet you" twice, firmly. She left. Then Jimmy and I haggled over who was to thank for ending the convo, him for thinking of it or me for doing it. He made me laugh so much. Man, is he funny.

Slept for nine hours, woke up and packed, then went back to the city. Ben has so many toys at the beach house, and I brought him a little plastic cake with which he'd spent a ridiculous amount of time doing cake cosplay during Covid lockdown. He was so happy to reunite with that little plastic cake! There was a meetup at the playground for all the parents and kids from his nursery school, and he brought the cake and then left it at the playground. I promised him when he goes back tomorrow after school, the cake will still be there. Jackie, Jeanne, and Fred came over for playtime with Ben and sushi.

## ⚏ MONDAY, APRIL 4, 2022—NEW YORK CITY

It was Bring Your Best Friend to Work Day: I started the day with Bruce on the radio, filling in for John Hill, and ended it with John Mayer behind my bar. It was also Pajama Day at school, and I put Ben in his cute set, but then he wanted to change into something with the solar system on it. I got him off that and out the door before he could remember he didn't like what he was wearing. Mom texted and said, "WHAT DID YOU TELL RYAN TO WATCH ON THAT MACHINE????" I guess Kelly and Ryan talked about Mark's dinner on their show today, and Ryan intimated that I told him to watch something unspeakable on his Oculus. I told her it wasn't important.

The little plastic cake was nowhere to be found at the playground today. Who would swipe a *little plastic cake*? I tried to teach him a lesson that he really didn't care to learn; he just wanted his cake. FaceTimed with George, who was at Memorial Sloan Kettering, in his second week of radiation for his glioblastoma. He said he's having a hard time following what people around him are saying, that he can't keep up with conversations. I said the truth is that no one is saying much of anything anyway, so just catch what you can, and I promise you're not going to miss anything important. He agreed. Put everything in perspective, that call.

There are three girly onesies hanging next to my desk, and Ben hugged them today. Made my heart burst. I was leaving to meet John for dinner at Via Carota, and Ben asked why we were having dinner. I said he was in town and I wanted to see him. He said, "Are you having dinner because you love him?" I said yes. I had to eat earlyish (seven thirty) because I had a live show. John wondered who my bartender was and said he'd love to do it, so we switched some Netflix women to tomorrow and booked him as a surprise. I said to him before the show that this was going to be so challenging for me, to see him standing there at the bar beyond Ciara and Andrea from *Summer House* in the blue chairs. He said he wanted to be Ed McMahon–ish and was only going to have four-word answers to everything I called on him for, which perfectly calibrated my expectations of him.

The audience and guests were floored when he came out. I started the show by offending nurses when I commented on how beautiful Ciara looked: "You're a *nurse* and you look like *that?*" By the first commercial break, my Twitter was clogged with mentions of what an asshole I am to nurses, and I flashed back to Joy Behar insulting nurses a few years ago and how it plagued her for several months. I think I cleaned it up. I asked John how I did, and he said his woke little heart was satisfied. He had some great lines and energized us all. The fact that he came and did that—*wow*.

## ::::: TUESDAY, APRIL 5, 2022

The construction next door is at a breakneck pace. I pitched Mom the idea of Lucy's middle name being "Eve," and she wasn't buying it. It's bad luck for Ashkenazi Jews to name babies after living relatives. That's how I came to "Lucy"; it's as close as I could get to "Louis" without giving my parents jinx-related heart attacks. Doctor's appointment with Kathleen—she is such a superstar. I'm so lucky, and *very* excited. It's odd doing this under a semicloak of secrecy. I want to shout it from the rooftops but I'm keeping it fairly quiet because I don't want anything to happen to her. I don't know what, and maybe I'm being too paranoid, but better safe here.

Didn't have a second guest to go on with Anitta tomorrow, so I texted Amy Sedaris this morning asking if she'd do it. She said she'd let me know later in the day. I got the sense she really didn't want to do it, so I said we were going to look for someone else but I might come back and beg, to which she replied that she had thought I was asking her to be in the *audience* of the show. I said, "*AMY?!?!* Not the *audience!*" (She really comes at things from another dimension sometimes.)

She said she really hopes we find someone else and that I would really have to beg because she's two steps behind right now. I said, yes, I see that. In other Amy news, Amy Schumer almost cancelled because she doesn't want to talk about the Oscars, but when I got there, she was fine. She had texted earlier that she was bringing her son, Gene, so Margot met me there with Ben, and the boys played. Ben watched the whole show backstage and apparently was laughing at everything I said. That's my son! He kept going up to the screen and kissing it when the doll of Wacha was on. That was his first time seeing the show!

Saw Sandra Bernhard at the gym—we'd been under the impression she was out of town. So we asked her about coming on tomorrow with Anitta, and she booked right in. Sedaris was thrilled!

## WEDNESDAY, APRIL 6, 2022

Anderson was ranked the most trusted person on TV. How cool is that? Now the downstairs neighbor is happy the ice maker was moved but is concerned that it may be bothering his neighbor next to him! As happy as the ending of the ice maker story is, the reveal of the new bar today in my apartment was the very best. Adding the studio apartment where baby Lucy will be, enabled me to expand my bar as a result, and it's just gorgeous. It's a good thing my new favorite watering hole in Manhattan is in my apartment, because I don't foresee myself leaving too much.

Kathleen and I are sending each other basically love notes. If you didn't know our relationship and saw the texts, you'd think we were in love. I think I *do* love her, anyway. She texted tonight saying she's putting together a playlist for the delivery and wants to include some artists that I like. I MEAN? Amazing. Also, it turns out we have the same taste in music. Then she asked if I'm opposed to any scents and if I'd be upset if there was a diffuser in the room. I said, listen, this is YOUR delivery, so diffuse away! She said this was just as much my experience, and making sure I was happy and comfortable would make her more comfortable. The kindness of this woman—and all surrogates—is next-level inspiring.

The *WWHL* taping with Sandra Bernhard and Anitta rocked our world! Before the show, Anitta told me to ask her anything. ANYTHING, she kept emphasizing. Anything. You don't have to tell *me* twice, Anitta! Within the first minute, I was asking if she'd had sex with Drake, and she said something like that she has sex with everybody—men, women, *everybody*. Sandra leaned in and was on fire all night. The show was electric. Brazilian Andy Samberg was there with his pals, and they loved it. We all stayed and partied after the show. It was the high point of a week of shows that included a taping with someone who was so nasty to one of our talent bookers that I thought the booker was going to cry, then came out and was as fake-nice as all get-out to me. That person is now on the (very short) BANNED list.

## ▦ THURSDAY, APRIL 7, 2022

Poured rain all day. Had some real adventures in potty training with Ben today that I won't include in fear of him going on whatever version of *Donahue* exists in 2040 to report what a horrible parent I was for publicly humiliating him. He'll be the B. D. Hyman of tomorrow! (Look it up.) Everybody is getting Covid again; SJ tested positive today, along with five other people I heard about.

After the gym, I had planned to go in my sweaty clothes to say hi to Caroline Stanbury and meet Nina Ali, both of whom were shooting their *RH of Dubai* show open on Twenty-Eighth Street. I stood looking for a cab on Seventh Avenue in the pouring rain for fifteen minutes, until I was soaked and actually screaming like a madman by the time a truck driver pulled over and offered to give me a ride downtown. First, he started asking me what I would pay a cabdriver, and I said I have no cash, so if this is about me paying you, I could Venmo you. He said forget it, but now you have to do a favor for someone else today. I was trying to convince him to let me put him on my Instagram, but he wouldn't let me. Then his wife called, and I asked her if she watched *Housewives*. She did, and she flipped that I was in the truck. We FaceTimed, and I gave them tickets to *WWHL*. He dropped me off right at my door!

Toured a school in the neighborhood that's a possibility for Ben. Balloons had arrived for my baby shower tonight, and Ben was frothing at the bit to play with them. The shower was a ball—Grac arrived early to set up games, which I immediately fought until she said, *you have to have games at a baby shower!* John was there with a woman he was on a second date with. I loved her. They couldn't figure out where to eat, and I wound up texting Waverly Inn for them, asking for a table "tucked away." He sang the cutest off-the-cuff song to Ben on the way out. Ben and Wyatt were total buddies and they were extra hyped about the party: Games!

Presents! Jackie gave me a few monogrammed items all with the big L, like Laverne DeFazio. Incredible. The bar is lit wrong, so we need to fix it fast!

Before bed, Ben kept asking for another hug and kiss. He was complaining that he couldn't hear the party. I said it was ending and everyone was leaving, which wasn't true. He didn't feel like he should have go to bed before cake was served. I said we would have it tomorrow, and he wanted to know if that meant we were having another big party tomorrow. Not sure most baby showers end with the same drunken energy as mine, but it was perfect.

## ⦙⦙⦙⦙ FRIDAY, APRIL 8, 2022

"Daddy, it's a *mess* in here!" was Ben's assessment of the living room when he went downstairs this morning. That and "John sang me a special song last night!" were his take on the whole thing. I'm trying to figure out lighting at the bar with the contractors. Texted with Lindsay Denman about *The Andy Warhol Diaries*. Watching the section about AIDS hit us both; since we were newbies in New York in 1990 we feel like we got through it by the skin of our teeth. I feel like I was the baby on the construction site, just blithely missing all the swinging hazards. Stopped by another intro shoot for Dubai to meet Chanel Ayan, who has major star quality (she brings a goat to a Thanksgiving dinner as a hostess gift!), Caroline Brooks (she's Phaedra's friend and responsible for her cameo!), and Lesa Milan (who was in the middle of holding her gold coins). By the way, they're either going to hold gold coins or sunglasses. I voted strongly for gold coins! I took a long nap, then watched *Peter Pan* with Ben: rife with horrible stereotypes about Native Americans, but also an alarming soliloquy from Wendy about the importance of having a mother, followed by a song on the topic. I was asking him all sorts of questions about the movie to distract him. Put him to bed and met my hot, bearded pals Martin and John for dinner.

When I left, I told Francesca, the sitter, I would be back either at eleven, at twelve, or in the two thirty range. Dinner at Cookshop, which was very gay. We got to the Eagle at ten thirty, which turned out to be wildly too early; the time to go is twelve fifteen, we discovered. They play porn there, and I was correctly predicting what was going to happen. (I cannot believe I'm patting myself on the back for predicting what happens in a porn movie, but I'm not averse to handing myself an accolade.) They had DJs on two floors. The heat is on in the upstairs bar, so it feels humid and kinda dank, like you're in the Florida panhandle in the middle of the day. "Love Hangover" never sounded as good as it did on that dance floor. Saw a sexy *Housewives* editor. Though it's really the time to arrive, I texted Francesca at twelve fifteen that I'd be home in the next thirty minutes and was quite pleased with myself when I arrived home precisely thirty minutes later. She said, "Did you have fun?" and I felt as if I was twelve and *I* was the one being watched by a babysitter. By the way, I was so tired I didn't even care that I left that place when it was just starting to get great.

## ⊞ SATURDAY, APRIL 9, 2022

We debriefed *Peter Pan* this morning while Ben was on the potty. He hated Captain Hook and the alligator, kept referring to Peter Pan as the "little green man," and was indifferent to Tinker Bell, which blew my mind. I kept showing him pictures of Tinker Bell and saying, "Don't you *love her*!?!" Not sure why I cared. By the time we got to Zazzy's for lunch, he was all ears about Tinker Bell.

Went to the playground after nap, and it was full of his school friends and their parents. It rained, like a light mist, and the place cleared out except for me and Maia and her mom. Late dinner with Shady Bill at Cafeteria, which is where you go to find the '90s gay scene. It's frozen in time, in a lively, good way. The bathrooms are unisex, and I guess I didn't lock mine completely—a woman half walked in on me, and then stood in front of my door absolutely flipping out that I didn't lock the door. When I walked out and she saw who I was, she quickly transitioned to apologizing for opening it. I had no respect for that. Don't give me a pass because I'm famous! We went to Loic's birthday party in Midtown and met some guys from Barcelona who'd never been to NYC. They were saying that every corner of the city is like it's out of a movie, and that's exactly how I felt in my early courtship with this place. Couldn't find a cab anywhere, and Lyft was doing that thing where they say they're three minutes away but you see they're coming from across town. So I was revving up for a fit when a sweet couple pulled over in their SUV. "Andy Cohen! Want a ride?" For the second time in three days, I said yes. How awesome. He's a doctor, and she's expecting a son in June. We got to know each other and took selfies. When we got out, Bill said, "Oh, you really had to keep the ball in the air in that car. You were so *friendly*." I said I was a car prostitute—I'm charming for a ride. Went to Motel 23, which I've been hearing about for a year. I can't think of another way to put it, but if you were looking for a twink, it was paradise. (AUTHOR'S NOTE: WHILE I HAVE NOTH-ING AGAINST TWINKS, I DID NOT GO TO THE BAR LOOK-ING FOR ONE.) It was so fun. I want to go back.

## ⬛ SUNDAY, APRIL 10, 2022

Ben got me up at seven fifteen, and it was rough. Absolutely no hangover—I was just tired. Visited Wyatt and Sebastian Cooper and family. Read Wyatt and Ben a dinosaur book. Anderson has been feeling like crap and slept eleven hours last night. Got Bus Stop Café to go and brought it home for lunch. We were both so tired by one thirty that we simultaneously crashed for naps. Matt and JJ came by to hang with Ben; he was in the hall with Matt at one point, and "Hung Up" came on, and he turned on the disco ball and instigated a dance party. I was BURSTING with pride. MY SON! He made up a dance that was all about flying.

Anderson texted that he has Covid. So duh. When someone tells you they feel like crap and slept eleven hours, they're telling you they have Covid. It's been two years of this bullshit, and I'm still too stupid to let it fully penetrate. Bruce says he found a note I wrote him for Ava's baby shower, when we thought he was going to name her Lola. In the note, I said I was excited to get her monogrammed clothes to look like Laverne DeFazio—which is exactly what Jackie got for Lucy. We like what we like! I always like when I show consistency in opinions; it makes me feel like I'm not losing my mind. Had dinner with Hickey and Jeff at Le Zie, which unfortunately tastes better when you eat outside than when you're in the dining room. We were in the dining room. Came home and worked on my Molly Shannon interview for tomorrow and got a massage from Adam.

## MONDAY, APRIL 11, 2022

Ben was driving me nuts today, and I was starting to lose it, which never happens to me. But the more he was pushing me against the wall, the more cheerful and cute he was, which fully brought me back into his corner.

The morning hot topic on NY1 was whether to accept rides from strangers, spurred on by my posting on Instagram about the two people who picked me up. People were tweeting at me about it, and then I brought it up on the radio, and the phone lines were jammed. People had *opinions*. It's not that deep, and I think I can tell if a pregnant woman and her doctor husband are going to kill me before I get in their SUV. (Famous last words.)

On to *WWHL*, where I taped two shows. My phone was blowing up with messages from random people: Countess Luann needs to talk, and Taylor Armstrong is pitching herself to be on *RHOC* because she lives there. That's not the worst idea. Then out of nowhere I heard from Wendy Williams, who has really been off the grid and hasn't returned texts or responded to flowers. She sounds like herself—Wendy Williams with the strong, booming voice. But the longer I talked to her the more she started to sound a little off. I asked her if she would consider coming back to radio—because wouldn't that be a coup, to have her in the morning on Radio Andy? She said she won't do it again and started mentioning something about having security at radio, which confused me. (Later I talked to Liza, who said there *was* security for Wendy at radio, so maybe I was the one not making sense.) Then I heard from Liz Rosenberg, calling to say she won't be there for the Michael Bublé taping. Hadn't talked to Liz in a long time, and of course

I only wanted to talk about Madonna, whom she represented forever. She indulged me.

After the taping, I raced up to Symphony Space to interview Molly Shannon, who was as wonderful as you'd ever want someone to be. It was a lively conversation inspired by my absolute devotion to her and her book. She is so pure of emotion—just inspiring. Met Jeanne and Amanda at Dragon Sushi on the Upper West Side, where we ran into Liza and Brian. Liza was at Café Luxembourg today and saw a very famous, *very* rich TV personality split the check with a young gay guy. We couldn't figure out why she didn't foot the bill. Amanda found a Hamptons rental for the summer, and her landlord's name is Nanette. She has rented homes from *three women named Nanette!* That's just nuts. I've never met one Nanette in my life, and she has three Nanette landladies.

## ⸬ TUESDAY, APRIL 12, 2022

This morning was a meeting with the contractors about how to properly re-light the bar, during which Ben was being utterly delightful. Went for a physical—I'm fine. There were no cabs anywhere around Columbus and Sixty-Sixth, and I was ready to hop in the car with the first stranger who wanted to pick me up. No such luck! I was, like, trying to advertise my face to the drivers. Pathetic! Finally found a cab and went to my lawyers' office to update my will. They brought in two witnesses to watch me sign, which reminded me that when I was at CBS News, I was pulled into a conference room by Andy Rooney to witness *his* will. Leaving the law office, a taxi cut off a guy in an Audi in order to pick me up. The Audi guy freaked out, and I started screaming at him to learn how to drive in Manhattan. I don't know why I fought so hard for my cabdriver, but it felt good! (Also, I was in the wrong, so there was that.)

Had a parent-teacher conference about Ben, which seems like overkill for a three-year-old who spends nine hours a week there, but I ate up every word. He seems to be doing great! *Us Weekly* found out that I'm having a kid, and now I can't figure out whether to announce it myself or what.

I'm worried for my surrogate's privacy. Jenn is going to try to get it killed. I'm eating like a pig these days. Back to my pre-Covid weight from last December—it's disgusting. Watched a subpar episode of *Atlanta* that I'm praying will get better, worked out with Stanny, took a twenty-minute nap, and headed to *WWHL* for two shows. FaceTimed with Mayer on the way; he's in a shitty hotel in Nashville that's trying to be super urban but failing. The first show was Molly Shannon and Craig Robinson. She was as delightful as ever, and he was super stoned and lovely. The live show was the woman from *My Unorthodox Life*, which I keep wanting to call "My So-Called Unorthodox Life." Literally, I messed it up so many times. Went home and looked at the temporary fix for the new bar lighting for ten minutes (I think it works!) until I got a headache and crashed.

## ⦙⦙⦙ WEDNESDAY, APRIL 13, 2022

Radio this morning, then a Covid test for *Today* at 30 Rock. Ran up to Bravo to see if I could kick up some trouble on the fourteenth floor. I didn't, but people are back to work, and there are new people on our floor, and I keep getting asked for pictures. I've never had that happen before at work. Caroline came to do my makeup, and Teresa called because she heard I was ragging on her on the radio this morning—that I said she's good TV until she's not. I told her that what I actually said was that *throwing plates* is good TV until it's not. Big difference.

Photo shoot at Cubbyhole for *The Hollywood Reporter*, which is naming me their Unscripted TV Player of the Year. Not sure why this is happening in April, but it's a good title. Daryn met me at the shoot to help me join TikTok for this live musical I'm hosting tomorrow on the platform. At home, the big buzz in the building is that there's gonna be a doorman strike starting next week. So I need to get all this shit for Lucy's room delivered before then—the crib and everything!

Taped two shows. First was Matt Rogers and Karen Huger. Matt did a rant at the end, in the style he does on his podcast. We let him pick the topic, and it turned out to be a savage anti–Gia Giudice thing that I had to recuse myself from, and when I went in the control room after the show Deirdre was concerned that it felt like an attack on a kid. Spoke to Matt in his dressing room after, and he wound up doing another rant, saying Mauricio isn't the hottest househusband, it's Evan Goldschneider. He was a real pro about it! The live show was Heather Dubrow and Garcelle. I think I inadvertently insulted Terry before the show. We have a running joke that I've never seen *Botched*, but maybe now that it's been on for so long it's not so funny to him. I asked Garcelle about her love life, and she said, "It's dry, like yours!" That got a lot of pickup, with people saying I was offended. I loved it. Banter! Repartee! It was our last show of the week (our proverbial "Friday night"), so I had JJ remind me in my ear to take an edible during the second commercial break, which I knew would kick in about twenty minutes after the aftershow ended. My timing was perfect, and we went to the Cubbyhole after the show with Danny, Nick, Anthony, and JJ. It was packed, and though it is an always-mixed lesbian bar, I felt like we were the only guys. Met Hickey at Corner Bistro and drank outside. Lots of laughs, and I solved a decade-old *WWHL* mystery that I can't put in print. Stayed up later than I wanted to before cohosting *Today*.

## ⠿ THURSDAY, APRIL 14, 2022

Ben woke me up at seven o'clock. Potty training is going well, and I can take none of the credit—it's all Margot. Thank G-d for her. Cohosted with Hoda, which is my idea of a great morning. I absolutely love her, and the whole vibe is easy and fun. Everyone tells you to have fun on their show, but on that show you actually do. During host chat I asked her something about whether she's dating, and she shut me down *hard*, which resulted in an awkward moment. We had the young women who wrote the *Bridgerton* musical; they told me during the break that they want to do a *Housewives* musical. I'm on it!

Everyone's talking about the doorman strike. I was opening a present and Ben cheerfully said, "I bet it's for my *sister!*" Looked at furniture for the beach house with Jackie, who found some very cool Brazilian stuff!

We found a pair of chairs and two potential coffee tables. I hosted a live musical on TikTok on Broadway in the '90s, then back downtown for dinner at SJP's.

## ⠿ FRIDAY, APRIL 15, 2022—NEW YORK CITY TO SAG HARBOR

Moving is so emotional. Today was the day. I packed all the pottery. Donated a ton of books and also kept so many I don't know that I *need* at my new house but that will make it feel homey, like Kitty Kelley's *Nancy Reagan* and *The Andy Warhol Diaries*. I need those at any home I'm going to be at, whether I crack them or not. I kept Susan Lucci's memoir but chucked Sally Jessy Raphael's that I found among the giveaway books at the Sag Harbor dump. I *love* the Sag Harbor dump. Wow, that's another thing I'll miss—my dump. I kept my disco Buddha, and the green felt Snoopy, and all the random As, which might go in the trash later.

I've lived in this sweet little hideaway on the Bay longer than anywhere in my life, including my childhood home. I began so many important friendships—with Bruce, the Perskys, Joe Mantello, Ricki Lake. I wrote all my books here, learned to DJ while trapped in a snowstorm, spent quality time with three boyfriends, witnessed the beginnings of the relationships of Grac and Neal and Dave and Ally. . . . I had Lyme disease here but thought it was a spider bite for weeks. I spent years hearing Mark and Kelly honk every time they drove by . . . went through phases where I ran by the water. . . . The *one* year I didn't attend the ceremony, I won my only Emmy from across the country and I watched from my living room with my mouth on the floor while my *Top Chef* colleagues climbed to the stage. I spent four months here during Covid with my son, seeing it all through his eyes, raising the blinds in his room to see the boats and waves and clouds and swans—and, after his bedtime, sitting on the deck alone, lights twinkling and waves crashing, listening to music and drinking rosé, which was glorious.

After spending all afternoon packing and reminiscing, I met Jeanne and Fred at Sam's. Graham is riding high off his triumphant bartending experience at *WWHL*. He said they got calls from all over the country wanting to know if they'd freeze pizza and ship it, with multiple calls coming from Mississippi, of all places! Mississippi needs good pizza! I'd just cancelled my order of a medium mushroom-and-onion to go, for me to freeze at home, when Graham came over to say he'd bought us dinner. I should've gotten the medium! Came home and blasted music, lit a massive fire, watched *RHUGT*, and had a party for one on my last night in my special love shack. Remembered being downstairs, sharing the two twin beds with John Shea one night (not sure how that happened)—we were just dozing off, and I guess he was breathing heavily, and I kind of mumbled asking him if he wanted a hit of my asthma inhaler, which he heard as, "Wanna eat my ass maybe later?" We howled for hours down there when we realized it, and still say it to each other.

Texted with Kathleen, who said tomorrow is the peak of the full moon, and it's called "pink moon." She said she had two of her babies on full-moon days and to start sleeping with my phone on! The future is now.

## ⠿ SATURDAY, APRIL 16, 2022— SAG HARBOR TO NEW YORK CITY

Jeanne came by to supervise all my piles of stuff that's coming to the new house, stuff going back to NYC, and stuff going to charity. She approved. Then the caretaker came by and we went through it all, and of course I'd forgotten a closet full of crap like stereo equipment from the early aughts (recycle pile). FaceTimed with Bruce and had one last look around with him. We talked about us sitting on the porch playing backgammon in the mid-'90s, shooting the shit and speculating about our future. If he'd suggested I'd still be in this place in my fifties, with a family, I would've shut the conversation down. It would've been too much to envision. All this reminiscing led to, as John called it, my Mary Tyler Moore moment, saying goodbye to the house. I did a slow walk-around, looking at the rooms and letting the years of memories wash over me. I worked myself into a really good heaving cry, but it was ultimately a happy one. For *years* I said to anyone who asked that the only way I'd ever leave this sweet little house was if I got a house on the ocean, never expecting I'd be able to afford one. The fact that I'm leaving for my dream house—which I'm filling with my own family—feels like a fantasy.

## ⠿ SUNDAY, APRIL 17, 2022—NEW YORK CITY

Easter Sunday wouldn't have been complete without Ben visiting Amy Sedaris's rabbit, Tina. When I got back to the city yesterday afternoon, I'd texted her (Amy, not Tina) hoping for a spontaneous late dinner. She was in, so we went to Il Cantinori, which lived up to its nickname ("Il CantAffordy")—*so* expensive. But *so* good—I ate like a pig at a trough, and shouldn't even be commenting because Amy paid. Anyway, Ben kind of terrorized Tina the rabbit. Had a low-key Passover Seder with Jackie and Jeanne at my place. We put *The Aristocats* on again, and Ben was transfixed.

## ⠿ MONDAY, APRIL 18, 2022

Doorman strike seems imminent. We'll know for sure by Wednesday night. I can't imagine the havoc this'll wreak: I signed up for a slot manning the door on Friday. I'm perhaps spending too much time thinking about the mechanics of the trash. Also, there'll be no deliveries at all. Not optimal for the days following a birth! Kathleen is in an Airbnb in the city waiting for Lucy. Bruce is supposed to come in on May 2 to be in the delivery room with me, but all signs point to her coming way before then. Ben is off school this week, and all his friends have Covid, so he had a pretty boring day. Potty training is going so well, but we keep him naked from the waist down as much as we can so he thinks before he does his business. He loves going into the new room and saying to the foreman, James, "So tell me about your day." James seems less amused by it than me. Now the ice maker in the kitchen is on the fritz, and Ben said to James, "The ice makers in here never work!" He's right! Interviewed Lizzo on the radio today and was asking her about her new boyfriend and whether it was hard dating someone when you're the superstar and he's the normal one. When she walked out (with her massive posse), I was told the boyfriend had been standing three feet from me in the studio. So then I felt bad.

## ⊞ TUESDAY, APRIL 19, 2022

The crib is in! The daybed is in! Lighting behind the bar is in! Ben's new dresser is in! And we found out at the end of the day that the doormen have reached a settlement! Just when I was kind of beginning to look forward to my shift on Friday. Ben keeps wanting to go in his little sister's room and play, which makes me excited. Went to the dentist. They said Anderson was there yesterday. (He turned me on to that joint.) Went on a walk around the block with George, whose spirits are just spectacular. He is facing glioblastoma as head-on as he can.

Sheree texted: "Hey Andy, I hope all is amazing! I hate to complain but I really dislike the tagline they have chosen for me this season: 'There's no OG greater than SHE!' I just I feel it's not as strong as the other option. Coming back for the third time as an OG, I feel like my tagline should be stronger, a bit shady but also something the people will relate to me. The one I feel is dope is, 'Spring, Summer, or September, I'm the one you'll ALWAYS remember!' What are ur thoughts?" I thought about it and agreed. The team did too; if we have time to replace it we will. Live show with Melissa and Jackie. Felt bad knowing Jackie's going to be demoted tomorrow. I really like her. Went to Hickey's for a nightcap after the show, then came home and stared at my new bar for an hour and wondered about Lucy.

## ⊞ WEDNESDAY, APRIL 20, 2022

Went to Midtown today with my zipper down and shoes untied. I dropped Ben off at school in this state. I realized it at Starbucks on Forty-Ninth. I love it there. Good crew work there.

Lucy is 8 pounds! Went to her doctor appointment. All seems to be going well! Today is the last day at the apartment for James (the construction foreman), and Ben told him he loved him. Not sure James knew what to do with that. At the end of the day I got word that NeNe is suing us for racial discrimination. What a sad end to a relationship with someone I adored and put on a pedestal for years and years.

## THURSDAY, APRIL 21, 2022

"Lawsuits! Tag, you're it!" That was the text I woke up to from Erika Jayne. That made me chuckle—me and Erika. Ben got me up at seven, and I felt like shit with allergies. Cynthia Bailey texted. Also heard from Garcelle, and got some voice notes from Kim Z-B. Harvey Fierstein and Matthew Broderick were on *WWHL* tonight. It was a lot of fun. Dinner with Liza at Morandi. Found out tonight that today is the five-year anniversary of Sandy Gallin's death. His departure still leaves a gulf in a lot of people's worlds, mine included.

## FRIDAY, APRIL 22, 2022

Got Wordle in two tries (the word was "plant"), which is even less interesting in a diary than it is in a tweet. Theresa came to sort through all the baby stuff we packed away two years ago. Felt very efficient. She is off duty with Sebastian the minute Lucy comes home from the hospital. Told some parents at the playground today about Ben's new sister, then I went to the gym and LOUDLY told Sandra Bernhard about Lucy's arrival. If I'm trying to keep this a secret, why I am screaming it in the gym?! Then Amy Sedaris walked in and started screaming "Racist!!!" at me. She knows exactly how to destabilize a situation for maximum effect. First time I've laughed about that lawsuit. Wyatt's birthday party was very sweet. Kelly is really great at a kid's birthday party—she knows what to do! Dinner with Jane Buffett, and my allergies were beyond terrible. Walked home from Via

Carota through a THUMPING West Village. It was electric. It's Florida here now—everyone is on top of each other, and there's a new variant, and it's fine; everyone is vaccinated and just dealing. Asleep by ten thirty.

## ⊞ SATURDAY, APRIL 23, 2022

Amanda came over, and I told her I wanted her to be Lucy's godmother. She taught Ben how to play tic-tac-toe. Lunch with the Cooper-Maisanis at Zazzy's, then the playground. Allergies still terrible. Ben fell out of his bed during nap, and that was a big roadblock. Visited Hickey. Dinner with Brazilian Andy Samberg at Cookshop at nine. Cookshop is coming back into my rotation after all these years. It's consistently good and, while there's always the possibility of a Sandy Bernhard sighting, we instead got Gus Kenworthy, which was fun in a different way. There won't be many lesbian farm-to-table joints where BAS is going, in Brazil, for a month. I "made" him go to Rebar after, at ten fifteen, which is I guess my new daddy-friendly time for going out. I thought it would be empty, and it was about a quarter full, which at first thrilled me. I felt like I was at the Met Ball. After about eight minutes that wore off, and it felt on the edge of sad. A guy came up to me and said, "I just want you to know that you're an inspiration in every-thing you do, *no matter what anybody says.*" Uh, thanks?! He continued, "You inspire me in what you do, *whatever it is you do.*" I said thanks and kept it moving. Was asleep by eleven thirty.

## ⊞ SUNDAY, APRIL 24, 2022

Today was a day when I wanted to bang my head against a tree by 11:00 a.m., and it made me wonder how I'm going to do with two kids. We were up so early—Ben started, guns blazing, at seven—and I was a hobbling, allergic, wheezing mess, and Ben was (adorably, even!) not listening to a word I was saying to him. While I sorted through my Wordle (got it in three), something instinctually told me I was supposed to be at Lu's cabaret last night. I texted her, and she said she was JUST thinking of me and wondering the same thing. She wants me to come in a couple weeks. And she wants me to post her tour dates.

Spent three hours at the more industrial playground down the street, and Ben and his pal Adrian just played in the dirt, looking for roly-polys, which is what I was doing in the leafy suburbs of St. Louis with Mike Goldman as a kid. So I feel like he's getting *some* nature. I was exhaustedly slumping around, magnetized to various benches around the playground, as he wandered (the cutest run ever, still) from one spot to the next. I felt like a cuck watching this dad who was super active with his two kids: *Running! Climbing! Hiding! Yelping!* (I'm trying to use more cuck references in polite conversation.) So the dad was already making me feel very old when I realized he *only had one leg*. The guy was a superhero. I have two, and I couldn't get off the bench. I did figure out a way to engineer chicken fingers from Bus Stop Café to the playground, though, so I wasn't all bad. After an hour nap (for us both), Jeanne came over to organize the new bar, and Jackie and Hickey soon followed. Hickey tested us all for Covid, then headed off to DC.

I had completely *had. It.* by five thirty. Wound up ordering sushi and folding: put Ben in front of *Encanto* at six thirty. He was riveted and said his favorite character was still the "princess"—who is actually just the vain oldest sister. He's susceptible to beauty tropes!

## ⠿ MONDAY, APRIL 25, 2022

Up early with Ben for his first day back at school. He told me I'm "such a good cooker" this morning over his toast with jelly, reheated quiche, and dry cereal. I felt like Ina!

Radio was fine. I often talk on the show about going to Toasties on Forty-Ninth before we go on-air, and so the last two weeks there have been listeners who've dragged their cameramen (husbands) along to offer to buy me breakfast and say hello. I say no to the offer but do take a pic.

Hopefully my killer isn't listening to Radio Andy. John made me download the new iOS so I could get the pregnant man emoji.

Stopped by Bravo to look at Atlanta taglines (Sheree's choice is in) and got an update on this upfront thing. It's at Radio City in a few weeks, and they're doing a massive number promoting BravoCon. They pitched me the creative last week, which had me doing a pre-shoot that I don't have time for and singing and dancing. Happily, the dream sequence has been killed, and I don't have to sing. I told them I *really* don't want to dance. Went to Dr. Gwen, who is the best throat doctor in the city and has helped Celine Dion and John and everyone else who sings. She happens to have the best machine in town for sucking out ear wax, and I should go at least once a year given that I stick an earpiece in every night on the show, which stuffs wax in my ear canal, which builds up and creates a mess. Sure enough, she looked in, said it was awful, and dumped something-oxide in my ear while I sat, head tilted, for twenty minutes, reading Bravo research on *Ultimate Girls Trip*. She moved me back and, over the course of five minutes, delivered what looked like a fetus out of my ear. I was carrying on so much that the women down the hall waiting for the throat scope portion of the appointment were alerted. They ran down the hall to see what all the yelling was about! Gwen asked me if I wanted to *take it home*. That's how big it was, that I should've made it a souvenir.

Lots of *WWHL* booking shit happening today, and I was at the show for a marathon of tapings. I held people all over the office hostage with my ear wax story. One A-list guest for tomorrow cancelled, and it was a whole domino effect. We're gang-shooting shows to prepare for me being off next week for Lucy: First was Gary Janetti and Margaret from *RHONJ*. It was a classic hodgepodge of notables—the drag queen Bendemic behind the bar with Brad Goreski, Marge Sr., and Marleney the housekeeper in the front row. Marlo Hampton was there getting ready for our "Marlo Gets a Peach Party" episode, and I brought Brad and Gary back to meet her, and they said it was like the Bravo version of them meeting Princess Margaret. The last show was Vanessa Bayer and Paige from *Summer House*, who both reported being starstruck from seeing Marlo in the hallway. Kathleen is coming to the show Wednesday night! That will be surreal. Got her tickets to *The Music Man* for tomorrow. Trying to keep her and Lucy entertained!

Raced home to kiss Ben goodnight. An hour later was high—and high up—at Jane Buffett's birthday party, seventy-something stories above Central Park, and wondering how our unbooked shows will resolve themselves. Then I got out of my head. The lighting is so great at Jane's, always. Felt great to see her whole crowd together after two years of the pandemic. People are so buzzed to be out. I told everyone I'm seconds away from a baby and my ringer is on. People really don't understand the basics of how surrogacy works, and then you put the words right to them, and they get it. There was apparently a love letter to Jimmy's retirement homes in the *New Yorker*. And Jimmy tells me he's launching a Margaritaville cruise ship. When he walked away, we speculated he could start a chain of cemeteries so people could get buried into a lifestyle, which seems like it would then cement the whole thing into a religion. Hung out with Leon Robinson for a long time. He's one of those people that I love seeing at the Buffetts'—always a great hang. He says Cynthia is thriving after *RHOA* and is getting a lot of acting stuff. Was home by ten thirty and fell asleep feeling light as a feather with my clear ear canals.

## TUESDAY, APRIL 26, 2022

I've been trying to unsubscribe from Domino's Pizza's email list for pretty much the whole year. I reached a new level of fury today.

## WEDNESDAY APRIL 27, 2022

I was an absolute disaster for the entire day today: sputtering, erratic, emotional, and totally exhausted. I blame the fucking toddler bed for my poor jump-off into the day. I hate it with every fiber of my being. I want to rip it apart with my bare hands. I want to reiterate that with his crib, Ben was trapped until I came in. Now he has total free rein. Ben had me up at six thirty today, which I've never been fully conditioned for but now I realize this is the new *it*. So we had two and a half hours of me being grumpy and him being full-throttle cheerful mixed with Dennis the Menace: dumping water on the floor, flicking light switches, demolishing towers we built—stupid shit, but I was *so tired*. I was so spoiled that he used to sleep until eight or eight thirty in the crib. In line at Toasties, I had one of those realizations that maybe I could be getting away with more than I am, in the way of *I'm talent so I'm gonna slightly be an asshole*. In the asshole zone for a moment, I realized I could ask for someone to get me Toasties and Starbucks every morning. I could just *expect* it when I get to Sirius. Then I realized it would be Scott or Lisa or one of them who had to get it for me and pictured them in this line, being annoyed at me about it, and that was that. (As I type this, I realize we could order it for delivery, so this is an example of how I'm ninety years old for not thinking of that already.) It was also my third time in a row at Toasties that someone has been waiting for me—a gal from New Hampshire. So I'm not only the guy who doesn't have someone get my food, I *tell people where I'm gonna be.*

The lady at the bank asked when NeNe is coming back, and I didn't know how to reply, so I told her unfortunately, NeNe hates me, so I don't know what to tell you. She didn't know what to say back! We took a picture. The Sirius lobby was buzzing when I got in: Jerrod Carmichael, some DJ, Bevy, and Kiernan Shipka, who was on with me this morning and coming back to *WWHL* later tonight. John and I were in midconversation on-air about the new *Wicked* movie being split into two parts when a text came from Kathleen saying she's two centimeters dilated and she thinks the baby will come later tonight or tomorrow, which made me completely freeze.

*She's coming.*

It was a slap in the face, a burst of complete adrenaline and exhaustion all at once. A wave of emotion, panic about logistics, and *oh shit, I'm on the radio right now—WAKE UP!* Apparently I kept just agreeing with John over and over. He said, what the *fuck* is going on over there? I said something big just happened in my texts that was about to change things and texted him the pregnant man emoji he'd made me download the other day. Then everyone thought I had to leave, and I was mouthing to them that it was fine. For the rest of the day, my whole system reverted to the day Ben was born: I was relatively speechless, wandering around in a state of vegetated emotion. Bruce said I was the quietest I'd he'd ever seen me that day. I felt numb to my surroundings and unable to move through the machinations of the day, knowing that my life was about to be spun on its axis. I cancelled Stan, went home, and tried to work and nap (unsuccessfully on both counts), packed my bag for the hospital, and went to *WWHL*, where I had three more shows to tape. Kathleen said she was resting all day in anticipation of coming to the 8:00 p.m. show, which had me in disbelief and excited.

The whole staff was brimming with sweetness around Lucy's arrival. It made me even more misty and short-circuited. Before the first show (Kiernan and Nikki Glaser), we had a creative call about Dubai, and all I could think of was my special guest's arrival at the show. She got there early, with her sweet husband. She is ready to go, she said. She told me they had their first date eighteen years ago, and right then and there, she told him her plan was for multiple kids, and then she wanted to be a surrogate to help people. Her husband pointed out that when I gave them the choice of which show to attend, he jokingly told her that they had to come see Elisabeth Moss and lean into the *Handmaid's Tale* of it all. We died laughing, and so did Elisabeth when I introduced them. Hickey met them too, and Deirdre and JJ. The whole staff knew who she was, an unusual situation indeed. The woman who was giving birth to my child the next day—the most important guest to sit in the Oprah chairs yet! Hickey was the other guest, and he was hoping she'd give birth right there: talk show history! On her way out, she said, "I might make something happen tonight. I always have my babies at night, so leave your phone on." I could barely focus on my live show with Jamie-Lynn Sigler and Jenna Dewan (though both are delightful), my head was so firmly in a delivery room—potentially imminently! They had a toast for me in the control room after, but I could barely speak (I sputtered) and went home in a fog, where I remained for the rest of the night, all eyes on my phone.

## ⸬ THURSDAY, APRIL 28, 2022

Super fitful sleep, up every hour looking at my phone. Nothing happened, and the morning plan was that unless something happened today, we'd reconvene tomorrow morning at seven at the hospital. Felt calm for the first time in a week, knowing work is finally wrapped, the shows are all banked, everything at home is in place, and we have an actual plan. Was supposed to have dinner with Hickey and Laura Linney, but she's a Covid close contact, so Hickey and I had lunch instead. It was Morandi, and we both had a festive rosé. Bolognese hit the spot. Worked out with Stanny. The gym ecosystem was in full bloom: the married JewFK Junior type whom I idealize; tattooed Elliot, whom I told about the cute Mad Marj party tomorrow night that I won't be able to attend on account of my new daughter; the handsy trainer, his arm around a woman's waist with fingers, *I swear*, resting on her situation. By day's end, Lucy liftoff was moved to 10:00 a.m. tomorrow.

Bedtime with Ben was extra long and maybe the best ever. I got in his toddler bed, and he tried convincing me to stay and have a sleepover as I pled my case about how the bed was actually too small to fit me. Tried catching green stars in his cloudy-blue ceiling solar system. Sang him "You Are My Sunshine," then called Bruce and gabbed until I had to go to bed. This boy house doesn't know what's about to hit us.

## ⸬ FRIDAY, APRIL 29, 2022

When the phone rang at six thirty this morning I figured it was baby news. Instead it was Wendy Williams. I didn't pick up, nor did I mind when Ben got up fifteen minutes later. We had the most delightful few hours together before school, punctuated by phone calls from Wendy every half hour. What did she want? Ben knew today was the day I was going to get his sister, whom he announced he was going to call "Lulu Bear." He also said it was very nice of me to go to the "hostable" to get her. He uncharacteristically held my hand for the entire walk to school, and I cried the whole way (somehow without him noticing). I didn't stop crying the entire way to the hospital. Watched George's Instagram story about his radiation journey, and as I got out of the Uber carrying a car seat that in twenty-four hours would have a new human passenger, I looked up at the hospital and really took in what a terminal it was, between people coming into and going out of this world. I felt heavy for so much pain and loss, and blessed to be entering probably the only happy floor in the joint.

Jackie was my emotional support pal in the delivery room, and when we got upstairs, Kathleen was ready for the day—she had a diffuser with lavender scent, motivational postcards on the wall, playlist in full effect, and super-cute delivery robe and shorts. The woman is a birth warrior! I, falling into the trope of useless men in delivery rooms, sat there carrying on about my TMJ, eating like an absolute pig, while she told us about the benefits of an all-natural birth. After three hours of waiting around, the nurses asked her if she wanted anything to move it along or any painkillers, and she said no, but bring me a breast pump, which is a natural birthing hack. Indeed, pumping her breasts generated really heavy contractions. She was in so much pain, and her husband knew exactly how to comfort her. I was feeling pretty helpless, but then between contractions she told me that Ricki Lake is her birthing idol. She owns Ricki's documentary, *The Business of Being Born, and* its sequel! (Ricki is something of a soothsayer in the birthing world.) I told her what pals Ricki and I are, and we left Ricki a voice note from Ground Zero, telling her how much her work had motivated Kathleen. Within minutes, Ricki, who is mourning the loss of her dog Momma, sent a voice note back saying this was exactly what she needed to hear today and cheering Kathleen on and telling her what a warrior she is, which made Kathleen cry and made *her* day. So it was one big love circle for everybody! And my TMJ felt better! FaceTimed with Ben, who wanted to know where his sister was. I said, I'm here at the hospital, waiting! He said to call him when she shows up at the "hostable." More calls from Wendy Williams throughout the day, and I finally texted and said, I can't speak today, and you'll understand later. Vicki texted saying she'd heard Taylor Armstrong had applied to be on *RHOC*, and she wanted to know what I thought about that. She said she was in Chicago, where Briana had just had a fourth child. I said, I'm about to have a daughter myself; I'm in the delivery room! She said, "Holy shit. Congratulations." I then realized I had only told two Housewives my big news in all these months: Kandi and Kyle.

As Kathleen's pain got more intense, nurses appeared, and suddenly we were in business. I watched the stunning miracle of birth through a mask of tears, my mouth gaping wide open. I noticed immediately how much Lucy looked like Ben. She was perfect—with big blue eyes! I know lots of babies are born with blue eyes, but these are *blue*. Blue eyes are not a big Cohen trait. I'm enchanted. Speaking of perfection, Kathleen pushed through immense pain and then was crying watching me have skin-to-skin time with baby Lucy—she said that sight was what she did it all for. What a heart!

Jackie took about sixty photos of Lucy that I planned to blast out on Instagram, and of course we settled on one of the first ones she took, which is always how it goes. I posted and waited for my phone to blow up in three, two, one. . . . It's always fun, but overwhelming, hearing from everyone you ever knew. And as my phone became its own ecosystem, friends of Kathleen and her husband started to realize that she was my surrogate. We FaceTimed Ben, who was so adorable talking to Lucy, and then my parents, who were over the moon. Kathleen watched her birth video and realized Lucy arrived as Richard Marx was singing "Right Here Waiting," about which I have mixed feelings.

Moved upstairs to my room, which was right next door to Kathleen's. I relearned how to feed a baby, and how little it takes to fill her little tummy. Conversely, Dave and Ally showed up to fill my *big* tummy with a feast from Elio's: chicken parm, pasta, and salmon—and a bottle of Casamigos reposado Dave hid in his backpack. Jackie got our traditional Covid-Saturday Sugarfish order for Kathleen and hubby (her choice, after going without for nine months). We had tequila shots toasting baby Lucy while she slept blissfully. I told Dave he was the godfather, so there was more celebrating before they all left and I had quiet time with my little baby girl. I spent the rest of late Friday night in a period of suspended time, gazing at my teeny daughter with the lights of Manhattan's East Side glowing around us—our first night together.

## SATURDAY, APRIL 30, 2022

The guy came to pick up the cord blood (blood from the umbilical cord that could be helpful if Lucy ever becomes very ill) at two in the morning, at which point I surrendered Lucy to the nursery only to wake like a shot at 7:00 a.m. Looked on Ben's monitor from my phone, and he was awake too. Grac came to meet Lucy, then Liza came by. There were greetings from Housewives near and far—Wendy Osefo, Erika Jayne (first to weigh in with a congratulations and a beer emoji), Rinna, Ramona. Caroline Manzo sent the rock jar that's a tradition in her family. I was feeling quite proud of my recall of burping and feeding and my general baby parenting instincts all day. I wasn't stressed out about handling her and took a lot of initiative—a stark contrast to my fear with Ben in Los Angeles three years ago. Made sure the baby spent some quality time with Kathleen today, both with and without me, so she could enjoy the fruits of her labor, as it were.

There were many challenges at the hospital, because the system cannot immediately recognize me as the parent of my child because I didn't give birth to her. Also, because I didn't give birth I'm not viewed as a patient, and all the paperwork initially connects the baby to the surrogate and not the actual parent. All that said, the hospital went out of their way to make both Kathleen and me feel comfortable. Lucy is one of the first surrogate babies born in the state of New York under the new law, so there is clearly a learning curve, although things aren't any better at Cedars-Sinai, where Ben was born. It's an interesting situation. Kathleen's obstetrician is also a gay father of two, and he was so moved by his surrogate's sacrifice for him that he went on to donate a kidney. Talk about passing it on.

Jeanne came to the hospital to help me bring Lucy home around five. I had an emo goodbye with Kathleen, who FaceTimed her own kids to show them Lucy one last time. Jeanne and I took Lucy home wearing the same white hat Ben wore home from the hospital in LA and wrapped in the white cashmere blanket Hamilton sent that's monogrammed *CHER*, because why not? My walking into the apartment carrying Lucy in her car seat was like a scene from a movie: Ben, who was sitting at the dining table wearing green corduroy overalls with a fresh haircut, looked up at us and cried, "My sister!" He ran over to us—his sweet little run, with both hands by the sides of his hips—and, almost as if he'd rehearsed, bent over, said "Hi, sister!" and gave her the sweetest kiss on her lips. I kvelled. He immediately accused her of crying (she wasn't), then picked up her pacifier and said it looked like a fire truck (it didn't). He was full of smiles and "hugs" (putting his head on her lap) all night.

The table was full of presents, including a big basket from Naomi Campbell full of real *fashion*. *Top Chef* alum Ed Cotton sent incredible food from Jack and Charlie's for dinner, and Simon Halls—who in my eyes started the whole wave of gay guys having babies—sent California gear for both kids. Of course Theresa was there, ready to receive Lucy and begin her baby-whispering voodoo magic on what will be the SEVENTY-EIGHTH baby in her care. Soon baby bootcamp begins, getting her on a schedule and sleeping through the night. Had an hour's kiki with Theresa at my new bar as Lucy intermittently cried herself to sleep, and we left her until she settled herself, which she did each time. I sat in the den listening to the Dead as deep-rooted feelings of *belonging* and *home* washed over me. It felt different, knowing now that there were *two* little people under my roof: the family I created was home. There was a party happening in Chelsea that I'd really been looking forward to—all famous faces and cute boys—but in my heart I knew I was in exactly the right place.

## ⬛ SUNDAY MAY 1, 2022—MONDAY, MAY 9, 2022

One week of paternity leave—the week everything changed. When I go to bed at night, I continue feeling the satisfaction and peace of having two children under one roof—a real family—but also the *weight* of it all. My goal is to stay present and peaceful and balanced, although that may last as well as my New Year's resolution to stay off Instagram. (Were you wondering if I'd ever bring that up again? Or if I even remembered?) This was also the week in which Ben somehow learned how to open every complicated knob and his vocabulary exploded. He possibly wants to love and kill his sister equally. His hugs are more than a hair too tight, and I have to keep him from completely manhandling Lucy while she sleeps (and snores a little!) on my shoulder. I don't want to begin every sentence to Ben with "Don't" or "You can't," but that's where I seem to be right now.

Theresa opened her door on baby's first morning home and said, "*That Lucy!*" She was up from twelve to three thirty. Here we go! Ben is so happy to have Theresa back. He quizzed her all about her morning pill routine. Lucy's first day home was actually a day I devoted to Ben—I wanted him to feel like the king of the castle so he doesn't start resenting Lucy (or me). And I guess Ben decided it was his day too, because just as Wacha marked *his* territory when Ben came home, Ben stood up and took a big leak all over the yellow gingham couch in front of the TV. We are all animals. I joined a playdate with Ben and a friend of his from the playground, during which the other parent's soliloquy about nursery schools, troubles with her grown stepkid, her children not getting along, and on and on spiraled me into a mild panic attack about what's coming up in my life. I'm pretty much walking into this blindly. A few hours later, at that cute playground in Washington Square, I had a delayed flash-forward of Ben and Lucy that was hopeful and bright.

I finally spoke to Wendy Williams, who was calling to pitch being on *RHONY*. Had this call come a year earlier, it would've been a brilliant idea. If she is struggling with mental health issues, though, this isn't the time. Her enthusiasm was infectious, though when I was explaining the idea of *Legacy* and the brand-new show, she just wanted to focus on the last version. So the conversation didn't go anywhere.

The rest of the (rather long) week involved holding Lucy, and an influx of nosh, gifts, and guests. There were just so many *people* in my apartment. How far I've come from living alone with a dog to doors swinging open at all hours and all kinds of shoes in the front hall. This place is alive! Regarding the nosh, it came from everywhere, and I ate like a total pig.

Just disgusting. The gifts were wild: Gucci shoes from Dorinda, two sets of flowers from the Hamlin/Rinnas (the florist screwed up!), a jewelry box from Gizelle—the list goes on and on.

The visitors were constant, and I tried keeping people relatively away from Lucy, since Covid is everywhere and Dr. R has me under strict orders. I got a scare after Kelly Ripa held her for a while and then found out a day later that she had Covid. All were fine, though, and it was a good lesson. Mom, Dad, and Em came, and Ben ran around to each of them saying I love you. Then he told Mom he was going to hit Lucy. That pretty much sums up his vibe this week. Oh, and he kept saying he's gonna put her in a truck. As the week went on, I figured out that the truck was an ambulance and it was taking her back to the "hostable."

## ▦ TUESDAY, MAY 10, 2022

After a morning doctor's appointment with Lucy (headline: she's doing great, sweetie!), it was back to work and reality. We taped a few shows today. It used to be a constant on *WWHL* for publicists to stretch the truth a bit about their clients' acumen regarding the Bravosphere in order to guarantee them a booking on a Housewives night, which are often our highest-rated shows. However, in the cold light of the clubhouse, it quickly becomes apparent who is literate at expressing opinions and who isn't. We had someone firing blanks today, and it not only took me back, it made the show feel twice as long. Conversely, after thinking for a couple weeks about how to address Jesse Williams's endowment, which is the talk of Broadway because he's naked in *Take Me Out*, I decided to just talk about the oddity of appearing naked onstage and people's reaction to it. It showed up as "news" everywhere. Came home and Lucy slept on me while I watched *Ultimate Girls Trip* and talked on the phone. Had dinner with Ben, then we played with his trains and watched *The Jungle Book*, which featured another prejudice disclaimer. At one slow point, I thought we were bored and getting sleepy, but when I paused it to pee, he said it was great! It's a whole different pace in 1967, but I wound up getting into it.

Brushing Ben's teeth, I asked if he liked my sweat suit—a green-and-white Camp High dot-art ensemble, hard to explain—and he said, "No, but I like your socks." I was wearing plain gray socks. I laughed out loud! I got in bed with him, and we role-played with a stuffed Hess train that lights up that was sent for Lucy. He keeps getting out of that damned toddler bed after his official goodnight. Each time I came in, I took away a toy: first the Hess choo choo, then all the Thomas trains. Then the camera went out and I had to go in there to reboot it, at which point he got extra cute and submissive and put his little puppy doll under his pajama shirt and kept saying it was a baby. So he delivered, and then we took care of the baby without killing it. Talked to Grac—she's excited about the Marilyn tote bag she got from the dinner for the Warhol *Marilyn* that just sold for $200 million. She *loves* a tote—always has. I told her she should publish a coffee table of her tote bags. I'd buy it.

## ⬛ WEDNESDAY, MAY 11, 2022

It's Natasha's heavenly birthday. (I love that term.) Along with Valentino and Nick Rizzo from *WWHL*. So I'm feeling bullish on Taureans! No pun intended. Ben woke me up at 6:00 a.m. and got in bed with me and just talked. Back on the radio this morning, and I taped two shows tonight, then did a live one with Kyle and Dorit Kemsley after the *Beverly Hills* premiere. The show before that was Bethenny, whom I haven't seen in a very long time. My team had worried it'd be awkward having both Bethenny and Kyle here, because Bethenny had unfollowed Kyle on Instagram a couple years ago (my team notices *everything*). I said not to worry, that if there is some problem, they wouldn't see each other. Sure enough, Kyle came a couple hours early to have her hair and makeup done, so they certainly *would* be seeing each other, and I then avoided asking Bethenny on the show why she unfollowed Kyle because it would've been awkward on top of awkward to have Kyle in airspace and seeing it, etc. I *hate* avoiding an awkward moment—it's not in my nature! Bethenny did go back and see Kyle after the show, and they hung for a half hour, and all seemed more than fine. The premiere of *BH* was the whole home invasion, and it reaffirmed for me what garbage social media is based on when I saw how many people doubted her story. No offense to Dorit, but she ain't that good of an actress to carry off the emotion she showed in the premiere.

Hung with Hickey and Sarah Jessica and Matthew. Had to walk through that rat alley under the construction on Eighth Avenue and Fourteenth on the way home. Saw TWO RATS.

## ⠿ THURSDAY, MAY 12, 2022

Drove to the beach for the day for a walk-through of the construction. Fought sleep the whole drive home. The frame is up, and I got to go upstairs to see my bedroom, featuring breathtaking views of the ocean and dunes. It's going to be airy and Fire Island–y and beachy and every damned-y that I was banking on. Well worth the five-hour roundtrip schlep! Got the script for the upfront, and it has me *dancing*. I sent them my notes and said I'm not dancing. They said, "But you will have danced on the stage of Radio City!" I said that doesn't mean anything to me and got another script back—dancing was still in there. They said I could just "move festively" if I wanted to. Isn't that dancing? I'll sway. I realized later that I've done one better than dancing onstage at Radio City: I was *dragged* (literally and metaphorically) on a leash by Britney Spears. That's the ultimate in Radio City stage work! Plus they made me a tux, and I told them I have so many beautiful tuxes that I could've saved them the trouble. Then I wondered whether I was just being an asshole and should shut up. So I did.

Micheál and Danny hosted their guncles, me and Hickey, for dinner for their mum's heavenly birthday. Micheál brought us gifts—for me, an old Snoopy diary of Natasha's, which had exactly one perfect entry, written on New Year's Day 1978, in which she declares her love for Kris Kristofferson and details meeting Steve McQueen while roller-skating. That diary is on my desk and won't move.

Friday the thirteenth opened with me finding Ben standing by the couch eating a buffet of orzo he'd dumped out for himself. Orzo everywhere! I'd put an alarm in his room that turns green when it's okay to get out of bed, but he's been ignoring it. On the way to a meeting at 30 Rock, I had a little fit at the Starbucks—a medium tea costs six bucks. It seems insane. I asked the guy about it, and he said they just raised the prices and they're higher at that location because "it's Rock Center." Um, okay. I'm trying to engineer a way to interview Britney in some capacity—the interview everyone wants. The scaffolding came down above Rat Alley, so I think it's gonna get better. It just seems lighter on that corner. Which, incidentally, is what happens *when scaffolding is removed*. An idiot and a master of the obvious: I will be the perfect embarrassment to my children.

Was sitting with Lucy and Theresa when Alan Braun called. I had him on speaker for what I assumed would be a fast Friday agent update. "Well, this is an interesting offer for the end of a day on Friday." "I'm listening," I said. He then named a very famous weight-loss company. As Theresa HOWLED in the background, I blew my top. "THIS is how they see me? Like the BEFORE picture in an ad? I definitely have thirteen pounds to lose right now, but am I at the point of holding my pants out six inches??" He said, "No, no, you're being body dysmorphic." I said, "Excuse me, body dysmorphic? They're telling me that's how I look!" He said it's more about lifestyle and fitness, and I said he's bullshitting me. Then we agreed we would hear the offer and talk. And wasn't that the beginning of Lisa Rinna selling diapers? I FaceTimed Anderson: "Would you care to know what company CAA says is interested in having me as their spokesman?" "No, who?!" he said, lighting up. He loves hearing about my adventures in sponcon. I told him, as Theresa continued to laugh and Lucy slept. He shook his head. "Wow. That's a blow." More calls followed—it was too funny not to tell the world. My mom said, "They think you're THAT FAT?! You better LISTEN." John Hill pointed out that I'm currently the spokesperson for Nathan's Famous Hot Dogs, which is a hilarious one-two punch.

Had a sweet dinner with Mayer at Raoul's; hilariously, I'd been thinking all day about how much I planned to eat there. And I did! Mayer drilled down on what I would and wouldn't do if I took the ad. (Would: fitness-based something, wouldn't: holding out bloomery pants to show weight loss.)

## SATURDAY, MAY 14, 2022

Ben stayed in bed till the alarm told him to get up! I was so proud of him. He and I had a blast of a day. I gave Lucy the lay of the land of her entire life ahead of her; she seemed happy but a little overwhelmed. Grac came over and was enchanted with Lucy, who was wearing a Gucci Ben-Me-Down courtesy of Karen Huger, then a summer dress from Naomi Campbell! She is two weeks old and feels a teeny bit more alive—still with blue eyes, which are a *major* topic of conversation in this household. Everyone has an opinion on whether they'll stay. I'm praying they do. I never imagined a blue-eyed girl! (Love blue eyes and I'm getting a kick out of the whole thing.) Lunch at Zazzy's, then rehearsal at Radio City for the upfront. It's a MASSIVE production number, a dream sequence bringing BravoCon to life in which I'm the ringleader of sorts. Just like when I was faux-humiliated by Britney in my last onstage appearance at Radio City, I'm basically being led from one spot onstage to the next by different dancers, then when words appear on the prompter, I just say them and move to the next stop. It's people from *Top Chef, Million Dollar Listing, Below Deck, Summer House, Southern Charm, Vanderpump Rules,* and of course the *Housewives* are the finale. I was happy to finally meet Captain Glenn for the first time, after interviewing him remotely from the bridge of his boat in Spain for the last few years. He's shorter than I expected!

All the waiting around was a good opportunity to kiki with the Housewives about their respective dramas. Garcelle and I talked about the *BH* premiere. Gizelle isn't getting along with Candiace and still doesn't speak to Wendy. Alexia said Lisa was totally blindsided by the divorce. Teresa is turning fifty but doesn't want anybody to talk about it, and I said she should shout it from the rooftops. Kenya is doing some Fox adventure series.

Went to Barbuto with Amy Sedaris, who made fun of my weight-loss offer all night and was doing a fake voice of a southern lady talking about the food items. "I love the *turkey tetrazzini* but the *fruit cup* always leaves me wanting more! I just want more of that *fruit cup!*" We were howling. At one point in the conversation I zoned out and then I heard Amy referring to something coming back and realized she was wondering aloud when HER attention span would come back. We are both zombies! Or stoners. Or both—zombie stoners. We laughed about that for a while too. Got in bed at ten and texted with Shep Rose, who was out with Tom and Tom Sandoval, Ariana Madix, and Austen Kroll. I hate skipping fun in order to roll over and go to bed, but I'm a tired daddy.

## ⠿ SUNDAY, MAY 15, 2022

Ben stayed in bed until his alarm went off again! I was thrilled! Went and met SJ's new adopted kitties. Ben put one of the kitty houses on his head and then had cat hair all over him. So I guess he's not allergic, because he lived, right? I, on the other hand, am still explaining the concept to him as it relates to me. Lucy looks JUST like Ben did two weeks in. It was 70 degrees out, and I got really stir-crazy at the end of the day and wound up meeting Loic and Antoine at the DL. Someone said, "TV makes you so much taller!" and I heard "You're short." Someone said, "You're so much better looking in person," and I heard "You're not cute on TV." Kept waking up in the middle of the night wondering what I'm doing at this upfront thing tomorrow. I forgot already!

## ⠿ MONDAY, MAY 16, 2022

Ben's reign of morning terror is back: came downstairs and found meatballs, scissors, and a (DULL) KNIFE on the couch. Then I hear Lucy scream bloody murder, and he's in there having HIT her. And then he just wants to give me hugs.

The upfront was first the red carpet where they were all asking about this (viral?) photo of Chris Meloni doing the splits. He was on the carpet too, and then it became all of them trying to get him to do the splits on the red carpet. His suit was so tight it would've ripped, so he didn't wind up doing it. I was happy to just *look* at the guy.

That woman from the *New York Post* who always traps me into saying something disgusting (see: *Music Man* opening night) seemed to be trying to get me to admit to spending all day on Grindr. I said I use dating apps like video games, as time wasters. So that's no headline news. The tux they made me turned out to be really cool, kind of blue sharkskin-y. I hung in the greenroom with all the Bravo folks, and it remains, even after all these years, fun to see everybody together—like when Laverne and Shirley showed up on *Happy Days*. As I stood backstage under a huge staircase, waiting for a double door in front of me to magically swing open, the stage manager told me to count to three after the doors opened and that the smoke I'd be walking through was thicker than in rehearsal. The doors swung open, so I counted to three and had the clumsiest entrance through smoke so intense I lost my way and almost tripped onto the stage. It felt like I ripped the suit a little—I felt fabric tear. The BravoCon portion of the event was chaotic but something of a showstopper, from what I'm told. People seemed happy. I can't tell what I did.

Came home and hung with Ben and took a nap, then SJ came to meet Lucy and play with Ben. Tonight, we're having Haim on, but one of the sisters cancelled five hours before the show with a bad migraine. So that was a bummer. The NBCUniversal upfront party was in the Pool Room at the old Four Seasons restaurant—where I had my fiftieth, and where (more famously) Bethenny peed in a bucket before her wedding. I never recognize *Below Deck* crew out of their uniforms and all made-up. I've talked to them relentlessly, but then when they're in street clothes with hair and makeup, I become idiotic. Only stayed a half hour and then raced to *WWHL*, where Haim wound up being delightful. I invited them to play at BravoCon in October.

## ▦ TUESDAY, MAY 17, 2022

Ben stole Lucy's cherry dress, and I had to chase him around the apartment for it. Interviewed George about his brain cancer for a podcast Justin is putting together. His clarity and peace of mind surrounding what
he's going through is so inspiring; he thinks this was G-d's will and is not
afraid of dying. Had lunch with Alex Baskin and we discussed the state
of *OC* and *BH*. Sure enough, the *New York Post* has an "exclusive" saying
I'm on every dating app and I play them like video games. The truth is I
do sit at home looking through Grindr like it's a video game, sending pics
to guys I have no intention of meeting—or whom I would *like* to meet,
but it seems logistically impossible to actually do so. But seeing it in print
always makes something seem criminal.

Taped a cameo for the new *Best Man* series before *WWHL*, which first
was Erika Jayne and Christine from *Selling Sunset*. Erika was so happy I
was putting Christine in the hot seat—like, literally *gleeful* it wasn't her.
The live show was the *NJ* husbands. Spoke with Jackie, whom I hadn't seen
since she'd been demoted to a Friend. She had simply the greatest attitude
and said she was going to be the best Friend there ever was on a Housewives
show. I love that. Brought a roadie home, and the street was blocked off
two blocks from my place because they were shooting *The Marvelous Mrs.
Maisel*. Without a care in the world, I ignored everyone and walked right
through the set with my red Solo cup. I had to get home, and stop messing
with my neighborhood, Mrs. Maisel!

## ▦ WEDNESDAY, MAY 18, 2022

Jacob Elordi was in my dream. I asked him out, and he seemed receptive.
Maybe that's why I woke up at six and couldn't fall back to sleep. I star-
tled Ben when he wandered out of his room looking for meatballs. Did
radio, then opened the "show" at a big UJA lunch honoring Scott Greenstein, where I had a quick kiki with Gayle King. At home I watched two
episodes of *Dubai*, which needs work but is going to be great, and fed

and held Lucy. Had dinner at Via Carota with Hickey and Allison Janney and a few of her friends. I once again made out with Janney. We're attracted to each other, what can I say? On the way out I said there was a 12 percent chance we would go home together. We didn't. The odds were against us!

## THURSDAY, MAY 19, 2022

Woke up at 4:30 a.m. stressed about life. Fell back asleep at 6:30, which was short-lived. This morning was Bennis the Menace getting into the jelly beans and an assortment of other petty crimes that pushed me to the limit. Sleepwalked through a workout with Stanny and then yawned my way through the *Below Deck Sailing Yacht* reunion, not because it was boring but I was tired. Bethenny was texting this morning about Erika, casually referring to her ex-fiancé as dead and how vile that was. Then Erika texted a few hours later, wanting to know why Bethenny was pissed at her. I left her a voice note explaining it, and she said well, Bethenny started it so she should get over it. Then I wondered who would win in a spar between the two, and I just don't know. Conference call about the weight-loss company. As my agent pitched, they are indeed doing a rebrand to have the campaign be more about fitness, which made me feel better about the whole endeavor. I don't know that we will ever agree on money, though. Held Lucy some more, then took Ben out for ice cream, which was the absolute highlight of my day if not my week. We counted taxicabs and commented on everything and everyone we saw. He was so sweet and funny. Oh man, it was life-affirming. Went to bed at ten!

## FRIDAY, MAY 20, 2022

Woke up fresh as a daisy to discover Bennis the Menace with a chocolate bar he found in the wee hours of the morning. Worked out with Stanny and told him I want him in the weight-loss commercial with me. We did a pretend commercial, and he was terrible. Picked up Ben from school and had lunch. Recorded a podcast for John Hill deep in the East Village, and it was such a beautiful day I decided to walk home. It was a great adventure. Was on the phone with Bruce and got stopped by a guy who said he was NYFD and in a bar with a bunch of firemen and wanted me to do shots with them—an invitation I didn't refuse! I did a single shot and loved every minute with those guys! Huge line outside Prada that I butted in on. They didn't have any tan suits, so I split. Got to the West Village and immediately had three paparazzi on me. I knew they weren't there for me, so I asked who was around. One said Irina Shayk was on the next block with her daughter at the playground and asked me to tell her to hurry up so they could get their shot. I ran right into her and had a festive hello (I haven't seen her since we were on a boat somewhere together five years ago). Her daughter is as beautiful as her parents. Had a lively dinner at I Sodi with Amanda, followed by a nightcap at the Hangar, which I didn't know is the only Black-owned gay bar in Manhattan!

## ⠿ SATURDAY, MAY 21, 2022

Who knew that a kid's birthday party would catapult me into an existential crisis? That's an overstatement, but it was a rough day, and this sweet little celebration of a three-year-old brought out a whole bunch of crap that I guess I've been carrying around with me but not accessed. It was an unseasonably hot Saturday, with a group of kids from Ben's little threes program and their parents. When I was "pregnant" with Ben, I speculated a lot about the ages of my fellow parents, knowing I'd be the oldest but not sure where they'd be. Turns out they're mainly late thirties into their early forties, which isn't *that* much younger. Somehow today, though, I decided that all these other first-time parents had their shit firmly together and I didn't. I guess it started with multiple people asking me why I didn't bring Lucy, and me wondering why I *would* bring her out in the 90-degree heat while I was chasing Ben around. So I was starting

New Year's Eve with
Anderson and the
legendary Leslie Jordan

Jen Shah showed up in purple velvet with a showgirl ring of feathers circling
her head and crystal boob embellishments, as easy breezy as I've ever seen her.

The King of Cutz saves my
credit card from the gutter.

My star with the real
star of the day

**So happy to be among a mix of old friends and business friends
(Not pictured: lady in the bright-pink pantsuit)**

**Had to get Bruce in with Patti and Anderson**

**Mini versions of AC²**

**Perfect night out**

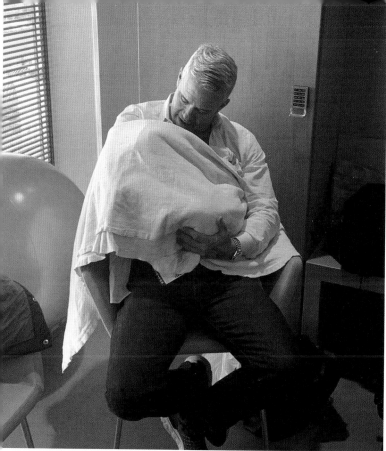

Meeting Lucy!

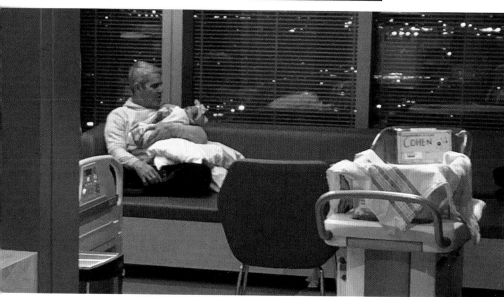

First night with Lucy

Ben meets Lucy.

Three generations of Cohens

Ben inspecting the construction

Someday this will be my living room.

A drive with Ben

With Bruce at Pride

This is a
Fellini movie.

Getting higher with the
Dead

My vantage point at the *RHOBH* reunion

The highlight of the US Open was Angus Cloud, by a mile.

My river guide at Camp Mayer in Montana

Cannes with Garcelle, Boy George, and Dorit

This is the thirst trap I contemplated posting after the *Married to Medicine* reunion. John Hill and Bruce said not to post, but they didn't say anything about me including it in this book!

Getting in shape for
BravoCon

Lucy makes her
BravoCon debut.

When he lifted the head off to reveal his translucent hair,
the audience and all my guests went wild.

BravoCon sing-along

Halloween with my gals, Jackie, Liza, and Lucy

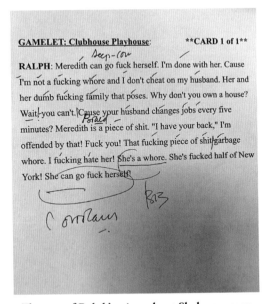

The text of Ralph's triumphant Shakespearean
performance of Lisa Barlow's hot mic moment

Dad pulled out Mom's engagement picture, which he's kept in his wallet for sixty-four years.

Mom helping me style Lucy

Actually made it to the Thanksgiving Day Parade

Date night with Amy

Happy 90th Birthday, Dad!

Ramona eyes and pickle juice shots to close out the year

to second-guess whether it was abnormal that I didn't bring her when the sprinklers turned on and all the kids magically raced into the fun wearing swim diapers. All the parents had brought them, along with changes of clothes, and I had nothing. The sight of Ben, so *hot*, in the wrong clothes, immediately sunk me into a pit of insecurities about my ability to do this alone. If I had a husband, we probably *would've* brought Lucy. And maybe one of us would've known to bring clothes? Watching the moms with all their gear, like Mary Poppins with the right thing for every situation, made me feel inept. The whole experience made me feel very alone, and I sank into a real sadness for the rest of the day.

The day ended with a movie night with Ben. We watched *Luca*, which made me WEEP at the end. During the movie, I was trying to pinpoint my discomfort from the day and realized that I was the only gay dad—and only single parent—today (and at the school). It's never registered to me before, but I think that was making me feel further like an odd dad out.

## ▦ SUNDAY, MAY 22, 2022

How do you get a three-year-old to stop saying "poopy"? You don't. (By the way, if someone told me to stop saying a word, I'd never stop saying it either.) It's 24–7 "poopy" in my universe.

I've been asking Ben to get pancakes with me one morning for weeks, and this was my lucky morning. La Bonbonnière was popping at 8:45 a.m., and my boy's optimism started everything off well. But it was 90 degrees again, and we were all melting, and Ben melted down again and again. He and I had a very chaotic burgers and fries at Corner Bistro for lunch.

I met a gay dad at that playground by the river. See that? I manifested it! Dinner with Cousin Josh and Melissa at Barbuto. I feel terrible about not letting people hold Lucy. Bruce called, having seen my food posts on Instagram, and said listen, you ate pancakes for breakfast and burgers for lunch and carbonara for dinner, so it seems like you WANT to be the weight-loss guy. Fair point.

# ⊞ MONDAY, MAY 23, 2022—NEW YORK CITY
# TO LOS ANGELES

Before flying to LA for a quick paid appearance, I went with Ben's class to let butterflies loose in the triangle park. When they walk on the street, they all hold the same rope, each wearing oversized shirts with the number of the school on them. It was so sweet letting the butterflies go.

On the plane to Los Angeles, I was seated behind the most in-shape, beautiful man in a white T-shirt and jeans; I clocked him pretty quickly as straight, with no wedding ring. Just a great package: olive skin, like a thirty-five-year-old Tom Cruise but taller. Simple beauty. Meanwhile, I'm in my loud floral Camp High sweat suit covered in mushrooms and pot leaves. I felt NOT simple nor beautiful. I asked the flight attendant if he knew who the guy in 1A was. He said he was on his flight last Thursday too. Then I said "Is that guy . . . an actor?" He didn't hear me say "actor" and said, "I don't think he is, no." I said, "No, I know he's not *gay*; I mean, is he an actor?" He said he didn't think so. I was fishing for him to give me 1A's name but didn't ask directly.

Away from kid-land, in the peace of the sky, I took some THC tincture and (stonedly) wrote forty-one thank-you notes. It doesn't sound like a lot on paper, but it took forever. The longer I wrote, the more high I got, so they were full of occasional excessive emotion, bad jokes, odd handwriting, and drawings.

The chocolate chip cookies appeared from the flight attendant. I feigned a *Should I?!*, took the cookie, then called him back.

"Did that guy take a cookie?" I pointed. "No, he didn't." *Of course* he didn't. That guy has a twenty-nine-inch waist, no fat on his abs, and pants that delicately cup his perfect ass. I handed back the cookie. See, the weight-loss company is already working on me in subliminal ways. When I felt more stoned in the air, I switched Mr. Seat 1A from Cruise to Christian Bale in *American Psycho*. (That's peak Bale.) When we landed, I had music pumping in my ear (*Andy Cohen's Kiki Lounge*, Sirius XM channel 312. You really should try it!) as I followed 1A's ass all the way to baggage claim, transfixed. As we walked out of the terminal, I didn't see my driver, someone called Marko, and called. Suddenly, in front of me I see a tall, blond, lean man in a black suit looking like he was about to walk a Tom Ford runway. He picked up his phone. "This is Marko. Mr. Cohen?" Marko! I *immediately* forgot about 1A and was blinded by Marko's eternal smile and bright eyes. "You're wearing what I'd like to be wearing!" he said, and smiled. I swooned! He liked my garish sweat suit! 1A who?!

In the car, I had Marko DJ for us. He loves hip-hop! He is twenty-nine. Oh, no, he's thirty and forgot! Oh, Marko! He's an actor from Indonesia and Santa Barbara! He's been driving for nine years. He surfs every day. He said 85 percent of women hit on him. He asked what percent hit on me, and I said, I don't drive a car but in life I am very gay, so only some hit on me, but they like me. He said you have to bring a baseball bat around in LA. He just likes to be friends with people. He is Norwegian. He said friendship is powerful and underestimated. In Indonesia, two guys or two women can walk down the street holding hands, as friends. I love that. Oh, Marko. He values friendship! I asked him how many men hit on him. He said pretty much all of the gay men, 90 percent of gay guys. (I vowed not to be one of them.) We talked about fatherhood for a long time. He wants kids. He is single right now and says it's hard to find a girl his speed in LA. He has a group of three surfer buddies who are like his brothers, and they have deep bonding over sporting exercise weekends. He said he makes music. He asked, "Do you want to hear my song? You have to want to go deep, though." I said, "I wanna go deep, Marko!" So we went deep (with his song), and he invited me to his gig Saturday on the beach in Malibu. On top of all that, as if he wasn't perfect enough, he works at a special-needs surf camp and offered me a lesson! (Not because he thought I have special needs but just because he was cool.)

At the end of the drive, though, I realized that we had only talked about *him* on our date—I mean drive—and that wasn't gonna work for me. I got out of the car feeling like we'd had a full relationship. Had dinner with Bruce at the Sunset Tower. We just laughed and laughed in a big booth. Michael Patrick King was at the next table. After dinner, Bruce went home, and John Mayer came, and we had ice cream sundaes for dessert. I felt like I was on vacation—a vacation to recover from my relationship with Marko.

## ⠿ TUESDAY, MAY 24, 2022—LOS ANGELES TO NEW YORK CITY

This morning's event in Santa Monica was painless, a Q and A at a conference for super-high-end Realtors. Got on the plane, changed back into my loud sweat suit, and settled in for five hours of killing time in the air. I decided to go through the file of double-hidden Instagram DMs; these are the ones I rarely look at because there are too many and nothing I need to see. As I was scrolling, I noticed a small picture of a guy, and the preview of the message said, "hope you enjoyed . . ." I clicked on it to find: "hope you enjoyed your flight, 2A," sent at six thirty last night. IT WAS FROM 1A! Christian Bale with the tight pants! I quickly dug into his Instagram to discover he is not only gay but married to a man of equal or greater beauty! *I was agape.* Seeing how picture-perfect they were, I downgraded the flirt I wanted to send to just me apologizing for staring at him for half the flight but saying I couldn't help it given how handsome he is. He responded that he was flattered and then went on with some random drivel that killed the conversation. We left it there. Looks like we have mutual friends (who I know I'm seeing this weekend), so I will get the full story.

Watched two episodes of *Dubai*, and it's great. Caroline Stanbury is an unapologetic bitch, and then you find out why she is from her upbringing. Chanel Ayan is a star like we haven't seen in a long time. Wow. Well, we've never actually seen *anyone* like her. People are not ready. Landed at twelve thirty and was in bed by one fifteen, watching Ben on the monitor. He was moving all around and gesticulating with his hands. I contemplated going in and chatting, then thought I didn't want to interrupt his sleep. Then I thought of the parents in Uvalde, Texas, who can't see their kids ever again. He tossed and turned some more, so I did go in. It turns out he was actually fast asleep. I kissed him and tiptoed out of his room.

Beautiful day. Ran around all day getting shit done before the long weekend. Took Ben to school and was greeted back at home by a BOUNTY of Gucci stuff from Brad Goreski and Gary Janetti. The Gucci sneakers for Ben are amazing. Took Lucy out for a stroll around the West Village. At Tea and Sympathy, Sean gave me a new kind of Yorkshire Gold called "Biscuit" that literally tastes and smells like biscuits. Got a pair of jeans at A.P.C., went to the ATM, and then in front of Equinox ran into Boomer Banks, who told me he knows Candiace from *Potomac*. Came home and tried the biscuit tea. I have a lot of thoughts about it; I generally feel it won't be part of my daily routine. Watched a long sequence from *All My Children* that that soap fan on Instagram posted. It's undeniable what a star Susan Lucci was, but every time each actor entered the scene, they seemed so iconic to me. Hickey watched too, and we were marveling at Erika's hair. It was amazing. She was so good. Did Julia Barr and she like or hate each other, I wonder? Going to ask Kelly. (I'm sure I've asked before and forgotten the answer.)

MTV offered me their Icon award at a reality TV award show they're doing, but it's taping in LA on my birthday. The thought of leaving the kids on my birthday to accept some random award wasn't enough to get me to say yes. If I didn't have kids I would've done it. Dinner with Jeanne at Pastis. We're supposed to go out for my birthday next Thursday. I want to stay home and have sushi; she thinks that's boring since we do it every week. I quoted Patti LaBelle and said, why block a blessing? She suggested that since I've been talking about a double-French-onion-soup dinner, I should finally do it. She makes a compelling point.

Had French onion soup as an appetizer and pined over not getting it for my main when I realized I was full from it, so maybe double French onion soup is actually a bad idea. Jeanne doesn't think I should give Ben the Gucci sneakers, but I promised her he isn't going to become label obsessed anytime soon, and she acquiesced. Came home and rearranged the bar.

This morning Ben asked me to tell him who the kids were on the front page of the *New York Times* today. Nineteen kids killed in their school in Texas. I read their names to him, and he looked on as he ate his bagel. I now understand the urge to put your child in a plastic bubble. And now I want to say something about *The Boy in the Plastic Bubble*, but it's not the place or time. But I *did* just mention it, I guess, so I'm terrible. So . . . traffic to the beach was easy breezy, and so was my cargo. Did a bunch of work calls on the Long Island Expressway, including a long one with Caroline Manzo about coming back. She is ACTIVATED about Teresa and feels a "moral obligation to tell this woman that she can't get away with her stuff." I know we won't be able to make a deal with her; the gap between her expectations and our reality is too wide. But I think it would be an incredible moment in what could be Teresa's last season, not to mention a major confrontation eight years in coming. I told Shari that I'd call Teresa and I thought she would be okay about it, and then by the end of the night I thought I was an idiot for thinking she would be okay with it. She's been texting me about officiating her wedding, which is a very sweet offer that I'm not sure I'm going to be able to accept.

Amagansett is such a vibe! Rented the house next to SJP's for the summer, and it's gonna be great. Hickey stopped by, and we went to see my construction. He is so fun to look at real estate with. My new place is just the right size. Before I go to bed, when I need something to think about, I think about the house. Swam with Ben forever. Our pool at the rental is so big! He started swimming at nine months and is going under and getting himself to the side of the pool.

After twenty-eight years of my Sag Harbor nucleus of stores—Cromer's for all my groceries and fried chicken, Goldberg's for bagels—I went to what is, as of this day forward, *my new IGA*. I loved it! They had super-wide aisles and Phil Collins's "Take Me Home" booming, and it never sounded better. Ben and I built sandcastles for an eternity during sunset. His words have exploded, and he's so spirited in conversation about anything. Read him the book of *Frozen* for the fiftieth time but really decided to commit this time. He wouldn't let me sing "Let It Go," but it was nonetheless a journey for us both.

After bedtime—around eight thirty—I went to Sam's (took me eight minutes, versus twenty-two from Sag!), which was packed! Like in a Nancy Meyers movie, a chair at the bar revealed itself, and I settled in to pig out. Graham knew exactly what this Weight Watchers gal needed to stay happy. There were two women next to me who were loudly auditioning to be *Summer House* people (I think—not Housewives, but they wanted *something*). My privacy screen once again saved the day, as I was looking down all night. Was texting Bruce and sent 🙂 and realized I really have no clue what 🙂 means. Asked Brazilian Andy Samberg, who said, "May need context. . . . I use it as a bit of a filler for multiple reasons but I can't really articulate . . . it's more on the smile side but maybe like a sly smile or like I'm smiling but not really or probably other uses too." I was as confused as when I asked. As I texted Bruce, I heard a familiar voice, and it was Katie Couric picking up a to-go order. (The Hamptons!) We had a powerschmooze for six minutes, and then she left and it felt like the restaurant had cleared out except for the *Summer House* rejects, who—as people do—turned out to be lovely. Before I left (I took two pizzas home to freeze), I said, "Well, I killed another one." "Number 766," Graham said. Took me eight minutes to get home, and I was asleep by ten thirty, hugged by the sound of the ocean.

## ⦙⦙⦙ FRIDAY, MAY 27, 2022, TO MONDAY, MAY 30, 2022— AMAGANSETT

The rest of the weekend was super-chill time with the kiddos. It should be noncontroversial to say that playing with your kids while a little high encourages incredibly concentrated, patient playtime. Ben and I spent almost the whole weekend in the pool, us best friends (he said we are, and I believe him), listening to *Andy Cohen's Kiki Lounge*. Streisand came on, and he said, "Is this Elsa?" Good call, Ben! During a different song he said, "Is this Madonna?" "Who *is* Madonna?" I asked. "She sings." I do not know how this boy knows that. He listens, I guess. He does know the Grateful Dead without fail, but this. Wow.

I think hearing my name on the *Kiki Lounge* has made him start thinking about my name. "Are you *Andy Cohen*?" he asked me on my way out to dinner one night. I said, "I'm Daddy." But he knows now the way to make me laugh is to call me "Andy Cohen" at really random times: "Throw me in the pool, Andy Cohen!" Everything in his world feels like something of joy, that's just who he is. Sitting waiting for the whistle of the choo choo (he calls every train the four thirty train) is joyful. Him turning to me in the middle of something, saying, "I just need to take a little *break*, Daddy," is a thing of joy.

Here's a conversation I had with Ben:

BEN: What are these?

ME: They're my nipples.

BEN: I thought they were belly buttons!

ME: What are those?

BEN: I don't know.

ME: They're *your* nipples.

BEN: Daddy, I have small nipples.

On Saturday night, I stayed home with Ben. Somewhere in Malibu, Marko was playing guitar on the beach for his friends.

## ▦ TUESDAY, MAY 31, 2022—AMAGANSETT TO NEW YORK CITY

Headed back to the city for three days of birthday festivities, which is ironic since I truly don't care and don't want anything. Drove by the new house—full of workmen, thankfully—when taking Ben home from the magic weekend. Ben was furious about leaving, just epically pissed. I would be too, if I was him. Spoke to Teresa on the way home from the beach. She was more receptive to the idea of Caroline coming back than I'd imagined. I told her I can't officiate the wedding. I saw a Tik-Tok of a woman impersonating Teresa on the beach and was thinking of that woman for half the conversation. It was tickling me! She needs an officiant now. I suggested Dina, since it should be someone close to the couple and she would come up with a great service. Picked up the new car on Long Island and went to a diner afterward in a parking lot full of cars with Trump and NRA stickers. I cannot imagine not only loving that man, but loving him and guns enough to slap stickers on my car for them. What sticker *would* I slap on my car, besides the Grateful Dead? I don't know. I got home to a box from Teresa and Luis, which I assumed would be a baby gift, but it was a big box of fresh flowers with a Lucite invitation to their wedding. I wonder what to do with the flower heads. For night one of birthday dinners, Amanda and Grac took me out to Via Carota, and it was fun not bringing my credit card out at the end. A novelty! Went to the Hangar for a nightcap. Ramona posted an unboxing of Teresa's wedding invite and revealed the location and showed the entire invite. Teresa is *pissed*: first, Ramona called her "the scarecrow," and now she doxxed her! I texted Teresa, who said it was "low class."

# SUMMER

IN WHICH I . . .

FACE MONKEYPOX

GO HIGHER WITH THE DEAD

DISCOVER THAT VACATIONS AS I KNOW THEM
ARE OVER

Walked up to a handsome man on the street and said hello to him. You would've thought I told him I had Covid by his response. PURE DISGUST! Then I saw a group of firemen at the supermarket—which as you may know is my thing—and THEY wanted nothing to do with me. Thus, on a day when I felt great about my hair AND arms, I learned that sometimes what you think you're putting out is not what people take in. I'm off work for another week, but Ramona texted to say she liked my tie on last night's rerun. I texted back, asking about the Teresa thing, and she called, doing her "apologizer" thing: "I just thought it was a beautiful invitation—*and I have seen so many*—but I didn't know!!! I'm unpredictable. *I guess that's why I'm good TV.*" She is pure chaos and still amuses me.

There was a new-parent mixer at Ben's new nursery school, and on the way I called Troy, another gay single dad who has been through this whole process, and asked for advice. Troy said listen more than you talk. I thought that was great advice! And not my normal inclination. There was wine, and the other parents seemed cool—looks like I'm the only gay dad (and single parent) at this school too. I listened a lot as parents and teachers alike took the opportunity to say nasty things about the threes program Ben has been (quite happily and productively!) attending, which didn't seem too far different from the curriculum at the new place. But everyone thinks their place is the best, and I was there to *listen*!

Amy came by for dinner, and we speculated about Lucy's eyes: still bright blue! We were going to the Polo Bar, and we took the subway at my insistence. "What could go wrong?! We'll wear masks!" What almost went wrong was a mentally ill dude beating the crap outta someone. He didn't, and we made it to the restaurant for a celebratory dinner in one piece. We saw Al Roker and his son, and Nate and Jeremiah. All night, Amy was loudly screaming at me: "Rashes disappear! Ointment makes them go away!"

## ⁜ THURSDAY, JUNE 2, 2022

Had the birthday glow all day. Today's highlight was that Ben slept till his clock went off, then I got to sit with Ben and Lucy both on my lap without him killing her for twenty minutes. She was very alert and looking around, and he was kind of screaming in her face but in a sweet way, if that's at all possible. Good workout with Stanny. Lunch with Dave. I was wondering what the right lunch would be to mentally gear up for a double-French-onion-soup dinner. I decided on a tuna burger with no bun. But I had fries, so that wasn't really a light lunch. Took Lucy to the doctor and kind of prayed to her that Lucy will keep her blue eyes. Doctor says she will, but I don't believe her. Lucy's ten pounds thirteen ounces.

I know several kids who share my birthday, and today celebrated Isla's second birthday at Deirdre's in Brooklyn. My real birthday present happened tonight, when I finally indulged my gluttony with the big double-French-onion-soup dinner at Pastis with Jeanne and Jackie. After I finished my appetizer, I was full and regretting ordering another soup, a feeling that was immediately erased when the waitress brought over a crispy and bubbling and *perfect* second crock. I DEVOURED it and, by the time we were walking home, started to feel a lump in my stomach that persisted through the night. My review: a lot of fun in the moment, with the consequence of an upset stomach.

## ⁜ FRIDAY, JUNE 3, 2022, TO SUNDAY, JUNE 5, 2022— AMAGANSETT AND NEW YORK CITY

This is obnoxious, but when Ben was born, he got more than one electric car, one from the Jersey Housewives at the end of a reunion show. I know, it's insane. They've been in storage waiting for the right moment, and now seemed perfect because Ben's been talking about wanting to drive. So we schlepped one of the big boxes out, and of course I couldn't get it to work on my own. I could barely put it together but felt like maybe over the weekend it would materialize. I'm hopeless.

At sunset on Friday night, I went to my new house and sat on the floor of what will be my bedroom and gabbed with Bruce, staring at the ocean and feeling the breeze. All I do is think about the house. The glass is allegedly on a freighter from Greece and due to arrive in a couple weeks. *What could possibly go wrong?* Dinner with Mark and Kelly in East Hampton was lovely, and seeing them that far east was like a mirage. We never seemed to leave Sag Harbor in all those years. Hickey took me into Amagansett to show me my new stores. I love my new neighborhood! My axis has been turned. Ben said, "Sag Harbor is the best for me," so he may not totally be where I am. At the playground Saturday, a man asked Ben his name. He replied, "I'm Ben," then pointed at me: "He's Andy Cohen." I died. On the way home he asked who sings for the Grateful Dead, which I thought was an EXCELLENT question. We had a nice chat about Jerry and John, and Bob. Had lots of super-chill pool time—played teacher and swim student, with Ben teaching, a lot. Of course by weekend's end, the car still wasn't working. Gonna show Margot next week.

Drove back to the city and went directly to Chelsea Piers for a combined five-kid birthday party—representing the summer birthdays while school is out—that I was kind of dubious about after the last one, but it was really fun. Ben wanted nothing to do with it until the dessert reveal (it looked like a cake, and the reveal was that it was cupcakes! I've never!) and the entertainer, Silly Billy, who *killed*. It was the same five jokes, but they didn't care. The kids couldn't get enough of Silly Billy! Ben's going to a different school in the fall, so it was bittersweet leaving the party and the nice parents. On the walk to the car, we saw Silly Billy, still wearing his red shirt, rainbow suspenders, and the garb, loudly screaming into his phone in a New York accent, searching for his Uber. Ben was starstruck and still, slowly repeating, "Hi, Silly Billy! Hi, Silly Billy!" Silly Billy totally stiffed him; it was a sad scene. As he walked away, dragging his roller bag toward the Uber, Ben mumbled, "Bye, Silly Billy," and told me he is a nice man. So the kid was unfazed. Lucy is so big and smiled at me a few times tonight—the smiles have begun! Had a live show, always a little painful for a Sunday night but made better when my favorite driver, Moussa from Somalia, picks me up. He is a gentle soul who always has the Sirius

Grateful Dead channel on for me, because that's the kind of lovely and considerate guy he is—and now as a result he's apparently a Deadhead. When he dropped me off at the end of the night, he paused and turned around in the car. He said, "Thank you for introducing me to the Grateful Dead. I never would've known about them, and now because of you I do." I felt like I'd done something right.

## ⠿ MONDAY, JUNE 6, 2022—NEW YORK CITY

Dear Hickey, SJ, and Matthew: Last night I dreamed I was in your play! I went up on my very first line, which was an entrance from the back of the theater. I was waiting for my entrance, looking everywhere for a script to find out that first line, but I couldn't for the life of me! Matthew saved me, and Hickey yelled at me backstage during the show. I kept saying to him, I am not an actor but I am really doing my best. It was all so thrilling. And I found that I had a little mailbox backstage, and there were candles and little opening-night presents in it. And I said to Hickey, I must be okay; look how full my box is. He didn't like that! I was in trouble! I loved being in the theater. Can't wait for the show tonight. See you there!

Dear Andrew: Today is Monday, your day off, but you have rehearsal tomorrow at 10:00 a.m.—Hickey

Dear Hickey: I do not feel supported by you and I don't know how I'm supposed to go on after you knocked my confidence out. We need to talk.

Dear Andy: Amazing dream! Welcome aboard! Just the bit of new energy we can use for our last weeks. See you tomorrow night.—Matthew

Those were the email exchanges that began my day, followed by three hours of radio—my show and then Jeff Lewis's. I think I got through Jeff's show without saying anything that can get picked up. Everyone has Covid, which is messing up all the talk shows, who are scrambling for guests. Colbert has two lead spots open. Today's show was going to be Sarah Silverman and Ryan O'Connell. Sarah had to cancel, so we booked Rachel Dratch with him. Then I get an email during radio saying Ryan has Covid, so can't do the show we're taping in three hours. Tried Jeff Lewis (he has a UTI!), Sedaris (shooting a movie), two of Dratch's castmates, Willie Geist (was just exposed to Covid), and a bunch of other random people. Wound up doing the show with Dratch solo and Mark Long and Beth Stolarczyk from the *Real World Challenge* universe behind the bar. Em was there and loved the show, so I guess it worked out.

Spoke to Anderson, who said he'd fill in anytime, and felt dumb for not asking him. Turns out he had a doctor's appointment at our tape time, so I felt better. Tamra started texting at dinner about something I'd said on Jeff's show about her coming back. She wants to. I said we'll speak tomorrow, which she read to mean she was in trouble or I didn't want her back. Sometimes "Let's talk tomorrow" just means *let's talk tomorrow!* Had a fun dinner with Em, Rob, and Abby at Morandi. Came home and started to watch *Fire Island*, which was really cute. I hope it doesn't cause people to want to come to Fire Island; it's perfect as is! I'd come home at the end of the night and was sitting in my room when Hickey showed up at my bedroom door, and we had a nightcap. I guess I left the door open. I wasn't mad!

## ⁛ TUESDAY, JUNE 7, 2022

Ugh, was I ever wrong about Jeff's show: "Andy Cohen Says Kids Can Defrost, Raise His Embryos One Day"—that was the headline on Page Six. It was *everywhere*. I was spitballing on the show and now I sound absolutely insane!

It was a whirlwind day. Potty training, field day for what I thought was Ben's last day of school (it's next week, duh), and then taped three shows including Melissa McCarthy, who I think left a little tipsy, in the best way. Spoke to Tamra about coming back to *OC* and my concerns with her podcast. She made some good points. Brandi Glanville texted wanting me to set her up with the captain from *Below Deck Down Under*.

## ⅲⅲ WEDNESDAY, JUNE 8, 2022

I spent an inordinate amount of time shopping for toddler undies online today, which is a sentence I never thought I'd write anywhere! They were out of Hot Wheels undies in Ben's size everywhere, and he is only mixed on *Paw Patrol.* Should I go on? Did radio. Went to Bravo. People seem to be coming back to the office. I did a rant about why Pride still matters and got a tweet this morning from some gay guy saying I'm a "wealthy cis gay white man who built his living off cis women" and on and on and on and on. All I said was why Pride still matters. I texted Brazilian Andy Samberg saying I hate millennials, and he said maybe you hate Twitter, and I said I hate millennials on Twitter, how about that. Mom texted and said "we need to talk about embryos—SHUT YOUR MOUTH!" I said I was grossly taken out of context and calm down. Got some Chersace merch with a personalized note from Cher, who at the end said either "Now *lose* the kids" or "Now *love* the kids"—I don't get either line, frankly.

We had Chanel Ayan on for her clubhouse debut, and Deirdre called as I was getting ready for the show to say that Chanel had brought chicks to gift me on the air, but that it's illegal to gift chicks in the state of New York (?!) so we couldn't do it on the air. This was all too stupid to comprehend, and after much back-and-forth with our lawyer, Chanel (after absolutely slaying for a half hour) brought out the chicks and said she *brought* them (not *gifted* them), and I said I had to send them right back to the farm. Not sure it was worth all the tumult, but people at home seemed to like it, and it calmed our lawyer down. I gave Ayan my standard "you're a new Housewife" speech, which mainly consisted of telling her not to buy into what people are saying on Twitter because they'll love you today and rip you to shreds tomorrow, at which point Sezin walked up and told her she should check Twitter because everyone was loving her. Ha! We all stayed and had drinks (it was our Friday!), and on the way out I ran into Tracey Baker-Simmons, with whom I worked in my early years at Bravo, when she produced *Being Bobby Brown.* It was all so random, and what was even more so was that *she had brought the chicks*! And there she was, leaving with them. Full circle?

## ⠿ THURSDAY, JUNE 9, 2022, TO SUNDAY, JUNE 12, 2022—AMAGANSETT

Ben's car is up and running, thanks to Margot. Ben kept saying he wants to "drive like Daddy," which horrified me. I don't think I'm the greatest driver, but we do always seem to make it in one piece. I told him to keep his eyes on the road, because—as he knows—our eyes are to see. He told me we need our eyes to *blink*, not to *see*. Also he was swiping at the windshield, saying, "This is my tablet." I didn't love that. I bought him *The Cat in the Hat* and then immediately regretted it. It's long! Too long!

Teresa called on Friday to say she didn't agree to filming with Caroline on *RHONJ*. I guess I took our quick conversation last week as a yes, but she heard it totally differently. I said I'd call her back, then got carried away with life stuff. I texted her Sunday, saying, "I got hung up—I'll call later." She replied, "I never got a call from you, what are you talking about?" I texted back that I said I got HUNG UP with other shit, not hung up *on*.

Had dinner at the Buffetts with a fun group including Don Johnson, who is the coolest and most fun. Was getting good mom advice from Jane and her pals. I am feeling the pressure of being a single dad and already having an expectation to show up to every event at the nursery school when I just can't. Also I don't know when it's okay to send Margot to, say, a playdate, if it ever is. There seem to be a lot of protocols. Ben had some Sunday fits, which led to me melting down too. I was shaking, saying, "Do you see how I'm acting?" I'm sure he was looking at me thinking, "I know I just lost my shit, but Daddy looks like a complete crazy person."

That being said, I had the absolute best drive back to the city—three hours from Amagansett—with Ben. (Lucy stayed in the city with Theresa— we aren't totally set up for her at the beach yet.) He wanted to watch me dance, then have both of us dance in our seats. We looked for airplanes in the sky. And I talked on the phone a bit, seemingly to his delight; he was listening to Hickey and me kibitz with the biggest grin on his face. Came home to discover the news that there are two new sets of gays in the building— sounds like a party! Went to the party for B. J. Novak's movie premiere, then to dinner outside at Morandi with Jason Blum. We had so many laughs.

## MONDAY, JUNE 13, 2022—NEW YORK CITY

Spoke to Teresa. She said, "I didn't hang up on you; I never got a call!" I said, "Teresa, I was *hung up*, I didn't get hung up *on!*" I told her I didn't think we'd be able to make a deal with Caroline but she should let us go through the process.

## TUESDAY, JUNE 14, 2022

We can't make a deal with Caroline, so that's that. I'm going to the South of France next week for forty-eight hours, representing NBCUniversal at Cannes Lions, and I realized my Spanish lover is not far away so I invited him to be my date. He's all in. Boy George is DJing on the yacht Bravo has for the week, and it will be so fun to have a date there. Ben met Kenya Moore at *WWHL*, and I told him she is a real-life Barbie doll. I don't think he knows what a Barbie doll is one way or another, but he seemed impressed. Iman Shumpert was the other guest. If there is a name, I WILL mispronounce it. I made him French. I think he was so high he was just laughing the entire show. Ben and I went for ice cream and counted cabs.

I got the news today that I've been nominated for induction onto the St. Louis Walk of Fame, which absolutely thrilled my mother. "FINALLY!" she said, as though I'd been suffering a complete indignity for years. Watched five episodes of *Severance*, preparing for taping a cast show tomorrow. Live show with Bowen Yang and Matt Rogers was a lot of fun.

## WEDNESDAY, JUNE 15, 2022

Wore flip-flops and shorts to radio, then wound up joining *RHONY* casting meetings at 30 Rock so I was walking around there looking like a fool. We have a shot at booking Madonna for *WWHL*. Apparently she has a new publicist who doesn't understand why she hasn't done the show. I told them I'd had a text exchange with her last year in which she referenced people dragging her on my show, so maybe it would be a good idea to put together a clip reel of all the pure devotion she receives on *WWHL*, from me and others. She would only hear about the bad stuff people say, because that's unfortunately what gets written about, but there's far more to this story! Taped *Severance* show with the cast. Ben Stiller loved me and Anderson on NYE! He couldn't stop gushing and couldn't believe how REAL it was. It made me feel so good to hear that. You just don't know who is watching at any given moment. Ran home to put Ben to bed. On the live show I accidently revealed Kyle's breast reduction. Whoops.

## ⁝⁝⁝ THURSDAY, JUNE 16, 2022

Texted Garcelle at 6:00 a.m. asking her to call when she woke up, and she thought she was in trouble. I was actually trying to add her to *RHUGT3*. Taped a show with Gloria Estefan and Andy Garcia to air while I'm in France next week. Had low expectations and then re-fell in love with Gloria for the fiftieth time. She has done it all, knows everyone, is a great storyteller, and spills the tea all over the place. Went to Ralph Lauren to get some suits. I'm now a 42, in my oversized, eat all the leftovers off Ben's plate, bring a roadie home from work in a Solo cup dad bod era. I'd been putting off going to the mean eye doctor (See: *The Andy Cohen Diaries* and *Superficial!*) since before Covid. While I was sitting in his waiting room today, Bethenny texted to say she was sitting next to Jill Zarin on a flight. I said I was sending a camera and Venmoing her a million dollars. Then I said, "B Strong."

I've been seeing double while watching TV and driving at night, which the nurse claimed is quite common. The doctor saw me and, as he was looking at my eyes, bluntly asked if I was the only person in my family with crossed eyes or if everyone had crossed eyes. I said, is there a way you could mention me being cross-eyed a little more? I didn't hear it those two times. I actually said that I am the only one with a *wandering eye*. He then told the nurse to dilate my eyes, asking on his way out the door if it was my first visit with him. I turned to the nurse in shock, saying I've been going there for twenty years. She said, well, it's late in the day, so maybe he's tired. I said, *it's three fifteen!* They called me back in to see him before my eyes had fully dilated, and he told the nurse to put more drops in my eyes. I said, are my eyes going to be *double* dilated now? They both said NO in unison. I felt like I was on *Severance*, in that weird torture office. They gave me new glasses to wear at night, and the lady at the glasses place said she loved watching me, and I said she should tell the doctor to be nice to me. On the way home, Bethenny called and detailed the flight, and I said that's a TV show—three hours of her trapped on a plane with Jill Zarin, and the credits roll as she exits.

Went with Hickey to see Paul McCartney at MetLife Stadium. He said he thinks the lady at the glasses shop is the wife of the mean doctor, and I said, good, I hope she tells him what I said then. Hickey is my concert buddy, and on the long drive to Jersey, we started making a list of all the amazing shows we'd seen together: Dolly at Irving Plaza and Newark, Cher at Barclays Center and MSG, Madonna multiple times (including Yankee Stadium, where she sang "Like a Prayer" in the rain and blew our minds), Pink, Dead and Company, John Mayer, the Killers, George Michael, the big Michael Jackson show at MSG the night before 9/11, Beyoncé, Britney, and I'm sure there are more. That's an amazing list! After navigating the nightmare that is MetLife Stadium, we finally arrived at what turned out to be killer seats, and it was a who's who: Lorne Michaels, Jon Bon Jovi, Whoopi Goldberg, and Mike Bloomberg, whom I implored to run for mayor again, and he said something to the effect of "It's your problem, not mine." The concert was outstanding. McCartney's voice is in the same key, and he knows how to use it for best effect, eighty years in. Seeing the show made me realize what a stadium band Wings was, and those songs were my highlights: "Maybe I'm Amazed" and "Live and Let Die" (with insane pyro in the rain to rival Madonna's Yankee Stadium moment). Oh, and freaking Bruce Springsteen came out and sang "Glory Days." Can you imagine?! After the show, we went to Corner Bistro for burgers and a nightcap. What a divine night.

## ⠿ FRIDAY, JUNE 17, 2022

Okay: I have something to confess that I'm not proud of. The truth is that we left the concert after the "Hey Jude" encore and missed Jon Bon Jovi coming out and singing with McCartney on "Birthday," Bruce coming back out, and apparently a "Helter Skelter" for the ages. And it was all my fault. I'd been burned so badly at MetLife before, having sat in the parking lot for *hours* after seeing U2. I vowed I'd never do it again! We felt pretty good about it last night, but Hickey says he would've sat in the two hours of traffic in order to have seen that encore. I agreed, but I'm secretly glad we got home in a half hour and got to have a burger, which sat in my stomach like a rock this morning as I got Ben ready for his last day of school.

Garcelle is out for *RHUGT*, and I'm hoping Shannon Beador can do it. She would be incredible with this group. Kathy Wakile sent me a huge amount of gifts for the kids. I was so touched, especially after not having spoken to her for years. I called her, and we had a great chat. Lots of Lucy time. Jackie came over, and we took the subway up to see *MJ: The Musical*. Forgot our masks, but the subway was empty. Drink at the Russian Samovar before, which brought back memories of intermissions past on Fifty-Second Street. Got to *MJ* and again realized we had no masks. They gave us some. The music and dancing were spectacular! We smoked a little of a joint before we went in and, during the (terrible—as bad as the music was good) exposition, my mind was wandering all over the place as I had negative stoned thoughts. On the edible they're all positive thoughts, which is a good note to stick with the edible. We left very happy, but the show proved that we as a culture have become happily immune to the fact that we are all cheering for fake Michael Jacksons and ABBA avatars. Are we becoming a "take what we can get" culture? But the versions are so good who can argue.

## ⠿ SATURDAY, JUNE 18, 2022—SUNDAY, JUNE 19, 2022

Father's Day weekend in the city started optimistically with Ben, on an unseasonably cool morning outside over pancakes at La Bonbonnière. Dan Patrick walked by and said hello. The big sports guy. Took Bryan, Billie, and Kingston to the playground and Lucy met us with Theresa, in what was her first visit of a lifetime of them. Full days with the kids. Had a lovely dinner with B. J. Novak at the Polo Bar. We laughed a lot. Had a Father's Day brunch at John and Adam's with several other gay dads. I felt seen! We watched a crane on the street for forty-five minutes. Took Lucy's new stroller to Via Carota for Father's Day dinner, with Ben standing on the little platform on the back. It was the first time using that stroller, and it felt chaotic and amazing walking down the street with them both.

## ▦ MONDAY, JUNE 20, 2022—NEW YORK CITY TO CANNES

Today was a hell race to get it all done that started with Ben wailing in his room sometime after 6:00 a.m. He's subliminally making me pay for going to France tonight. Did radio from home, and the equipment wouldn't work, so I was broadcasting via Zoom from AirPods, which put me in a horrible, shit frame of mind after spending half the weekend reading two books so I could do great interviews with their authors. They turned out fair. I just didn't have my mojo. Then taped two *WWHLs* and spent quality time with Ben and Lucy, cleaned out my bathroom, and got through cleaning about one-eighth of my closet before heading to Teterboro Airport for the ten o'clock flight. It was just me and Jenn and Imani on the private plane. Having the PR team with me made me feel like I could spend the next forty-eight hours lobotomized and they'd get me where I needed to be. On that score, I had some rosé, took my Ambien, and was asleep a half hour into the flight. (The women gave me the big bed.)

## ▦ TUESDAY, JUNE 21, 2022, TO WEDNESDAY, JUNE 22, 2022— CANNES

Landed completely refreshed after seven hours of sleep—more than I usually get, at this point. The second you get off the plane in France you remember that French men are all wearing the tightest pants. Specifically, tight around their asses. My driver didn't speak a word of English but was so cute. I attempted speaking Spanish to him but that didn't work. Got to the hotel, freshened up, and headed to the Bravo cabana, where I did a live *WWHL* with Dorit and Garcelle as guests, with Captain Sandy and Kate Chastain in the audience. At the cocktail party after for clients, I met two reporters from Page Six who were telling me which Housewives leak the most to them, and the top two are exactly who I would've expected and are also the two who are constantly telling me they never leak stuff, that they don't care about the press. (Clue: they are both in the *RHONY* universe). I should start leaking stuff. I've never leaked a story!

Went home to take some tincture, and Garcelle texted that she, Dorit, and Captain Sandy were next door at Hermès, so I joined them and bought a bright yellow swimsuit that I'll never wear. Five hundred bucks down the drain. Garcelle got a keychain, and Dorit didn't buy anything because there "wasn't time." Watching her in a store is something—she's ravenous. We all had cocktails and dinner together on the NBCUniversal boat, site of our Wednesday-night party. Conversation turned to the old chestnut of who likes a finger up their butt, with Kate and me leading the discussion. It turned out to be a beautiful and fun evening. I was sitting between Dorit and Garcelle and across from Kate Chastain. Dorit, with all good intentions, was giving Kate dating advice, and gave Kate a mantra she didn't ask for. (It was also too long to even remember and therefore not a mantra per se.) Her assessment of Kate led with all negatives, like, "You're not unlikeble. Actually, you're not unlovable." It absolutely felt like an episode of *Housewives*, and I was dying not to be hearing a confessional from Kate about what was going through her mind. (I did get the confessional later.) Went to a huge Spotify party right on the water where Dua Lipa performed. Post Malone was there, and Jemele Hill (not together). Also, there were a ton of Swedes, who apparently all take the summer off and go around Europe. Hung in front of the stage with Kate and the Housewives and danced our asses off to Dua Lipa, who was dancing *her* ass off and, I'm pretty sure, lip-synching. It was great fun, and I love her. A surprisingly deep talk on the way out with a handsome stranger who turned out to be engaged. We told each other all our secrets and I'm pretty sure we'll never cross paths again. Romantic!

Woke up Wednesday feeling like I got hit by a truck. Ran over to a client lunch on the yacht. Did work in my hotel room. Met Dorit and G at Dolce, where they were getting their packages wrapped. Garcelle had been offered a ride on the corporate jet but was waffling because she hates small planes. Dorit and I told her she was nuts and talked her into it. Headed to Chanel, where I witnessed the fact that Dorit literally buys shit off the rack, retail, full price. She got a jumpsuit, shoes, and three other things—she had to have spent fifteen to twenty thousand bucks. Garcelle got a thousand-dollar scarf, and I was flirting with this cute little egg-shaped purse for Grac but found out it was five thousand dollars, so I left empty-handed to my panel. Walking out of the panel, I ran into Paris Hilton and her new husband, who clearly is madly in love with her. He was telling me how booked she's been all weekend and how she made a ton of money, but he jokingly calls her P2D2 because they go home, unplug her, and then plug her back in before her next appearance. *P2D2 is funny!* He asked me if I'm going to protect his mother-in-law when the shit hits the fan on *BH*. I did the Oprah thing of kind of not answering but joyously yelling, "Protect Kathy Hilton at all costs!" They're going on the plane with Garcelle tomorrow. So that will be spicy.

My Spanish lover met me at the hotel to spend the night. We have a really easy vibe, got right back into it with a great catch-up dinner outside before heading to the party on the boat, where I found a cushion on the bow for us to perch ourselves on. When he left for Spain, it was to figure things out, but it's clear he is staying. Boy George was a brilliant DJ, and he had a mic where he was singing along to some of the songs, then sang "Time (Clock of the Heart)" and "Church of the Poison Mind"—we all lost our minds. Dorit was behind the DJ stand, dancing with him. Garcelle stayed on the floor the whole time, we lost Kate Chastain and Captain Sandy, and I was so happy to have a man I was into to dance with. And I cannot overstate how great a DJ George was. (If I ever get married, maybe PK will give me a little discount.) In a night of many highlights, the best was getting a video from Theresa of Ben singing the ABC song to his sister, who lay there staring at him (I'd like to say adoringly, but who can tell with a baby).

Anyway, the headline is they had what I think was their first extended quality time together where he just wanted to be *nonviolently* all over her.

After the set, we hung out with George in the master suite of the boat, which was incidentally super modern. Had a lovely chat with him that's been wiped from my memory by the tequila and edible, but I do know we talked about Madonna (I always bring her up whenever I can, as one may have already figured out). Dorit and my man were speaking in Hebrew and French together, so theirs was a love match. We got back to the hotel around two thirty, and there was a huge party in the suite right next to mine, so we went in and hung out for a while before going to bed.

## THURSDAY, JUNE 23, 2022—CANNES TO NEW YORK CITY

Woke up wildly hung over, not having packed, with a driver waiting downstairs to take me to the plane. Flew home alone. Who am I, Taylor Swift?! There's a major rush for monkeypox vaccines, as it's starting to spread just as gay pride is beginning this weekend. My architect, Gordon, sent me a listing for an insane penthouse in the West Village with gorgeous outdoor space. I made a beeline to see it tomorrow. FaceTimed with Anderson, who was in DC and brought Wolf Blitzer on to say hi. He reminded me of his *Housewives* tagline, something about being a Wolf in a Situation Room? I can't remember, but it's good. Back in New York, I put Ben and Lucy to bed, had dinner with Bruce, and crashed.

## FRIDAY, JUNE 24, 2022

As John Hill and I were broadcasting from the Stonewall Inn, we got word that *Roe v. Wade* had been overturned. So we tried not to let that sink the festive vibe of the show. Saw new penthouse, which had outdoor space like I can't believe, but my gut was that it's not big enough. It's certainly not as big as my current place, which is—minus the lack of outdoor space—my dream apartment. Outdoor space is the one thing in life that's eluding me. And love. But outdoor space I can buy at least. It's also insanely priced. Like, *crazy*. Architect Gordon is going next week to make sure it's not enough space. Tonight was Bruce's party at DiscOasis, the new roller disco installation at Wollman Rink in Central Park. Though I was a rollerblading FIEND in the '90s, I was a lil wobbly the first time out on skates. A few hours later, with more liquid courage and the safety of nightfall, I reached an emotional high gliding around that circle, bathed in beautiful lights, in the shadow of midtown Manhattan. I felt like I was on Molly. (That's euphoria.) Went with Bruce and Bryan to the new restaurant on Seventh and Perry—the guy came from Café des Artistes and so it's the same kind of super-thin pizza.

## ⠿ SATURDAY, JUNE 25, 2022, TO SUNDAY, JUNE 26, 2022

Happy Pride! It was a real Daddycation, because Ben went to spend the weekend with his grandparents in St. Louis, so I spent the bulk of both days in bed—literally just holding court horizontally. Lucy would come lie with me, and I was grateful for her inertia. Went to Planet Pride at Brooklyn Mirage with Bruce. Did I get monkeypox? I guess I'll know in two weeks! Sunday was once again spent in bed, listening to the parade and madness fifteen stories below me. Hosted a fantastic sunset Pride party for Mujen at the Skylark and went to Café Cluny after. The streets were chaos, and downtown was locked down. Because of that, no one could get to the Mobil station on Thirteenth and Eighth Avenue, so in walking home I discovered it had been shut down and converted into an outdoor rave. There was a rave *at the gas station*. It was so surreal I had to walk right into the thick of it to feel the vibe, which was less than stellar.

## ⠿ MONDAY, JUNE 27, 2022

Jill Zarin was on *WWHL* with Brandi Glanville, who told Jill she was thirsty, and Jill was incredulous about it. After the show I took every variation of photo with Jill; her boyfriend, Gary; the dog, "Bossi"; and daughter, Ally. It was like we were at a wedding and had to get the shots. I will say Jill is one of only a few Housewives speaking out against the overturning of *Roe v. Wade*, and I commend her for it. Where are the women? After putting the kids to bed, I had dinner with Amanda and Grac.

## ⬛ TUESDAY, JUNE 28, 2022

Taped a show. Lucy was so fussy all day. Looked at fabrics for the beach house tonight with Jackie.

## ⬛ WEDNESDAY, JUNE 29, 2022

Today was nonstop. Woke up and Howard was raging on the *BH* women's faces. On the way to Sirius, I called in to his show from the cab and wound up fighting with Chris Wilding on and off for a half hour as I stood on the corner of Seventh Avenue and Fiftieth Street. Good radio show and meeting after with Tim and Megan about the future of Radio Andy. Gordon called from the potential apartment, telling me I had to look at it again seriously. Pinged Hickey to meet me there, and as we walked out he said, "Buy it." It's so freaking expensive. I went home and had a total breakdown over it. I cried. Having completed what I thought was my dream apartment, spending all that money, having to gut it, and now having two mortgages at once and a new beach house, not to mention while *raising two kids*—I just buckled at the thought. Had a *WWHL* conference call, then met Alan Braun for tea, and he said don't do it. That's my agent telling me not to do it, so I listened. But I cancelled my workout with Stanny and met Debbie the Realtor at my place to see how much she'd sell it for. She quoted a high price. Gordon sent a revised plan for the apartment with a much more exciting master suite, and that tipped the scales and got me excited. Taped a show with Dorinda and Phaedra, who brought Ayden and Dylan, with whom I had a sweet reunion. The live show was Garcelle and Ziwe. Met Bruce, Bryan, Kevin, and Simon at Café Cluny after the show, and they all were very enthusiastically telling me that I absolutely HAD to buy the apartment. It is a truly one-of-a-kind penthouse in the very small radius of the West Village that I've deemed the perfect spot in Manhattan in which to live. I'm going for it.

## ⠿ THURSDAY, JUNE 30, 2022, TO SUNDAY, JULY 10, 2022— AMAGANSETT

Around nine fifteen on the morning we were to leave for ten days of family vacation in the Hamptons, I was in a feverish rage in front of my building, covered in sweat. My transformation into the person I never thought I'd become was complete. There I stood in front of my new SUV, the one with three rows (*I never wanted an SUV, let alone one with three fucking rows!*), fighting with inanimate objects in front of my two helpless children and nannies. This is what we tried jamming into the car that was supposed to fit everything: Ben, Lucy, Margot, Theresa, two car seats, three coolers full of breast milk (Kathleen is pumping for us!), a baby bathtub, a stroller, and mounds of luggage. The result was that it all certainly did *not* fit, and I almost threw one of the car seats down the street. Marcos the doorman, watching from the side and trying to be of service, was actually scared of me at one point. We somehow jammed it in and began a three-plus-hour trek to paradise. Toward the end of the journey, everyone in the car hit the wall and started crying. And that was the moment I philosophically connected with Kyle Cooke's prescience. Summer *should* be fun. This was *not fun*. Not one bit of fun!

Buying the new apartment was an underlying cause for stress the entire "vacation," and I pooped no fewer than twenty times in the first four days alone. It's the cost, renovating it for two years with jacked-up pricing, and then selling my current (former dream?) apartment in whatever market that would be—and then the size of the apartment (smaller than mine). If I was playing a game on *WWHL*, it would be "How! Much! Can He! Take!" I was a wreck. Thinking about leaving my current building, where I've been just shy of twenty years, makes me want to cry. Also, this is the place my kids will grow up, full stop. And probably my last stop on my stay in Manhattan. All huge life decisions here. The thing that tipped it toward happening was when I visualized living in the apartment, and specifically using the outdoor space as much as I know I will. While I was renovating this current apartment, I rented with a wraparound terrace (see *Superficial*), and I left there saying that even though I had just built my dream apartment, I would leave for outside space. The new spot has sunsets every night of the week. That's PARADISE!

Spent lots of great quality time with the kids this week. Ben is so sweet to Lucy. Ben and I had long swims either before or after dinner every night. We looked for roly-polys by the side of the pool, under the watchful wonderment of his sister, and we would swim to her and tell her things (Ben is like a fish and fully underwater now). Ben spent lots of time driving his Audi down the street in Grateful Dead gear, and a neighbor stopped by one day and said, I guess I don't have to wonder who your dad is. "My parent is Andy Cohen," Ben replied. Spent at least an hour a day looking for darn roly-polys. (It felt like my job!) Had a great Fourth of July barbecue over here (grilling is the only cooking I know how to do), and Ben was the consummate host, asking the Brodericks and anyone who would listen if they had everything they needed. Had dinner with the Buffetts one night and showed Jimmy how serve yourself Froyo places work at Buddhaberry.

So there's this weird Housewives phone hack that's been happening for many years, but I'd forgotten about it because it stopped. It's back. Here's how it works: my phone will ring, and it looks like Jill Zarin or Caroline Manzo is calling me. I pick it up, and there's no one there. Concurrently they—and others—get what look like calls from my phone. It's been going on for years, and they'll text and say, "Did you call me?" and I say "It's that weird hack." This week I heard from Bethenny, Cynthia Bailey, Caroline Manzo, Marysol, and Ramona—and had to re-explain that it's that "thing" that happens (they all know what it is). Got a text from Carole Radziwill with a screenshot of missed calls from me and Luann, saying, "What is going on?" We had a businesslike exchange, our first time communicating since we didn't pick up her contract and she told me to never speak to her again. In other Housewives stuff (there was a lot this week), I had to slap Jill Zarin's wrist about something, and then in making conversation I said, "I'll see you at Luann's Fosé party," and she didn't know anything about it. "Wait, I thought Luann was in the *city*? I didn't know about a Fosé launch. Do you think she didn't invite me?" I felt like I had stepped in shit. Or an episode of *RHONY*. Or both.

I rarely go to Housewives events, because I feel like if I go to one I should go to all of them, but there I was in the middle of vacation at Lu's Fosé launch with Bruce, and indeed it felt like stepping into the show. Jill was the first person I ran into, looking really GREAT. The *RHONY* women should give a MasterClass in how to stay looking incredible. Lu got up and spoke about Fosé. In a galaxy of shitty products launched out of the show, this one seems like a real winner, especially after you hear her speak about it. From there, Bruce and I went to a big gay benefit, and being with him in the Hamptons felt like we were back in the '90s until we looked around and saw how old everyone had gotten. Then we turned to each other and said, "Do *we* look like that?" We do.

Barry Diller invited me to Europe on the boat this summer, and John is doing John Mayer summer camp in Montana for the month of August. I don't feel like I can do either. I can't believe how much my life has changed, and how much I'm building for my family's future—it's a heaviness I've never felt but also a sense of sureness that feels good. I often turn to Theresa, or Margot, or Ben, or whoever is in the room with me (and there is *always* someone in the room) and say, "I used to be alone. I used to do *whatever* I wanted *whenever* I wanted it." They nod.

Came back to the city after eleven days totally recharged. A bounty of packages awaited me, and the one that stood out wasn't from Cher but from Jen Shah, who is in town for her trial. Not only was there a mini-microphone for Lucy, she also got her a baby Dior dress and headband. On the one hand, I was touched that she thought of me with all she has going on (like facing thirty years in jail), but on the other, I didn't love how much she must have spent. And, like, is that money coming from people she ripped off? Do I need to turn this baby Dior dress in to someone? Are there elderly fraud victims who should have it? It's sitting on my desk in a state of limbo. Had a wonderful night with Bruce and, walking home, met one of the new hot gay guys who moved into the building. He introduced himself to me, and suddenly New York seemed full of possibility all over again.

## ⬜ MONDAY JULY 11, 2022—NEW YORK CITY

Back to business! I was on the radio interviewing a documentary producer who mentioned his next project is about a "female" robot that is super smart and can do anything. "Can you fuck her?" I asked. I regretted the question all day. (You can't fuck her, it turns out.) During the show, Jen Shah's guilty plea was announced. I had so many emotions. First I was pissed. She spent two years lying on camera about it, crying racism because people were questioning her finances, and advocating for the wrongly accused. Then I felt horrible for her victims. And I felt just *bad* all the way around because I'd really grown to enjoy her on the show; it always struck me that there was something about her that radiated optimism, of all things. She's likeable, and there's something bright about her face (when she isn't throwing wine or yelling). Anyway, I said none of that on the radio because I was processing it all and didn't want to speak until I'd thought about what I wanted to say. Instead I said I didn't know what to think and marveled at the fact that she'd just sent the gifts. Lunch with Jason and Lauren Blum at the Mark Hotel. Ben said "oh shit" today. Oh shit.

The other day, I got an offer to play myself on *Gossip Girl*, and the shoot is tomorrow. They came for a fitting today. I don't understand the script at all. They have me playing myself, but as a horrible human being—like at the end of it I say I hate teachers. Or that no one cares about teachers. I said, I know you guys think I'm a bottom-feeding reality television producer, but can I not lean into that trope in this appearance? They're taking another whack at the script.

A new *RHONY* cast member dropped out. I need to call her, but she's in Italy. Oh, and Tamra is on *WWHL* next week with Vicki, and Bravo wants me to announce she's coming back to *OC*, but I don't want to make Vicki uncomfortable. I gotta call Tamra and make a plan. I don't want to tell Vicki that Tamra's coming back now because I don't want it to leak. We heard from Madonna's people that it's not looking likely that she'll do *WWHL* for the remix album but that they'll let us know this week. I asked Dori to get a *reason* from them, so I at least know what the issue is.

Trying to get a monkeypox vaccine. They're releasing more doses at 1:00 p.m. tomorrow, and I've got Daryn on triple standby. I am not going to LOOK at another guy until I get one. Dinner with John Mayer and Naomi Fry at Barbuto before the live show, and John agreed to another spontaneous bartending gig. The audience lost their mind when he came out. He was perfect. And looked very cute.

## ⁞⁞⁞ TUESDAY, JULY 12, 2022

It was 90 degrees, and I was clonking around Minetta Tavern in a velvet Tom Ford tuxedo shooting a show I thought I didn't care about but became riveted by as the day went on. It was a big group scene for the *Gossip Girl* finale, when "Gossip Girl" is revealed to the cast after the Met Ball, and I was sitting in a booth with this adorable kid, Eli Brown, who plays Obie. We shot all day, and I decided I looked like Eli's fat grandpappy sitting there next to him. I'd last about a day on a scripted show. They shoot the same scene from every angle, so you're there all day for what will amount to maybe two minutes of TV time. It felt very dramatic, though! And as bad an actor as I am, I didn't totally stink up the room. At 1:00 p.m., I looked around and saw every gay man on his phone trying to get a monkeypox vaccine appointment. I would've been too, but Daryn was hitting refresh for an hour until she got me one in Queens on Friday. Gordon is dealing with the new building, figuring out if we can really do everything I want to the apartment.

Ben said "shit" again, but he *did* use it correctly in a sentence ("Oh shit, there's bird poo on this chair"), so does that count for anything? Oh, and he was on a playdate and he asked his friend Reece if *her* daddy has a Kiki

Lounge. Oy vey. In today's Housewives news, Alexis Bellino and Meghan King are texting to get on the next *Ultimate Girls Trip*, which (as I told them) leaves in two days, so that's not going to happen. Porsha is joining, and I'm so excited she'll be back on our air. We'd originally talked to her, and for some reason the conversation fizzled, so this is the best possible solution. And my noncomments about Jen Shah on the radio yesterday are getting picked up all over as "Andy Cohen Reacts to the Jen Shah News: He Doesn't Know What to Think"! So by not saying anything I sound like a complete fucking idiot who doesn't know *what* to possibly think about her scamming all those poor people. Twitter was making fun of me for not being able to muster a thought, and Meghan McCain wrote an editorial saying she needs to be fired, quoting my bumbling comments where I marvel that she got me a gift. Tomorrow I need to say something on the radio about how disgusted I am.

My parents are coming to town next week, and I texted on the family text chain asking if they'd bartend on Tuesday when Tamra and Vicki are on (I need to call Tamra!), and they said fine. Mom said, "Just don't have us do anything dirty," then Dad asked if Tamra's implants are still in the clubhouse. So that's mixed messaging! We had two shows tonight, and Jamair, the hot trainer from the gym, bartended. I hugged him before the show, and he'd oiled himself up, and I got it all over myself. I wish I'd gotten it all over myself doing something more fun.

## ⁞⁞⁞ WEDNESDAY, JULY 13, 2022

The day started with a shock as I woke up at six thirty from a nightmare in which I had to tell Beanie Feldstein to stop singing at a party. (Don't ask.) I went to pee and, as the bright morning sunlight streamed into my bathroom, I got a glimpse of my back and what I thought was a monkeypox lesion, which then caused two hours of tossing and turning in my bed. The next time I looked at it, at eight thirty, it looked like . . . a red mark. So that was time when I could've been panicking about a multitude of *other* things! I said my piece about Jen Shah on the radio. Then we were giving relationship advice, and a woman from Philly (a regular caller) called in to say she wants to have a three-way with me and her husband, and her husband (who has never messed around with a guy) is fully on board. The woman wants to take my gold star status! As if that wasn't enough, she's coming to the show next Tuesday night and wants it to happen then. I told her that's not happening because a) I'm on sexual lockdown because of monkeypox so I'm suppressing any horny urges right now; and b) even if I *was* horny, Tuesday wouldn't be the night because my parents will be at that Vicki/Tamra show and I can't be looking at them behind the bar and then my hetero *lovers* in the audience. But it was good radio. And she's sending John pictures of them for him to vet. I am intrigued!

Had a cab that smelled like dead animals and proceeded to get in a huge fight with the driver, who took me the wrong way. I called Tamra from the gym, and we agreed she would call Vicki and tell her she's coming back and see how she responds. What could go wrong? Spoke to the woman trying to drop out of *RHONY*. It turns out she is already in my phone, having asked me and SJ to be someone's guest at the Met Ball a few years ago. Then she said she was one of the people in that weird phone hack involving all the Housewives! Which is crazy. Then she said she ran into Sutton Stracke getting gelato last night in Italy. *These are signs!* Got a text from Vicki saying she's so happy for Tamra but had hoped the tres amigos would be back together, and she couldn't stop crying and wondered whether it was a good idea for her to come on *WWHL* at all. I said we don't have to announce it with you sitting there, we can do it another way if that makes you uncomfortable; this is a marathon, not a sprint. We got you on *UGT*, and you're coming to BravoCon, and we are family whether you like it or not. She said she'd rather not be there for the announcement; she won't be able to stay composed. Then Tamra called and said there is no way Vicki won't ruin this and bring it up on *WWHL*, and I said then THAT will be an interesting live-TV moment and we will deal with it as we can.

Speaking of interesting live-TV moments, Caroline Brooks and Nina Ali from Dubai made their clubhouse debut tonight. Every night during commercial breaks, the hair and makeup teams rush to the guests to "fix" whatever movement happened during the seven minutes they were sitting still in chairs on TV (it's totally ridiculous). Brooks's hair person put a piping hot curling iron down on my little table to my left where I keep my cards and, reaching for the cards, I moved it with my fingers and burned them. I was in immediate pain and anger, while the hair person was remarkably unbothered, unrepentant, and unmoving until I screamed at her to LEAVE. I never scream. I'm not a screamer. I was physically shaking for the rest of the show and held ice for five minutes until Deirdre calmly said in my ear during the next act, "Ice doesn't help." I asked on-air for them to bring me whatever *does* help. They brought cream and I-don't-know-what during the next commercial break. I was shaking the whole time. Shaking! Came home in a *mood* and, after struggling to get my tie and shirt off with one hand (I need a boyfriend), got in a Twitter fight with Kari Lake, this psycho running for governor in Arizona.

## THURSDAY, JULY 14, 2022

Woke up at 6:00 a.m. with throbbing fingers, which gradually got better as the day went on. Brooks DMed me, apologizing. I feel bad if she feels like it was her fault; it clearly wasn't. After I yelled at her hair person to get out, she apparently went running from the studio straight out the front door! Also heard from Stanbury and Ayan, who I'm sure were secretly happy it wasn't *their* hair person who burned me on the air! Upgraded my Tinder subscription, and the men are really handsome on there. In the same vein, since I've been on a total sex lockdown because of monkeypox I've been hearing from a collection of the hottest guys on Grindr, guys who six weeks ago would never have been interested in me. It's odd. I feel like I'm being tested. But I will not waver.

We taped a show with Lizzo today. She is an A-plus guest; it was so fun. She taught me how to twerk. I feel like people are always teaching me how to twerk on TV, though I'm not sure what the audience is for that. I tried to kill the segment before the show, but the team thought it would be funny. They were right. My ass is so small. We're gonna have Tamra ring the doorbell on the live show next Wednesday to announce she's coming back to

*OC*, thereby saving Vicki any embarrassment. (That is, *if* we can close her deal, and *if* Vicki doesn't blurt it out on Tuesday's show, in front of my parents and my new hetero lovers in the audience.) Negotiating with the owners of my new apartment, who want to stay living there for six months and are being tough about what I'll get in return. I feel like I'm being punked in this negotiation, given how expensive it all is. In celebration of his tour wrapping up Saturday, Jordan Rubin put together a group dinner for John at Jack's Wife Freda in SoHo. As he sat in front of me, looking extra hot, I said, "I have to take a picture of this man candy." I took one shot, which might be the most beautiful pic of John I've seen, and immediately posted it, causing panties to bunch from coast to coast. No joke, he looked *that good.*

## ⁜ FRIDAY, JULY 15, 2022

Usually the day of a Dead show is all happy, but today was high highs and low lows. Madonna officially once again passed on *WWHL*. Then Jill Biden's office called out of nowhere asking if she could be on before the end of summer.

I missed Ben's first time on a pony and was going mental about it. My heart sank when I opened Margot's text and saw the picture, knowing that I wasn't there. I texted Bruce for wisdom and help. He helped a lot. "This is going to be the back & forth . . . You can't be there for all . . . No parent is . . . You're working. He's where he should be . . . You'll have many firsts with him . . ." That made me feel better. Got the monkeypox vaccine, which actually hurt! The line was all gay men, and the man behind me was a handsome Australian who engaged me in a really scandalous flirt that started in person and continued on Instagram DM while we waited in separate rooms to get a shot. You simply cannot keep gay men away from the flirt!

I was already in Queens, so I stayed there and did some work in my car (I had a driver) before taking an extra-huge dose of liquid THC and heading to Citi Field to meet the Camp High folks to help them sell T-shirts in the parking lot before the show. I figured all I had to do was just *be high* for the next eight hours, so why not go jumbo? Once in the madness of Shakedown Street (where all the merch is pre-show), the THC hit me like a Mack truck, and then I got a text from John saying, "How would you like to introduce the band tonight?! I just had the idea and Bob loves it! Mr. New York." My heart almost stopped from excitement, and highness. I've been onstage in front of massive crowds before, but this was onstage *with the Dead*. At *Citi Field*. I was legitimately so high and so nervous. Then I realized of course that everyone in the audience—and probably everyone onstage—would be high, so if I *wasn't* incredibly high to introduce the band, that would be more of a problem. The text came as we were in the middle of summer heat and the madness that is Shakedown before a show, people selling balloons to suck up the nitrous oxide (overheard: "the nitrous in LA early in the tour was *trash!*") and many, many kind, enthusiastic Deadheads who wanted selfies (despite having no apparent knowledge of how to take one?), all while I was trying to figure out the perfect three lines to say to introduce the band. And in the midst of texting with John's crew about logistics, I get an incoming rampage of texts from Vicki, who has heard secondhand that I've been asking guests what they think of her being antivax, which she found totally inappropriate, along with a diatribe about her medical conditions and beliefs about the Covid vaccine, which in my state I was not ready to process and didn't even skim. I texted her back and said I asked guests about a fight that occurred *on the show she is on*. I was asking about the show! I got more paragraphs back about not wanting to discuss it on Tuesday night, and I said I didn't either and that I was at a Dead show and didn't want to fight with her right then. She said, "I love the Grateful Dead! Have fun!" and that was that. See how the Dead makes everything better?

Greg, Annemarie, and I tried to navigate getting into Citi Field and found an amazing security person who helped us and wound up mistakenly bringing us to John's dressing room, where I bothered him about my intro, forgetting he had a show to play. He said, "If you say, 'Ladies and gentlemen, Dead and Company,' is that going to offend people? Like, would it be misgendering them to say 'ladies and gentlemen'"? I said, "Don't worry, I'm going to say, 'Give it up for Dead and Company!'" He kind of flinched in a way that made me think maybe I should say "ladies and gentlemen," but I got side-tracked, asking him over and over if I look fat and my boobs look big in my T-shirt, to which he said, "No, you look muscular," until I asked him again.

We headed to the stage on his golf cart, and that's when everything got real fun. Seeing Bob Weir on the side of the stage made me completely adrenalized; I floated on air. We hugged, I thanked him, we said other stuff I don't remember, and Matt Busch told me the band were going to go out first and then I'd come and intro them so they could slam right into "Bertha" after the intro. So smart! I made them point out my mic four times, and they said there's a little switch on it that I should turn on before the intro. I said, "I am incapable of turning that switch on, so please do it now, and I'll just step up to the mic and do my thing." My brilliant intro was: "New York City! [Saying "New York City" to an NYC crowd guarantees rapturous applause.] New York City! [I said it twice.] Are you ready to have a real good time? [I meant to say are you ready *for* a real good time, which is a Grateful Dead song lyric.] Give it up for Dead and Company!" Then I literally skipped off and danced on the side of the stage to "Bertha" with Natascha and her daughter Monet Weir. Stayed on the floor dancing by the spinners (look it up, it's worth seeing) with Greg and Annemarie for most of the show, which was really fun. Highlights were: "Sugaree," "Terrapin," and "I Know You Rider," but the boys feel like they're slowing down a bit. Seems like tomorrow night is gonna be the last stop on this road. After the show, we rode out of the venue with John on his bus, rockstar style, and had incredible pizza on a sidewalk in Tribeca from I don't know where, and absolutely laughed our asses off until 2:00 a.m. I felt like I was on a cloud. Belly laughing! It was *magic*! All verrrrrrry high.

## ▦ SATURDAY, JULY 16, 2022

When we planned how to announce Tamra's return to *RHOC*, we didn't factor Jill Zarin's mouth into the process. Exactly one week after I asked her to think before she speaks publicly about anything relating to Bravo, she blew the news on Instagram, adding that Vicki is pissed. Texted her asking WTF, and she said she is only repeating things she heard online. I said, I'm not debating this with you. This all led to Bravo being furious, then both Tamra and Vicki being furious, and Vicki texting saying maybe she shouldn't do the show on Tuesday. I said to stay, but now she and Tamra seem to be furious at *each other* for some reason. So this promises to be very messy. At least my parents and a couple trying to have a three-way with me will also be there, so it won't be weird at all.

Night two of Dead and Company at Citi Field absolutely blew last night away. It was maybe the best show I've seen. Highlights were "Dear Mr. Fantasy" into "Hey Jude," "Jack Straw," and "Morning Dew." If that was the last Dead and Co. show I ever see, I went out on a real banger. We spent most of the show with the spinners and their considerable body scents. Before the show, we wandered backstage and schmoozed with a lot of the crew and band support I've been seeing for the last six years of this band iteration. Visited with Bob Weir in his bus, and he was sitting in front of a portrait he made of Jerry's mugshot, which they wound up showing onscreen during "Truckin'," and the crowd went wild. I learned from Greg that the only other people to ever introduce the Dead at a gig are Bill Graham, Ken Kesey, John Belushi, and—believe it or not—Donald Trump in the '80s somewhere. Not only do I feel honored, I'm starting to second-guess my whole intro: Was I too loud? Should I have said "ladies and gentlemen" instead?

After the show, Greg got us a ride in someone's Sprinter (I still haven't exactly figured out who the group was that was kind enough to take us), and we wound up trying the nitrous in the parking lot. Everyone said it's like poppers, but it wasn't as good. In the Sprinter home, Greg gave me Wacky Packs and gave my friend Austin a set of *Gremlins 2* cards that had one of those hard sticks of gum in it, which, in my very stoned haze, I ate and then proceeded to evaporate on my tongue. We wound up in a bar in Brooklyn (John was already on a plane home) and Googled *Gremlins 2* and determined those cards and gum were from 1990. So the gum was older than Austin and from the year I moved to New York City. No wonder it disappeared on my tongue! By the time I got to bed, I felt like I'd lived.

## ⊞ SUNDAY, JULY 17, 2022

Today I got to be with Ben all day. Went to Omari's first birthday party and met more gay dads, one of whom I dated years ago and who now seems to live in the 'burbs with two kids. He was doing a hard sell on my moving to Jersey, and I told him not to waste his time. Took Ben to Billie Lourd's birthday dinner. Ryan Murphy was wearing the coolest Prada terry cloth set. I sat next to Leslie Grossman at dinner, and apparently our *RHOBH* casting people reached out to her to see what her level of interest is in being a Housewife. Who knew! It was a magical night on the terrace, and I couldn't stop thinking about the Dead show the night before. I'm feeling that music like crazy! I can't explain it. If you know, you know.

## ⊞ MONDAY, JULY 18, 2022

After that weekend, it's no wonder I overslept this morning; Ben came and woke me up at eight fifteen. My car was already downstairs to take me to *Live with Kelly and Ryan*. Traffic was so bad I almost didn't make it. Went straight onto the air, and all the wear and tear of the weekend was all over my face; I looked so gross in the monitors. From the Upper West Side, it was straight to radio, where I'm sure I looked equally gross behind the microphone. On the radio I discussed the couple who are coming to the show tomorrow. John shared their pictures with me, and they're cute. This is all too much. Somehow managed to work out with Stanny in the afternoon. Bob Weir texted asking what time my show is, saying that maybe he'll come by. How do I say no to *that*?! Spoke to Vicki, who said she and Tamra aren't speaking. I don't know what the hell is going to happen on this show tomorrow night. Also found out that a few moms from Ben's school will be in the audience, along with—of course—the potential hetero three-way and my parents.

Had dinner with Mom and Dad, and Mom was remembering me road-tripping to Wisconsin for some Grateful Dead shows when I was eighteen and sleeping in my car in the parking lot. "Why THE HELL did I let you

DO THAT?!" she kept saying. I figured out that she let me do that because she trusted me, which is a beautiful thing. Would she have trusted me if she knew I'd be doing mushrooms and LSD all weekend? Probably not! But I am so grateful for the experience. It informed the man I am today! I've been trying to sell them on seeing *MJ*, and they're so indifferent. I'm getting them tickets to the Wednesday matinee whether they want me to or not.

## ⁣⁣⁣⁣ TUESDAY, JULY 19, 2022

Woke up to annoying news from the people I'm buying the apartment from, which made me face the entire rainbow of emotions about the apartment all day. I know it's one of a kind, in the West Village, but the price makes me a little embarrassed, frankly. Interviewed Jane Fonda for radio, and she cried talking about her dad. I asked her for advice in raising a daughter to have a ton of confidence. She said to make the relationship so that I'm the person she goes to for answers and goes to with her fears and questions. "Spend a lot of time listening. Open your heart and listen from your heart. If she sees you as a parent who is totally present and listens from their heart she will come to you." Thought that was great. Met with Gordon and Steve, going over their plans for the new apartment for ninety minutes, while my mom occasionally chimed in with newly invented points to worry about, mainly about the kids. After really discussing the ins and outs of it, I ended the meeting feeling bullish about the purchase again.

Tamra hasn't signed her deal, but it's close, so we decided to go with the doorbell tomorrow night and we just won't mention a thing about it tonight. The first of two shows was Austen Kroll and the Miz. Mom and Dad were bartending on the second show, and I introduced Austen to Mom as "a cad" and then had to explain the definition to him. He said he had dinner with Vicki last night, who was lamenting not being asked back, and instead of saying, "Well, you have this other show you're on," he said, "Yeah, you're right." I said, you said exactly the wrong thing to her; thanks a lot. Later, Tamra showed Mom and me the latest iteration of her boobs, which had some kind of covers on them. "What are THOSE?!" my mom wailed. Tamra said you put them on, and they make your boobs perk up. Mom said she needed them, and Tamra offered her hers right off her boobs! Generous! I told my mom how many times I'd seen/touched/felt/discussed all the versions of Tamra's breasts, which made Tamra wonder aloud if she should show my dad her boobs on the air. Mom shook her head, and I muttered, "Maybe?!" I asked the control room, and Deirdre said not to put my dad through that. Then she ratted out my parents, who've apparently been bitching to everyone on my staff that I'm "making" them see *MJ* tomorrow. "And there's an UNDERSTUDY!" my mom kept saying.

Vicki was in good spirits, despite the staff and audience having to all mask up because of her lack of vaccine. It all felt a little hysterical to me, but they're corporate Covid policies. The show was fun, as predicted, and the two of them got along great despite a dustup about Teddi Mellencamp, which I found amusing. During the pre-show Q and A, I flagged my amorous couple when the wife lowered her mask and gave me a look that revealed herself—not a lustful look, more like intense focus. The husband was just sitting there. My first impression was that I wasn't physically attracted to her but the husband was cute. (This is another reminder that I am a homosexual.) During a commercial break, things got a little heated when she stood (they were right next to camera 4) and beckoned me over. The music was pumping, so no one else could hear her say, "You need to talk to us. I heard you talking about us on the radio yesterday." I motioned to her husband, asking for some kind of recognition of what was going on, and he shrugged back. He was cute in a conservative way. "*You need to pay attention to us*," she said to me again, with a strength that made me realize how she could convince a straight guy to participate in this. I pointed out, also strongly, that I was *in the middle of hosting a show*. That turned me off the whole thing. I motioned to her a few other times during the show, to make her feel like I was communicating with her in some way so she wouldn't torch the joint on the way out, and waved when I left the studio.

After the show, I explained what was going on to Tamra, who seemed kind of floored. There are some Housewives that I have—or have had—sexual energy with, and Tamra is definitely one. "But you won't fuck her, right? That's not happening." If the window to me fucking women is open, wouldn't that shift the dynamic of our interactions? I explained that if the guy was involved and I was attracted to the woman, I might. I'm titillated by the idea. I said it was clear from my eight seconds eyeballing the husband that he wasn't going to be the Jeff Stryker I was looking for. (Look it up.) Had a fun hang with the (hammered) school moms and their cool husbands—a great foursome. Hoping the parents from Ben's new school are as cool.

After everyone had left, I sat with my parents and relatives (also in the audience!) having a nightcap as the PAs cleaned up around us. I get a text from Tamra: "the couple are waiting outside. She told me they are waiting to have a threesome with you." OH MY G-D. I asked her what the guy said. "I told him he had to participate. And he said oh boy this is what she wants. Andy, I don't think she's hot enough for you." I said, "I love that you said that." I went back to the people in front of me, at first alarmed to think they were waiting down there. Then I started to think that I wanted to have a five-minute conversation with them on the street, to just satisfy my own curiosity about these two: hear their story and ask them everything I was wondering, and most importantly, hear from the guy! After fifteen more minutes, I sent my parents and the rest off and went to my dressing room to remove my makeup, so I'd be exiting the building alone and could talk to them in private. When I got outside, they were gone. So that ended with a thud. I have a feeling I'll hear from her one way or another.

## ⠿ WEDNESDAY, JULY 20, 2022

Had a great radio show. Told the whole story of the couple and the night, and the switchboards lit up with comments galore. (A polyamorous married woman said to do it. A gay dude said not to lose my gold star status. Lots of people from Michigan had opinions, randomly.) During the show, the woman DMed John and said she almost went to Toasties to try to find me getting my bagel. Callers then started saying she is a stalker and I need to get away. Then she called and told Jordon she didn't want to be on the air, that I had gotten great radio out of all this but "*this is very real to me.*" That gave me cause for pause. But I saw her Instagram, and she looks like a very nice mom with a nice family. I prefer to think she is passionate and not a stalker.

Parents went to *MJ* and, as I predicted, loved it. "That UNDERSTUDY was GREAT!" As we debriefed about Mr. Jackson, my mom asked how radio was, and I told her not to listen to today's show because it was too dirty for her, which led me to telling them about the couple. My mom just shook her head the whole time, and Dad looked titillated and confused. It *is* titillating! And confusing! I still can't get over that I introduced the Dead the other night, and texted Bob, telling him so and thanking him again. "The last person who did that was Mr. Trumpsky—and he got elected president; let's see how're you gonna top that—I bet you can . . ." I MEAN!

Tamra signed her deal and came into the live show with a doorbell and skintight bodysuit, reclaiming her orange. Greg from Camp High was bartending. We played Would You Smash Them: Housewives Edition with a few of my crew guys after the show, and their picks were fascinating. Here these straight guys have watched a parade of Housewives, year after year after year, and I never thought to ask who they were attracted to. It was endlessly entertaining! Vicki sent Tamra the sweetest text after the show, saying how happy she was for her and how she was going to kill it. Very classy. It actually made me emo.

## ⸬ THURSDAY, JULY 21, 2022—AMAGANSETT

Solo weekend with Ben at the beach. The glass arrived all the way from Greece to my construction site in the Hamptons. For a house that's mainly glass, this is an important event! During an otherwise ordinary summer afternoon, Diane Ronnau's son Aidan called with the news that Di was in hospice and this was looking like the end of the road for her. To have that conversation with her son, whom I visited in the hospital when he was born (!) and who twenty years later was calling, with strength and clarity, to share this news . . . It was just too emotional. After he called, I sat on my bed honing in on all the good memories we had, starting when we worked together at CBS News in the '90s. Thankfully, Dave was here for twenty-four hours, so I felt like I was with family. We went to the Crow's Nest in Montauk, which is a real scene but fun. Took Ubers, and they were close to a hundred bucks each way. Insanity prevails. I can't decide whether to go to John Mayer camp next weekend.

## ⠿ FRIDAY, JULY 22, 2022, TO SUNDAY, JULY 24, 2022— AMAGANSETT TO NEW YORK CITY

The weekend was swim time and bug hunting with Ben. There was a big birthday party at the Fallons' for Winnie. I ate everything, and Ben was pretty social. Got a ride back to the city on a famous person's helicopter (someone who probably doesn't want me to mention their name) and landed into an inferno, feeling like a hot sponge. Had dinner with Amy Sedaris at Pasta by Hudson. I hope that place makes it. It's so good, but there never seems to be anyone there. We both talked about how fat we are, but that didn't stop us from killing *two* pizzas. She's going to be in a Beyoncé video this week.

## ⠿ MONDAY, JULY 25, 2022, TO THURSDAY, JULY 28, 2022— NEW YORK CITY

I generated a ridiculous amount of content this week; I felt like a robot. Was so glad Ben was in the Hamptons at camp, because I wouldn't have had a second for him. In four days, we made seven episodes of *WWHL* (including with Kevin Hart, who was spectacular), five hours of radio (including a town hall with the cast of *Uncoupled*), and shot the *Real Housewives of Dubai* reunion, plus I signed my contract for the new apartment and squeezed in as much Lucy time as possible in the midst of unexpected roadblocks like Ben having rough drop-offs at camp, the refrigerator at the beach going out, insane traffic in the city, and waking up at 6:00 a.m. every day stressed out. The one week Ben's not around, and I got no sleep!

On Monday, I shot the second scene from *Gossip Girl*, where I'm at the Met Ball and run into the sweet kid who plays Obie. I had a terrible time remembering what seemed like a long monologue that was actually four lines. They shot my part, which was me and Matt Doyle blabbing to this character Obie, and then they shot his side of things, and the director said, "You want to get away from this conversation." . . . So it turns out we look like old queens trying to galvanize this kid's attention at the Met Ball while he's trying to get away from us! I loudly and humorously complained to the director, who had him tone it down a little for the next take. Decided to pull the trigger on John Mayer camp; I'm gonna go a week from Friday.

Remember the Housewives phone hack thing? It's still happening, but on Wednesday I got a call from an unknown number and randomly picked it up. "Who is this speaking?" said the unmistakable voice of Joy Behar. "Who is *this* speaking?" I responded. "It's Joy; you called me," she said. I said okay, well, this is weird, but I *didn't* call you. She said her phone was calling and ringing with all sorts of people, and that it was happening to Sunny Hostin too. I explained what's been happening with the Housewives hack, and we left it there and started schmoozing. "Do you still have that show?" she asked. Then she said she'll come back on. I love her. Later that day I got a text from Meghan McCain saying her phone was hacked and this is her new number. Should I be changing my number? I love my number! I might be too lazy to change it.

During audience Q&A one night at *WWHL*, a woman raised her hand and said, "I just wanna say I saw you helping your dad at the frozen yogurt place in Sag Harbor a few weeks ago, and I thought you two looked so cute together." "That wasn't my dad," I shot back, "it was Jimmy fucking Buffett!" The audience howled.

The Dubai reunion was great, and began with a surprise call from Naomi Campbell as I sat on-set with Stanbury and Ayan waiting for the other women. When her name came up, I thought it was part of that hack thing, but I picked it up and realized it was indeed she, calling as she randomly does, to discuss Housewives. She wasn't just calling to discuss Housewives, though; she wanted to discuss Ayan, who was sitting next to me, and get her contact info to book her for a runway show in Qatar! We rolled on the whole thing, and it's going to look completely set up because Stanbury is sitting there like a stone, but it was all real! After the taping, I raced home to say goodnight to Lucy, and then the car took me directly to Amagansett. Ben stayed up waiting for me, and all the stress of the week rolled off as we lay in his bed. After he slept, I had a big tequila outside and looked at the full moon.

## ⁞⁞ FRIDAY, JULY 29, 2022, TO SUNDAY, JULY 31, 2022— AMAGANSETT

The weekend with Ben was the highest highs and the lowest lows. Friday was just he and me alone, squeezing out every ounce of summer we could. We swam, looked for bugs, made sandcastles on the beach, visited Ava at Bruce's, and had dinner at the Lobster Roll, followed by ice cream at John's Drive-In. I was able to view the livestream of Diane's funeral during his nap. I remember her first cancer diagnosis (she had pancreatic and thyroid) almost twenty years ago, and her wish that she would live long enough to take the boys to college. She did live to see that happen, in the face of impossible odds. Listening to her son Aidan speak crystallized that she raised both her boys with the knowledge she was on borrowed time, so she deliberately crammed in a lifetime of adventure and knowledge for them before she left. Food for thought.

Saturday was another story. Ben gave me every hard time he could—not listening, not sharing, talking back. It was a day that tested me in every way. By evening, I was at the end of my tether when I called from the front door that it was time for a bath, and he informed me that he wasn't interested in his bath and that he intended to continue playing with the gravel in the driveway in front of the house. "FINE!" I screamed. "YOU KEEP PLAYING IN THE DIRT, AND I'M GOING TO BED! YOU CAN DO WHATEVER YOU WANT! I'LL SEE YOU IN THE MORNING!" With that, I slammed the front door, hard. I froze there for five seconds, wondering what kinds of thoughts were going through his head and reflecting on how the potential for complete freedom at the hands of his maniacal father might not have landed well. I flashed to the terror I felt as a little kid on a car trip, when my parents got in a huge fight at a gas station in the middle of nowhere, and my mom screeched out of the parking lot with me in the back seat, leaving my sister and dad behind. *I'm going to traumatize my son!* I quickly opened the door. He was sitting frozen in his same spot. "JUST KIDDING!" I yelled, sounding even crazier than I had twenty seconds before. "You didn't think I'd leave you out there?! That is SO SILLY!" I cannot imagine what a lunatic I must've seemed like to him. (I will say, though, that he relented and took the bath.) When I put him to bed, he wanted me to lie with him and chat. "Ben . . . this day wasn't great. Let's just end it, and both of us will go to sleep, and tomorrow will be better." He agreed. I went to bed at 9:00 p.m. *Nine p.m.* Not since I had Covid the first time have I gone to bed at nine.

On the way to the helicopter Sunday (I got another ride—Ben stayed for camp), he said to me, "I'm sorry for being a bad boy." And everything was erased.

## MONDAY, AUGUST 1, 2022—NEW YORK CITY

It would've been Jerry Garcia's eightieth birthday today, so he was on my mind all day. Isn't he on my mind a little bit *every* day? Well, yes, but today people were posting about him. I had so much quality time with Lucy (eyes still blue!), and late this afternoon we were sitting staring at each other, as one does, when my phone rang and it was Bob Weir! I couldn't believe my good fortune to be getting a call from *him* on this day of all days. We kind of aimlessly shot the shit, and I started to wonder if this was that hack thing again, like the call was a mistake. I asked him what I could do for him, and he realized he, in fact, had butt-dialed me. I turned it into an opportunity to try to book him on *WWHL*, and we're looking at a date in late September. *No butt-dial goes unutilized!* In other booking news, we are *this close* to getting the First Lady on next week. Her people think she'll even play Plead the Fifth!

Saw the firemen from Squad 18 at the supermarket today. The big handsome Cuban firefighter was making them Cuban food for dinner! (If you're questioning why this merits an exclamation point, just know that for some odd reason firemen all cooking for each other brings me joy.) Last night I spoke out about monkeypox and said the federal government had so far done an abysmal job responding to it, which generated a bunch of headlines and hopefully didn't mess up FLOTUS coming on the show. Trying to get Madonna for radio. Could happen next Tuesday. (It won't!) Speaking of monkeypox, I'm still avoiding any physical contact for fear of infecting myself or (far worse) the kids, which has left me feeling like . . . is "a caged animal" too dramatic? It probably is, but when you tell someone they can't have candy, all they want is . . . (This also applies to when you tell a kid not to say "poopy.") So I'm feeling so repressed that I somehow had a dream that Cynthia Nixon gave Craig Conover a hand job. I didn't *see* it happen, but she told me about it in the dream, and I woke up thinking I really need some sort of *release.* It's summer!

Went to see the new apartment with Bruce and Bryan and felt so much better about it. Then Bruce showed me a listing for a huge place in Tribeca with its own private *pool* that was way bigger and less money than my new place. I don't want to live in Tribeca, nor is that place my style. But seeing the listing kinda messed me up.

Nick Rizzo does a series of cooking videos on his Instagram called "the #GayfootContessa" that Bruce and I love. So he hosted us for "Streisand Ribs" tonight in Brooklyn with Anthony and Danny Vee. (Streisand *loves* ribs!) It was phenomenal, and these kids made every damned thing from scratch, including *tablescapes* (paging Bugsy! *IYKYK*). On the way home Bruce and I recalled what idiots we were in our thirties compared to these boys. Well, we weren't *idiots*, but we certainly weren't making any food from scratch. What *were* we doing? I for one was making mixtapes. Constantly.

## WEDNESDAY, AUGUST 3, 2022

On the radio this morning I talked about monkeypox and my crazy dreams. Mom called later in the day and said, "I didn't realize how much SEX you're having! It's THAT HARD to just ABSTAIN for a SUMMER?" I said, I'm not hooking up, I'm just sexually frustrated right now. Speaking of frustrating, doesn't look like the First Lady is going to happen in August. Hopefully, in September.

Ramona texted asking if I'm going to Teresa's wedding this weekend, and I said I'll be in Montana. She said, I've never been to Montana, but it's supposed to be fab. I said, *Ramona, didn't you go there in Season 4 or 5 when Aviva didn't go because of her asthma???* "OMG, yes. I forgot." She is always on-brand. Had dinner with Bill at Morandi and met a handsome Scottish guy at Julius' after. We're going to go for a drink. *No contact, though.*

## THURSDAY, AUGUST 4, 2022, TO SUNDAY, AUGUST 7, 2022— JOHN MAYER CAMP FOR GIFTED CHILDREN, LIVINGSTON, MONTANA

My Daddy Time pre–family vacation vacation dropped in my lap in the form of John hosting Ricky, B. J. Novak, and me for a beta test of the monthlong "camp" he's hosting for his friends. The setup was a little campus of tents along the river, with cooking areas and hangout pits. He always goes the extra mile, and there were bags from L.L. Bean waiting for each of us filled with supplies for our tents and—giving new meaning to "limited edition"—camp "merch" from Online Ceramics: incredible T-shirts and hoodies! A *limited* limited edition. The first day was lunch in town with a little shopping (I bought towels at a hardware store).

John is the absolute king of gear on any day of the week, but he was in a real groove with all that being a camp director entailed. Night one was hibachi night (Grade A proteins!) followed by a fireside hang in which we relentlessly quizzed John about what happens if there are bears, a possibility he discounted eighteen different ways. We gave him every scenario that would attract a bear ("But we have tons of raw meat here; what if we drop it? What if they smell how gamey we are?"), but he very confidently explained that we were in the wrong area for bears, that they weren't looking for people—in truth I now have forgotten everything he said because I was high, but I remember he was rational and convincing. Also that I ate everything in sight, and tooted up a storm because of the altitude.

By the end of the night, I was happy, high-er, and completely cocooned in a sleeping bag for my first tent experience in at least thirty years. I felt heavenly sleeping in that tent, in the crisp air of the August Montana night, next to the rushing river—which makes a *delightful soundtrack for sleep*. It was the greatest night's rest.

Woke up and found John, who'd had a sleepless night. Hilariously enough, at some point in the night, John had gotten psyched out about the bears! Isn't that what happens in a bad sitcom—the guy telling the horror story winds up getting spooked in the night? This IS camp! Camp is about facing your fears head-on.

It seems like just yesterday I had to pass a test at Camp Nebagamon, "swamping" a canoe—where you rock back and forth until you flip the canoe over and swim under it. I *think* it was a simulation to teach you what to do if your canoe capsized, so you didn't panic if it actually happened. You had to get under it so you could push it out of the water and flip it back over (which I'm now told is nearly impossible for any child under twelve—and wasn't I under twelve?). The entire exercise was further lost on me *because I had no plans to be in a canoe whatsoever*. I'd be better off learning what to do if a plane crashed. The point is that I was in absolute terror at the mere thought of being in a canoe as it flipped over. I thought I was going to hit my head. After many sleepless nights, letters of worry home and, I think, even a call between my parents and Nardie, the camp director, it was negotiated that my counselor would take me out privately. This happened on a (cold) Sunday morning, and we did it together, and the exercise was inevitably followed by an obligatory—but true—"See, that wasn't so bad, was it?"

I don't know if it wasn't so bad, the hysteria of it still gives me a pit in my stomach enough to write about it now. (I'm embarrassed to say this incident may be mentioned in *Most Talkative* as well. I'm sorry. It's not even anything worth retelling.) My point is, camp is about facing your fears, and thus we glided confidently through the rest of the camp experience. The next day, we rafted the Yellowstone River, which was like four hours of meditation under big skies, lazily winding around the vastness. Our guide, Kelly, jolted us when she reported that yes, there *are* bears nearby where we are. Mwa-ha-ha!

Okay, camp fear flashbacks over. Back at camp Mayer, we talked all weekend and pondered life's big questions, like, "Would the *Ghostbusters* song have been a hit if there was no movie attached?"

The guys hyped me up to get me on Raya, so I joined. Had drinks with the Montana Man I met in New York a few years ago. He has a phobia of driving but said it was worth the two hours in the car! (Also that two hours in Montana is like forty-five minutes everywhere else.) I left camp mentally and emotionally stimulated, hypnotized by three nights of tent sleeps, a little fatter (which is fat on top of fat at this point), with a big L.L. Bean bag full of merch.

## ⚏ MONDAY, AUGUST 8, 2022—NEW YORK CITY

I had the greatest reunion with Ben last night. And today was a lot of hugs and playing doctor and hugging Lucy. The only pop culture that punctured my Montana bubble was the only story that mattered, and that was Teresa's wedding hair. I woke up and texted Teresa asking to book her hairdresser on the radio, which turned out to be a highly fulfilling interview. I had so many questions. (The fifteen hundred bobby pins alone!)

Raya seems like all people who *say* they're a creative director, or a photographer, or a director—big titles!—and then when you ask them about it they reveal that they're no such thing. So, it's a members-only app that bills itself as accepting only highly vetted people but seems to be all hot influencers or hot impostors. The keyword being "hot," though, so, I'm engaged! Speaking to a "model" from Berlin, an "interior designer" from North Carolina, a "choreographer" from Brooklyn, and a "fashion designer" from France. How in the universe could this lead to anything but a fulfilling, non-monkeypox-ridden relationship? Had to tell the doormen I'm moving, and I couldn't tell if they'd already seen it in the *New York Post*. I get so emotional thinking about leaving this place. Knowing I won't be moving for a couple years makes it sweeter. On that note, I got an email out of the blue from a TV writer who said he heard I'm moving and he saw my apartment in *Elle Decor* and might be interested in seeing it.

## ⠿ TUESDAY, AUGUST 9, 2022

It was an old-school morning of torture courtesy of Bennis the Menace. He had me up at the crack of dawn, banging on his door trying to get out (the kid's lock thingy is installed still), and wound up locking *me* in his room this morning. Serves me right!

Filling out forms for Ben's nursery school might wind up being the thing that mentally does me in. I have never seen so many consent forms: consent to photograph your child, consent to agree that they do/don't have allergies, consent to take them out of school. All make perfect sense, but you'd kind of like to have the option to skip it and sign something that says, "Please take care of him, use your judgment, and go with G-d." Does that seem lax or irresponsible? Bought two new suits from Ralph Lauren and, in a moment of personal physical defeat, had to get 42 Regulars and have them altered a little bit, as opposed to the 40 Reg I've been my entire life. My suits are too tight! I'm not pleased about it. I had a half-hour window to nap around three o'clock, and two of the guys out my bedroom window were having a kiki. With music. I was so annoyed. But it's too funny.

Mindy Kaling was on the show and we quickly connected during a commercial about the intensity of being single parents. Really just about the weight that comes with the responsibility of being the only parent. I need more fellowship with other single parents. I don't meet many.

## ⦙⦙⦙ WEDNESDAY, AUGUST 10, 2022

This day would be called "cramming it all in before vacation." With three weeks off coming up, there's a lot to cram in. It started with me waking up at 3:30 a.m., stressing about the universe at large and, locally, my new apartment. An episode of *Heartstopper* calmed me down and put me back to sleep. Radio was good until PR texted me screenshots of a round of tweets about what a horrible person I am. I will never get over someone I loved so much coming after me. On the one hand, it's embarrassing, but on the other, it's also just sad. As much as I'm used to the noise of Housewives publicly going at each other, I've never had one publicly, or even privately, go at me.

I was distracted for the rest of the radio show, but I had a long day ahead of me so I vowed to stay off Twitter and move on. It worked! Put the phone down, and it doesn't exist. Shot a commercial for Fresca all afternoon in Long Island City, then a quick shotski for a commercial for Peacock at Chelsea Market. Feels like forever ago that Ike Barinholtz asked me on the plane to play myself in an episode of *History of the World* for Hulu, but I finally did it this afternoon before shooting two episodes of *WWHL*. Marlo was on the first one, and I gave her what I hope was a pep talk for tomorrow's reunion. I said it felt like she's been walking around on the show with an AK-47 and randomly firing.

The live show was Kathy Hilton. We played Will! Kathy! Know Them!, where we showed her pics of people and guessed whether she'd be able to identify them. Lizzo popped up, and Kathy guessed "Precious." It was bad. In fairness to her, she also couldn't identify the Rock or Justin Timberlake. And she famously thought Garcelle was her own sister. Suffice it to say, Twitter was not kind to her.

After the show, we had cocktails on the terrace to celebrate the last show of the summer. I vowed I'd stay till midnight and drink slowly. I stayed until two and drank slowly. My phone was lit all night with people sending the "Precious" clip: Chrissy Teigen, Cheyenne Jackson, other Housewives, John Hill—it was a real who's who. Had such a fun night I hated ripping myself away, but I did an Irish goodbye.

## ⊞ THURSDAY, AUGUST 11, 2022

Six hours of sleep and a long Atlanta reunion ahead of me. We didn't start filming until noon, which made me totally nuts. The set was Jamaica with a moat around it and some birds, a (confusing) reunion first. They had to put a bridge up for us to walk on and off, and then for glam and audio and . . . the day resulted in a lot of bridge work. I knew from my visits with the Housewives in their dressing rooms that it was going to be a great day. And it immediately reminded me how much I used to love doing *Real Housewives of Atlanta* reunions. I hated the last two, but this felt like old-school Atlanta reunions and reminded me of how I always loved bantering with that group. They were firing on all cylinders—so electric and sharp. There were some great, engaging back-and-forths. We spent almost ninety minutes on Marlo, which Kenya thought was damage control. It was interesting to hear about her background in the system, looking for acceptance all her life, which explains why getting a peach was so meaningful to her. We wrapped at 10:00 p.m., and I was exhausted and still in stress mode from the week. I raced home, took an edible, and grabbed a bag that's maybe packed with what I hope is the residual stuff that's not on Long Island already that I need to spend three weeks there. Was driven out to Amagansett (Lucy and Theresa join us tomorrow). I'm finally on summer vacation, for real.

## ⊞ FRIDAY, AUGUST 12, 2022, TO THURSDAY, AUGUST 18, 2022— AMAGANSETT (VACATION WEEK ONE)

Picked Ben up from camp on day one and he's got this boil thing he's had which has become much worse, so I took him straight to the doctor, who said he needs to stay out of the sun for the next week! So there went my plans for lazy days with Lucy while he was at camp. Spent the first five days keeping him out of the sun and ultimately drained the thing with his babysitter, Hariette, holding him, Theresa putting a compress on it, Hickey being "Dr. Pimple Popper," and me taking a culture of it. It was a four-man job. We felt like we'd delivered a baby or something. A proud moment! Ben was excited too!

There is insane price gouging here. Went to Dopo La Spiaggia in East Hampton with Amanda, and the Caesar salad appetizer was twenty-seven dollars. Insanity. Along those lines, I went for a tea at that cute place in Amagansett the other morning and waited so long for the drink after paying that I stood there muttering loudly to myself and ultimately left in a huff without the tea, barking, "It's *fine. I'm fine*" to the overwhelmed and underpaid barista as I stormed off. I understood that I looked like a restless bloviator and wasn't proud of it. Sure enough, it was in the "Sunday Spotted" section of DeuxMoi ("what your favorite stars have been up to this week"). Thankfully it wasn't reported that I had a hissy fit but simply "looked like he was in a rush—left before his coffee was ready." Maybe it wasn't so bad?

My favorite thing out here is taking Ben to Montauk for beach food—all the best burgers, ice cream, lobster rolls, fries. So many fries. I ate everything. I'm his personal valet and vacuum cleaner. At this point I'm so far gone to seed that I just pile it all in. The social highlight of this week involved a dinner at the Buffetts' (Jimmy and I are now referring to each other as "Dad" and "Son" because of the woman thinking he was my dad). Dinner there is under a sheet of twinkly purple lights Jane has hanging from the trees. So it's already magic when you step in, but then Paul McCartney is five feet away and it's electric.

At dinner, a mogul told Bruce I really need to lose weight. Bruce said, "He knows—he's going to start a diet after Labor Day and be thin by Bravo-Con." That is indeed my plan, and I love Bruce for knowing that. Got my second monkeypox vaccine. It takes two weeks to be fully effective. Lucy is *waking up*. We're putting her in a different dress every day, so she can wear every gorgeous thing she got when she was born. I've never seen a parade of sundresses like this. Did I mention that a recurring issue for ME this summer is that Ben won't eat a hot dog on a bun? It drives me nuts. I think the fresh bun makes it so GOOD. I want him to experience it so much, but he refuses. And while we're on the subject, he is a fiend for ketchup but refuses to dip a burger in it. What am I gonna do with this kid? I don't want him to miss out!!!!

Bennis the Menace is indeed on vacation with us too, and testing every boundary. Margot keeps reminding me that he is a three-and-a-half-year-old. You just have to keep repeating that to yourself. The poor guy hasn't been feeling great either. In other upbeat vacation news, I've never had much self-doubt and now am suddenly experiencing areas of stress and worry I never imagined. "If I don't fall in love, are my kids gonna hate me for being a single dad?" "Is he mad at me because I went out to dinner the last few nights?" and the eternal question I ask myself after spending four hours with him: "Did I spend enough time with him today?" I lived my life for fifty worry-free years. *What did I worry about?* Now I can't even remember. Now I'm making shit up to worry about. Am I becoming my mother? I think we know the answer. Wow—this vacation is not turning out as planned. And the term "vacation" may not apply.

## FRIDAY, AUGUST 19, 2022, TO FRIDAY, AUGUST 26, 2022— FIRE ISLAND (VACATION WEEK TWO)

If Fire Island can't turn this vacation around, there's no hope at all. What happened in the island paradise? Everything and nothing. I love the guys at the liquor store. Sloppily played Simon Says on the beach with Amanda and Grac. Hickey ran into his dog's optometrist at tea. Heard some great new Olivia Newton-John (RIP) remixes. Also at tea, I heard "I Feel Love" remixed and mashed up with "The Night the Lights Went Out in Georgia," which doesn't sound like it would work but did, *ferociously*. Not sure when's the last time Vicki Lawrence was booming over a dance floor. Good for her! On the topic, also heard Whitney's "It's Not Right, But It's Okay" mixed with the theme from *Soul Train*, and it also worked very much.

Ben loves it here and can run down the boardwalk and do anything on the beach. His swimming is next-level. But he is really ready to go back to the city, and saying it a bunch. And I don't think he's 100 percent better. Poor kid. The week was an otherwise beachy, flirty, fun romp, but monkeypox killed the possibility of anything sexy actually happening. The vax distribution on this island seems to be happening regularly, a few doors down from us, in fact. Bill and Chris took me to that Bette Bathhouse and Beyond party to see the great Amber Martin. We were looking around at the guys, and someone quoted Bette Midler: "You fuck the wrong person, and your right arm falls off!" Grindr was a good way to flirt with people, with limits. One day I was talking to someone desperate for his second shot, and Ben and I walked to the vaccine station next door to see if I could get him in. I was like the monkeypox USO, only less successful (they had sixty people on the waiting list!). The week was interspersed with BravoCon questions already coming in over email. I cannot believe it, but Anderson got approval from CNN for us to reveal him as the gay shark. It will be a hilarious sight gag. I am so heavy I can't stand it. Like a gut hanging out all day at the pool.

## SATURDAY, AUGUST 27, 2022, TO MONDAY, SEPTEMBER 3, 2022—AMAGANSETT (VACATION WEEK THREE)

This "vacation" is bullshit. It's anything but. I am finally, and fully, stressed out. I feel overwhelmed by life. I feel *heavy.* I've been *grinding my teeth.* Ben, who has long been ready to split town for the city, has had *every* ailment, the poor guy. And he is a full-on threenager, or a three-*rager.* So there's a . . . volatility there, and it's not his fault. He's just going through it—and putting me through it. *Wild* fits about I don't even know what—wearing PJs? It boils down to control, I guess, if you want to go global. And then he switches back into being the smart and funny boy he is. One day, I put him down for a nap, and he marched out five minutes later announcing it had been canceled. That's my guy! Had a lot of great pool time with SJP talking about parenting stuff. A whole new window of conversation has opened up with my old friends who are parents. I'm like a sponge for their opinions about shit I've never considered—a lot about schedules, nanny protocol, and discipline.

Lucy was the star of the week. We just stare at each other. I've been singing a lot of Grateful Dead to her and kinda slowing it down, then taking her for a ride. She smiles, stares, and bops side to side!

As weighted down as this week was, I started every day like Willona on *Good Times*, barging in next door to SJ's in the morning with Lucy on my arm and a cup of tea in the other hand. Meanwhile, I'm on the grill every day—it's like a hot dog factory here. (Ben still won't eat a hot dog on a bun.) I got Matthew to do an early evening ocean swim with me almost every day. Early in the week I met Dave and Ally at the Crow's Nest and decided two things: this would be my last drink till BravoCon (thus beginning my weight-loss journey), and I have no desire to bring toddlers to the Crow's Nest. It doesn't seem fun for *me*. And of limited fun for them!

My house was a revolving door of people coming to park for the ocean or to swim in the pool, and that was a real bright spot: Amanda, Jim, Jeanne, Fred, Jackie, Hickey. I've been loving having Montauk right down the road. Though I wasn't drinking, I continued to indulge in father-son garbage meals with Ben. (The weight loss journey begins in stages.) There are so many places for me to discover in Montauk. Had lunch with Scott Greenstein at Duryea's, which I loved. Ran right into Dina Manzo, which was a joy. On the way home she called, and I picked up, and she said she hadn't called me. So it was that Housewives hack again! She said it happened to her and Teresa while Teresa was on her honeymoon. *So* weird. I had a security guy look into it and discovered nothing.

Speaking of Housewives, I went on a hysterical morning beach walk with Bethenny. Showed her my property, and she was a hype person for it. We were literally walking down the beach screaming at each other, that's how loud we were talking. Thank G-d we were by the ocean because we covered a lot of ground.

Spent a lot of time by the pool, and Ben had an abundance of nature to keep him entertained in the form of bugs and grass and bushes. One day I was lounging on the phone with Hickey, who was in terrible traffic. I guess I was responding very dramatically, and Ben said, "Daddy, did someone *die?*" I said, "No, Hickey's in a lot of traffic." "Oooooooh," he said, continuing playing with his trucks and—as I discovered later—dumping a big pile of dirt in the pool.

I think not drinking this week caused me to look inward, in a way. I put the kids to bed and retired to my room at about nine o'clock, ready for bed, pretty much every night. I discovered lots of shit on YouTube killing time before I fell asleep, the best of which was an immense treasure trove of *All My Children* episodes from the eighties. Outstanding—with like *weeks* of shows in full sequence! There's also a bunch of "Best of Erica Kane" montages. I slept so well and was up super early every morning, with Ben sliding into my bed begging for *Bob the Builder* at times that started with the number six. In those moments, though, we were probably each in a suspended state, me trying to sleep next to him while he was in absolute heaven, watching TV and looking adorable in his PJs.

Last week Surfin texted me "how are you," which is often his way of starting a conversation in which he's going to give me some news— something bad about my apartment or a neighbor mad at me, or the guys out my window. This news was so sad: the incredibly sweet woman I've lived next door to for my nineteen years here suddenly passed away. Out of nowhere. She was my age. Texted a lot with the doormen this week; all were so upset. I often marvel at the amount of life, in all its stages, that you come in contact with living in New York City. And in a big apartment building you see life pass you by through the faces of neighbors. I counted seven people who have died on my floor since I've been there. *Seven.* In other life news, Sherman texted a video of Wacha on a lake somewhere, looking really happy. Ben insisted we watch it five times and called him "our dog." The whole scenario made me really misty.

I need to re-emphasize how much I really hit the wall this week. I feel like I'm going into the fall a changed person, sober for now (Cali sober), and feeling things I've not ever felt before. The *weight* of life. Have I ever equated life with weight? NO. Also, call me the most recent new parent to find out that I'm on a *trip* and not a *vacation*, and that it's gonna be this way for a long while. This was an intense range of emotions—this three weeks—for me and my family.

On the last night of my summer, I threw a big barbecue. Hickey added a bunch of people and then spent a day bitching at me about making him prepare a big salad (we bicker, have you noticed?). I got a ton of Cromer's fried chicken, and the night was a great vibe. Before bed, I carried Ben out in his PJs to look at the stars, which were bursting over the ocean. He kept whispering, "The galaxy!" At that moment, it finally felt like a vacation.

# FALL

IN WHICH I . . .

IMMERSE MYSELF IN BRAVOCON

HOST THANKSGIVING

GO SOBER FOR NEW YEAR'S EVE

# ::::: SUNDAY, SEPTEMBER 4, 2022—
# AMAGANSETT TO NEW YORK CITY

I was so strict with Ben's TV time up until this year, when he got *Sesame Street* on weekends, airplane iPad access, and occasional movie nights. Today he watched *Bob the Builder* from 7:00 a.m. to 1:00 p.m., and I felt like I was getting away with the best kind of murder! (Is there a good kind of murder?) I had so much work to do all day and needed full focus to pack up the rental with stuff going back to the city and some going straight to my never-gonna-be-finished Barbie Beach House. I should actually start calling it Chateau Sheree for the amount of time it's taking. Got it all done with a huge assist from Theresa. Brought Lucy over to the Brodericks' to say goodbye for my final visit as Willona Woods. Ten minutes before departure, I treated myself to one last ocean swim—the water was bliss, and I got out and meditated on the fact that the next time I'll be in this water it'll be just down the beach at my very own house.

The story writes itself, but Mr. Ben did NOT care for me shutting off the TV—even though he got to watch for HOURS—and telling him it was time to come back to the city. He had another massive fit in the fully loaded car, which caused Lucy to have a fit, which then caused ME to have a fit. I quietly lost it. No wonder I have TMJ. We hadn't even gotten to the end of Further Lane when he calmly asked, "*Why does Lucy cry so much?*" Ha! I love when he lands the plane.

Suffice it to say I haven't been this happy to see Manhattan in a while. Went to Gourmet Garage to find something healthy, to switch things up for Ben, and asked a fellow customer how to weigh the buffet veggies. "I know what you spent on your new apartment; you're gonna be okay for the veggies," he cracked. I felt like I was back with my people (not that they're not the same people on Long Island). I said, I'm not *complaining* about the price, I just want to *know* the price. He told me to ask the lady in the front. When we got home, I collapsed on my bed as Ben reunited with his toys and attempted to cover every inch of his room with anything he could find. Soon he was lying next to me on my bed. He earnestly turned to me: "When are we going back to Amagansett?"

This is the first Labor Day I've willingly woken up in Manhattan in . . . I can't remember. I am so happy to be HOME. And so is Ben. It feels GREAT. It feels HOPEFUL. I feel CLEAR.

I have a set of books that tell you what your kids are like at every age. I've been schlepping the threes book around all summer but haven't read the cover beyond the "3," much less cracked the book itself. The subtitle is: "Friend or Enemy?" I laughed out loud! After the three weeks I've had, I'm *just* seeing this?! I felt *heard* reading that three-and-a-half-year-olds are essentially demons who take a lot of shit out on their primary caregiver. The advice in this book ("get a babysitter as much as possible, don't leave the house with them, ignore them when they won't eat") had me look-ing to see when it was published: 1985. Hmmmm. Does that stuff still apply? They go on to say spanking is basically okay. Fascinating, but I'm gonna keep my hands off Ben. We went to Anderson's this morning, and Ben and Wyatt played well together. I tried to get some fellowship from AC about how tough it is with these kids, but things are hunky-dory over there, so it was more of me warning him of bleak times ahead.

Had a Covid Labor Day Sugarfish sushi hang with Jackie for dinner. Ben was lovely and thrilled to hang with her as I went through a month's worth of mail. It must say on some Reddit thread somewhere that I RSVP to wedding invitations, regardless of whether I know the couple or not. I have done this for a few years (if there's an SASE!—anyone get this refer-ence to the old PBS show *Zoom*?), and now I get stacks of invitations both at *WWHL* and home. I love looking at the locations. Tonight's batch was from everywhere: Maryland, Texas, New Mexico (!). The invitations are also WILD. People make BOLD style choices! Boring to read here, but hey, it's a little acorn for me for opening the envelope.

In going through papers I discovered my high school algebra teacher, Bev Nance, died of Alzheimer's, an extra-tragic end given her brainpower. I just couldn't get algebra, and she knew I could get it and made me come in a couple mornings at some ungodly early hour so she could jam it into my head, and she simplified it so much I got it all. Couple years ago, I read she was denied housing by an old folks' home in St. Louis because she was married to a woman. I hope she found somewhere nicer to live; she deserved it.

## ⊞ TUESDAY, SEPTEMBER 6, 2022

I need to get mom and dad something for their sixty-third anniversary tomorrow. Sixty-three fucking years. No wonder they are so concurrently cute, yet verging on mariticide. Poured rain much of the day, which was a perfect opportunity for me to work in my office at home until *WWHL*.

Watched two episodes of *RHOBH* where all the Kathy Hilton shit goes down. Kathy just did her interview for the episodes, so these were without her point of view. Friday is going to be an intense reunion. I feel like it's going to be very ugly.

Endless emails from the nursery school with Covid protocols, schedules, parent stuff, and on and on. We have to make him a book about his family before Thursday. Got a lot done and cleared off my whole desk, which was positive, but couldn't shake feeling the weight of the world on me all day. I felt heavy. By the time I got to work I kind of felt like crying, to be honest. I'm in my head about everything—the weight of being a single dad, carrying two apartments, the never-ending beach house, finding a new nanny (for when Theresa leaves). I haven't had a drink in ten days. *Could it be that when you stop masking your feelings, your actual feelings come out?* (I couldn't help but wonder . . .) Anyway, I'm *feeling* a lot of shit right now.

Turned it around with some energy because Hillary and Chelsea were on the first show, though I marveled that none of my friends were coming. Then I wondered whom I'd actually invited. Texted Brazilian Andy Samberg an hour or so before, and he made it happen, for which I was glad. We had a female firefighter behind the bar. Before the show I said, when are you gonna set me up with a gay firefighter? She immediately thought of someone and left him a message. Showed me the photo—he is indeed a big, tall fireman. Why do I want to date a firefighter? I think it's such a statement of a human being to be a firefighter. Who doesn't want a big, brave husband?

Within two minutes of the show beginning, I mentioned on air that Jackie (firefighter) is setting me up, then segued into telling Hillary I'd had an affair with her Secret Service guy when she was FLOTUS. "TMI, Andy!" she howled. Chelsea looked a little stunned. It was a really good show. They were both *on*, and she is obviously fun to talk politics with. (If she had been this loose before . . . ?) She asked me if I have enough help at home and I said I do, but as a single dad, it doesn't matter how much help you have, you're always *the one*.

Got home just as Margot had Ben in his fireman PJs (I mean, if I brought home a fireman, wouldn't it be a poetic moment for this house?), freshly bathed, with pristinely parted hair. ("I like your clothes, Daddy!" he said upon seeing me in a suit for the first time in a month.) He and I played in his room for a half hour, then lay on the floor looking at the solar system. The hangout brought me back down to earth in a way I didn't realize I needed. Talked to Mom for thirty-eight minutes, and we sorted through a lot of family and St. Louis events. I got invited to some Elton John AIDS Foundation event with a concert on the White House lawn, followed by a day of conversations with some pretty heavy hitters. I immediately discounted it because of leaving the kids, and Mom of all people said I should go. Now I'm thinking about it. After spending three straight weeks together, I'm feeling better about leaving for a weekend. Had a productive, Cali sober night at home.

## ⦙⦙⦙⦙ WEDNESDAY, SEPTEMBER 7, 2022

Em and I wound up getting Mom and Dad nothing for their anniversary. Isn't that terrible? Did radio, then hopped over to 30 Rock, where I went foraging for stuff in my office for the "museum" at BravoCon but started feeling overwhelmed by all the crap after a minute, so I stopped. Aviva Drescher emailed out of the blue to tell me that based on the videos I've been posting of Ben, it seems like maybe he's not getting enough sleep. So there's that.

Now that I'm back in the city I've added to my no-drinking routine by changing my diet to mainly protein, low carbs, eating a light dinner early, and no snacks or sugar. Had two *WWHLs* and was exhausted and depressed after. Met Bruce and Liza for a late dinner at Café Cluny, which was the tonic I needed to turn my mood around. Three cute girls in their early twenties came over to the table to sweetly fan out to me, and I took it in a bad direction: "If I was straight and you were older, would you date me?" They glossed over the question, and I realized that is PERVY of me. What was I *doing?* Like, what *is* that?

## THURSDAY, SEPTEMBER 8, 2022—
## NEW YORK CITY TO LOS ANGELES

When you don't drink, you need less sleep and feel less horrible when you get none. So I felt fine this morning at 6:45 puttering around before Ben got up. We had a meeting at his new nursery school at nine o'clock, and I wanted to have plenty of time with him to get him out the door. He wasn't psyched when the word "school" was mentioned, so I kind of conned him into going out for pancakes with me, then said we had to stop by somewhere on the way home. He was super shy sitting with the teachers, and it was over in a half hour. Told him this morning I'm going to LA and will be back in two sleeps—he asked me to bring him food back from California. I don't know how to manifest that in a meaningful way. Got to the airport, and Anderson texted that Queen Elizabeth died. I texted about the queen with anyone I know who would care and then worked the whole way on the plane—watching *House-wives* cuts, working on tomorrow's reunion script, playing Word Chums (that's work!), and watching a highlight reel for next week's *Southern Charm* reunion.

The Beverly Hills ladies are ACTIVATED about tomorrow. Beyond whatever drama is happening on the show, there's a world of stuff happening online that's causing all sorts of mess. Garcelle is especially stressed out. Diana is apparently really sick and won't be there, which is a shame because she has a lot to answer for. I don't understand her at all. I've never even met her in person! Everyone was out of town in LA—Mayer's in Chicago, Bruce is in New York, and John Hill was busy (that's everyone!), so it was a room service night. Also, I'm double-dosed for monkeypox and in a hotel, so I had a little rendezvous with an old friend.

## ⠿ FRIDAY, SEPTEMBER 9, 2022—LOS ANGELES

*RHOBH* reunion day, and I feel like I shit the bed. My Twitter feed has been full of rage from impassioned fans of the show who would like me to roast Kyle, Rinna, and Erika, and I knew that no matter how far I pushed them it was never going to be enough for the Twitter crowd. So the idea that I was a failure was playing somewhere in the back of my head. And the sequence with Kathy Hilton and Kyle was so sad, layered, and deep that by the end of the day it had me wondering what the point of all of it really was. Garcelle turned to me a couple times as Kathy and Kyle were at odds and said, "Why are we doing this?"

The bigger question was why Rinna had made a federal case about it on the show. By the day's end, it seemed that Kathy and Kyle's relation-ship was irreparable. I hate when family become collateral damage of the Housewives, and I had the same pit in my stomach at the end of the day as I did in early seasons with Kyle and Kim, and several times in New Jersey. Also irreparable seemed to be Rinna's relationship to the show. All us producers ended the day wondering if there was a path forward for her. We wrapped a little before 10:00 p.m. (!) and I went back to the hotel and got very little rest. Didn't even have my usual post-taping tequila(s). My head was spinning, though. I thought of a lot of things I *should've* said. Got a text from Rinna after midnight saying she's leaving the show and eight years was a good run. It sure was. She is smart to leave now. It absolutely feels right. I wish she could've gone out on a better note. Not sure this is the last of this discussion. Diana will be gone too, so she will be the first Housewife in the history of the show that I never met in person. Now THAT is a statistic!

## SATURDAY, SEPTEMBER 10, 2022—LOS ANGELES TO NEW YORK CITY

Eight o'clock flight with a very hot pilot who was aggressively straight and who I bet is very boring in bed. Probably selfish too. Very regimented. So fuck him! I am still preparing for the *Southern Charm* reunion. I will say I don't know *why* I find it so entertaining watching this trio of tall fops (Austen/Shep/Craig) argue, but I smile watching it. Overly emotional men are often entertaining.

Ben gave me a wonderful welcome home, which I matched with an immediate trip to the ice cream store and a movie night. He wanted to watch "something with dogs," so we saw fourteen minutes of *One Hundred and One Dalmatians* until Cruella De Vil entered the scene and, eyes full of water and fear, he demanded we shut it off. Instead, it was a second viewing of *Cinderella*. I had the same issues as the first time I saw it: too much cat-and-mouse content, no payoff at the end seeing the evil step-mom and sisters in misery after Cinderella gets the prize. Put him to bed and called Anderson, who was bored in his hotel room in Dallas after a *60 Minutes* shoot. After I told him all my problems with the movie, he said, "Would you ever have imagined we'd be spending a Saturday night on the phone talking at length about *Cinderella*?" The answer was a swift no.

## SUNDAY, SEPTEMBER 11, 2022

I can bring Lucy to Ben's room and she is fully entertained watching him play. She can't take her eyes off him. It's amazing. And she's really resilient to him lightly pummeling her. Ben and I had a West Village day today—the fun playground (met a super-hot, but straight, dad) and Corner Bistro. "The queen is dead, but she lived a very big life," Ben told me, biting into his burger. Jackie and I continued our US Open tradition and went to the men's finals as guests in the Ralph Lauren box. It was quite a group: Anne Hathaway, Zach Braff, James Marsden, David and Andrew Lauren, and—the highlight—Angus Cloud from *Euphoria*, who was hysterical. I'm gonna guess it was his first tennis match, and his (loud) color commentary was not what you're gonna get from the guys on CBS. He was a trip top to bottom: big white sunglasses, drinking a purple drink that he told me was Sprite and grape juice. Everyone thought it was cough syrup, but he let me try, it and it tasted as he billed it. I told him it was peppy. He didn't know from the word "peppy." I felt ninety. Diplo was in the next box and was not only very handsome but also super chill and nice. He had a set in Brooklyn starting at seven but didn't seem in any hurry to get there. He has good swagger. Oh, and Angus Cloud was rolling a very smelly joint, and I saw all the RL folks trying to figure out what to do. His handler told him to put it away. Zach Braff looked amusingly uncomfortable. Cloud left early and pronounced to the group that he had thought the tennis was gonna be really boring but he loved it! It was an incredible night of game play, won by the nineteen-year-old Spaniard. Anne Hathaway graciously explained what was happening during an endless deuce. I guess that's the point—deuces can often be endless. I don't know what I'm talking about fully here. We tried out a new nanny while I was gone, and she was wonderful. Praying she accepts the job offer.

## ▓ MONDAY, SEPTEMBER 12, 2022

I didn't realize I had a photo shoot for an ad campaign at eight o'clock this morning before radio, which meant I couldn't walk Ben to his first day of nursery school. My heart sank. Ben didn't seem to notice, but I was upset. He was only there for an hour, by the way, but still. There's a picture in the *Post* of Anne Hathaway talking and me looking confused, like she's explaining tennis to her grandpappy.

Ben had the best time at school and said he can't wait to go back tomorrow. He also loved soccer. Taped two *WWHLs* and one live show tonight. Had a great gossip session with Rosie O'Donnell before her show. We talked kids, Madonna, Britney, talk shows, and the miracle weight-loss drug that everyone in Hollywood seems to be on. Then I turned on the Emmys and saw how thin everyone is, and that proved it. People suddenly were thirty pounds lighter! When they stop taking this Ozempic junk they're gonna gain it all back, right? It's tempting, though. On the live show I had two Real Girlfriends in Paris behind the bar, who I was trying to hook up with the *Below Deck* boys who were guests. Then we came back from break, and I told the women, "You're so cute that I want to date you!" And then I realized I'm fifty-four and sounded, yet again, incredibly pervy saying that. My second time hitting on young women in a week! *Who am I?* I *think* something is going to come out as a compliment, but it just sounds gross. Oh well, it's not like it gets broadcast on television or anything.

## ⸬ TUESDAY, SEPTEMBER 13, 2022

I got no sleep last night. I'm so stressed out by a merry-go-round of the same topics. Another day, another reunion show—and not my last of the week! This time it was *Southern Charm*. I love that group, and the taping was a breeze, all things considered. I cried twice! (Once when Austen was talking about his sister who passed away and once when Shep and Taylor were going through it.)

Ben and I got haircuts early this morning, and I walked him to school, where he ran up the stairs to enter without a care in the world. Asked JJ and Deirdre if I seemed pervy with the Paris girls last night, and they said it was fine but they didn't like my "full bush" comment to them. Oy, I'd forgotten that one! We wrapped at seven, and I spent some sweet time with the kids and then worked all night. Diana Ross was playing Radio City and I missed it. Too much work. I'm exhausted.

## ⸬ WEDNESDAY, SEPTEMBER 14, 2022

*Once again* got no sleep last night. Not drinking is supposed to help sleeping, but I have a list of a thousand worries and hanging chads. I've been trying to engage with Tinder and Raya in a meaningful way, meaning following through with meeting people who look great. The problem is finding the people who look great.

The potential new nanny called during radio to say she'd accepted another job offer with more regular hours. Worked a bunch of the other stuff out, at least: met with Gordon about plans for the new apartment and felt good about the progress on the downstairs. Still have to figure out where to put the bar. My new scripted show for NBC was announced today, based on my first book—like a *Wonder Years* kind of show with a gay kid in the '80s in St. Louis. Also decided to go to that Elton John thing in DC next weekend, and Dave said he'd love to come. Taped three shows, and they were all great! Came home and put Ben and Lucy to bed. Watched a bunch of *Housewives* cuts and crashed early.

## ⊞ THURSDAY, SEPTEMBER 15, 2022

Feels like yesterday that I was walking in the snow on Thirty-Seventh Street in a white suit before the Miami reunion. I was back on the same block this morning for the *Married to Medicine* reunion. It was great. I love those women and that show. Got home JUST in time to put Ben to bed. I was so bored after that I took a *Risky Business*–like thirst trap in my closet (shirt and jacket but no pants) and asked John Hill and Bruce if I could post it. Both said no. Bruce further said, "You have to ask yourself *why* you're post-ing it." The answer was that my legs looked good, and I wanted attention. I didn't post it but it's on page three of the second insert.

## ⊞ FRIDAY, SEPTEMBER 16, 2022

I got my life back today. Dropped Ben off at school and picked him up, and we went to the playground with his new friends. Had real quality time with Lucy. Went through a stack of bullshit with Daryn. Watched three *Housewives* cuts. Worked out with Stanny. It kinda seems like Rinna *isn't* quitting, based on some correspondence with the team. This is going to be a journey, on both sides. Tonight I cohosted a memorial for Diane at the Campbell at Grand Central Station. Saw old CBS colleagues I hadn't seen for twenty years. Interesting being one of the few sober people in the room.

## ▦ SATURDAY, SEPTEMBER 17, 2022

Spent almost an hour at a birthday party in a playground on Twenty-Second Street flirting with a dad with deep green eyes who turned out to be straight. When he revealed it, Ben threw dirt at his daughter! Literally, he mentioned his wife, and Ben threw the dirt! So maybe he DOES know what's going on here. Getting texts from a lot of people in St. Louis who think the scripted show that was announced the other day is happening and will be on in a minute. The development announcement was confusing, I guess. Watched and enjoyed *Mulan* and went to bed at 10:00 p.m. *On a Saturday night!* And I had a fun party to go to! What has become of me?

## ▦ SUNDAY, SEPTEMBER 18, 2022

All kids, all the time. I'm going to DC on Friday with Dave for two nights, so I feel like I won't be horribly guilty about leaving them given what a marathon the weekend was. Negotiating guilt is a new, unwelcome emotion. Watched *Bros* tonight. It's such a funny script. I texted Billy that he was giving me "The Gay We Were," and he said that was one of his inspirations and no one was getting it. So I felt smart for a second.

## ▦ MONDAY, SEPTEMBER 19, 2022

Texted Monique to get her binder for the BravoCon museum, and Bethenny to get something. She has her roller-skating outfit and her dress from her wedding to Jason. Chrissy Teigen texted that she's coming to BravoCon with a bunch of her friends. They bought tickets! Had radio, taped a *WWHL*, and did a live one. Is it wrong to say the show is a little more fun when I'm tipping it back?

## ⸬ TUESDAY, SEPTEMBER 20, 2022

Everything is BravoCon right now. It's in three weeks. Gonna be huge—twenty-five or thirty thousand people. Last time was so intimate, but people were shut out for tickets. Was at 30 Rock today for a hype fest about everything going on at the company, being broadcast from Studio 8H. Hung with Jason Blum and Jamie Lee Curtis; they're hyping *Halloween Ends*. Up on the fourteenth floor, Daryn and I found stuff for the Bravo museum, which I learned is called the Bravo Experience. Gave them hundreds of question cards from early *early Housewives* reunions. I'm hoping they make a big wall of them. A colleague at Bravo offhandedly asked me if Lucy ever smiles. That, on top of strangers commenting the same thing on Instagram, made me feel a certain way (annoyed). She *does* smile, and beautifully—but always at *me* and not at a camera. Which is what I told my Bravo pal; we agreed that was the better option anyway.

Had lunch with Ben, who has finally accepted eating the hot dog on a bun. Hallelujah! Worked out with Stanny, and it was squats squats squats. My face looks thinner from the no booze, but the rest needs work. I still feel great, noticing that the diet is starting to work. I matched with the most handsome guy today on Tinder; he seems to live overseas but is here for an extended period of time. I am visualizing a husband here. He looks like a Jewish Superman.

The UN is in town, and you can't get anywhere aboveground. Took the subway to Shari Levine's goodbye at L'Avenue (not to be confused with Le'Archive). It was a wonderful gathering of Bravo pals. I noticed, in my sobriety, how chic all the women who work at Bravo are. They *dress*. Took the B train home by mistake so had to get off at West Fourth and walk. It was deceptively humid, but that was forgotten when Ben met me to put him to bed. We had a dance party, three stories, and five minutes under the solar system. I promised him we could have a breakfast picnic on the floor of his room in the morning. Is that a fun or terrible idea? FaceTimed with Brazilian Andy Samberg and crashed.

## ⠿ WEDNESDAY, SEPTEMBER 21, 2022

Woke up in a panic because I'm throwing a big roller disco party for the staff of *WWHL* tomorrow in Central Park, and it's supposed to rain all day. That's depressing me. Also, Mom, Dad, and Em are coming in for a baby naming for Lucy next week, and I've planned nothing. Does playing phone tag with the rabbi count as planning? No message back from the Tinder guy yet! Time is of the essence here—he's visiting!.

## ⠿ THURSDAY, SEPTEMBER 22, 2022

Ben woke up saying he wished he was two again. I explained all the things he couldn't do when he was two (ride his scooter, go to school, *communicate effectively*) but he wasn't deterred. The staff party is postponed to next week. They can't get the rain off the roller rink in time. I'm so bummed.

Got so much done today. Planned the baby naming with the rabbi, found a great potential new Housewife for *RHOBH*, initiated insurance for my new apartment, dealt with contract negotiations with Sirius, and had a call about the next *Ultimate Girls Trip* and came up with a fun list of ex-Housewives for the next go-around. We all decided maybe Scary Island wasn't the greatest place to send them, that maybe we should do it on *RHONY: Legacy* but we should get Alex McCord. Emailed Alex and said, I know it's a long shot but can I propose something to you. A dad with a sick baby came up to me in the pediatrician's waiting room and said, "You have to fire Rinna." A dad with a sick baby! Tired of waiting for a response on Tinder, I took matters into my own hands and DMed the Jewish Superman on Instagram.

## ▦ FRIDAY, SEPTEMBER 23, 2022— NEW YORK CITY TO WASHINGTON, DC

Dropped Ben off at school. Worked out and was on my phone the entire time with agents. My Sirius contract is up next Friday, and I can't tell if we're going to make a deal. I'm very stressed about it. Heard back from the Jewish Superman: he heads back to the UK on Sunday night! I don't get back until the afternoon, so I proposed meeting in the playground, and we can at least get to know each other while Ben's in the sandbox. An unconventional first date, but he seems game. Heard back from Alex McCord, who said if it's about *RHONY: Legacy*, the answer is no. She wants to focus on her growing psych career. I said this is a proposition she's going to want to consider. We're going to talk next week. Train to DC with Dave, and we were in the same car as Bruce, Bryan, and Gayle King. We were supposed to go to the Elton John thing at the White House tonight, but on the train we wound up with an invite to Bruce and Bryan's fancy dinner that included the vice president, Julia Roberts, the Clooneys, and Tom Hanks. (We're seeing Elton tomorrow night at Nationals Park anyway, so we will still get our fix.)

We hit the ground running in DC, with Covid and security hoops to jump through before going to meet Gayle to ride as a trio, but it all was well worth it. The whole thing was private, so I can't blab about it, but I will say I fell in love with the Second Gentleman, Doug, who I think should make a movie based on his life. Also really enjoyed Amal Clooney, who seems to want to set me up. I'm ready. (On that note, I made a Tinder date for Monday with another gay dad.) We debriefed the dinner in the car home with Gayle, and I dragged Dave to a gay bar called Number Nine. I forgot how cute DC guys are. Took a lot of selfies, happily. What a fun night.

## ▦ SATURDAY, SEPTEMBER 24, 2022—WASHINGTON, DC

I went full-tilt tourist today, and my feet aren't happy. Dave and I (and Jeremy) had a three-hour private tour of the National Museum of African

American History and Culture, which was moving, educational, and fun. Also, any time I can see original clothes from *The Jeffersons*, I'm happy. From there we had a spectacular private tour of the White House. We were alone walking around, and we got to see the bowling alley and the screening room and got to stand in the door of the crown jewel: the Oval Office. You stare into that room and try to picture everything—it feels too big to comprehend. We had naps, then went to Elton John at Nationals Park, which was superb. Our highlights were "Rocket Man" (with four minutes of new content at the end!), a surprisingly jamming "Levon," and "Funeral for a Friend." His voice sounded excellent (we were expecting less, and that's not a slam; the man is seventy-five).

It was hell finding a ride home, and we wound up paying a cabdriver fifty bucks to get us to our hotel. Let me detour to say that I met so many nice people all day, and probably took seventy-five selfies by the time we got to the Hotel Washington roof for a nightcap (I broke my no-drinking policy for this weekend alone and will be back to Cali sober tomorrow). The bar up there is great, and I figured I'd say hi to Candiace's husband, Chris, who is the manager there—or, I found out, *was* the manager there up until two weeks ago. I could've used him because I walked into a fiasco of my own making.

We got drinks, wandered around the bar unsuccessfully looking for a spot to stand (took ten more selfies), and wound up by a table in what I guess is a no-standing zone. A woman came to tell me we couldn't stand there, and after a day of being so kind to everyone who came up to me, I was not to her. I just reached my limit, faced with what seemed like an arbitrary rule when I just wanted to stand and have a drink and enjoy the view. I kind of snarled at her, wanting to know *why* I couldn't stand there, and she kind of backed away from me. Two minutes later, security was there telling me I was being kicked out of the bar for speaking disrespect-fully to the hostess, who apparently was in the back in a puddle of tears. I had made someone cry, after a day of going out of my way to be extra kind to everyone. The manager (not Chris) appeared and when she saw it was me who was the nasty person she had come to confront, said, "I am so disappointed in you, Andy Cohen. I wouldn't expect this from you."

I felt incredibly defeated, and begged her and the security guard to let me apologize to the crying hostess before I left. She said she would check. I explained that I was at the end of my rope at the end of a long day but affirmed that there was no excuse. Thankfully, I did get a chance to apologize to the hostess, who seemed to accept it and said my context about my headspace helped her understand where I was coming from. I felt terribly and said again that there was no excuse. I went up to my room feeling like I'd really blown it. I made someone *cry*—how do you get over that? Watched *Saturday Night Fever* until I fell asleep.

## ⠿ SUNDAY, SEPTEMBER 25, 2022— WASHINGTON, DC, TO NEW YORK CITY

The whole train ride home I beat myself up about how last night ended. I contemplated sending the woman flowers but wondered if it would be overkill. *I'm not a bad boy!* Your head goes everywhere. Got back to New York City in time for a drizzly mix, as they say, which killed my playground date with Jewish Superman. Instead I took Ben out on his scooter, and we met in the little park down the street with enough time for Ben and me to determine he was worth inviting home for tea and general play in Ben's room. I can't say I've ever had a first date while playing with train sets, but there was something really sweet about it. He's a keeper. But when will he ever be back? Dinner with Bruce and Bryan and Kevin Huvane at Via Carota. My Sirius deal is hanging by a thread. I have a serious offer from someone else, but I don't want to leave what I've spent seven years building.

## ⠿ MONDAY, SEPTEMBER 26, 2022

Ben woke up and barfed but then seemed fine. Called Candiace and got the name of the woman who I made cry so I could send her an orchid. I was stunned she hadn't already heard about me getting kicked out of the bar. Wouldn't that have been juicy tea for one of Chris's ex-coworkers to tell her? I think she was a little flabbergasted to hear my tale. ("You did WHAT?!") She said that place has a lot of rules and they're always moving people away from that area. I feel a little better now that I'm closing the loop. I could've made my *builder* cry after the way I screamed at him while I was walking to the gym today. All the pent-up frustration and sleepless nights erupted into one noisy rant that filled the length of Fourteenth Street from Eighth Avenue to Fifth Avenue. Had an early drinks date (I had seltzer) with another single gay dad. It was really great connecting with him about our shared experiences. I'm feeling thin for a change, and it feels really good. My suits all fit perfectly again.

## ⠿ TUESDAY, SEPTEMBER 27, 2022

I woke up and barfed immediately. So maybe I have what Ben did yesterday. Man, I was SICK SICK SICK all day, but talk show hosts aren't really allowed to get sick. I had commitments (and today's were personal to me), so it was a balancing act between attempting to be charming on-air and constantly running to the bathroom. I took Ben to school and raced home for a half-hour nap. Woke up in time for my Alex McCord conversation. She has the same jaunty energy. She seemed intrigued by *UGT* and said it's her "fiduciary duty to discuss with Simon." Cab to Sirius, where I taped an hour-long town hall with Kelly, whose wonderful new book comes out today. Thankfully, Kelly is a great talker, so she did all the heavy lifting. Then I blearily walked through Times Square (of all the days for my car not to show up!) hunting for a cab. Raced home for another half-hour nap, then to *WWHL*, where I taped another show with Kelly. The amount of support she and Mark have given my books in the past made me want to be there for her in a big way, but as I was running to the potty during commercial breaks, I realized I was never going to be able to make her fancy dinner tonight honoring the book. She said, "Can I not go too?" Very her! Went home to sleep another hour, then had conference calls, did the seating for the ballet gala tomorrow night, and got insurance for the new apartment, all from my sickbed. That wrapped up at five, and I slept on and off while Ben tried to "take care of me."

## WEDNESDAY, SEPTEMBER 28, 2022

I'm still sick. My stomach is still shaky. Did radio from home, drinking ginger tea and eating saltines the whole time. Taped two *WWHL*s. Mom, Dad, and Em arrived for tomorrow's baby naming. Tonight was the New York City Ballet gala that I was a cochair of, where SJ was being honored. I was hosting a table of my friends. SJ texted that she was on her way to the hospital to care for her father, who has taken a turn for the worse, so she would not be at the gala tonight. I felt terribly for her and got my shit together, put on a tux, and went. I couldn't have fit in that tux four months ago, by a mile. Amy was my date, and it wound up being very magical, but Sarah Jessica was very missed. It's her baby, this fashion gala, which she came up with ten years ago. There were three brilliant, brand-new ballets, one with music composed by Solange. Had lovely chats with Bryant and Hilary Gumbel, Michael Patrick King, and Kristin Davis.

## THURSDAY, SEPTEMBER 29, 2022

Thank G-d I woke up well enough for Lucy's baby naming. I'm not sure baby namings are an actual thing, but since Ben was "welcomed" into the Jewish religion with a bris, I wanted to share the love for Lucy and figure out something ceremonial my family could attend. It was at my place, small and special. Rabbi Kleinbaum presided, with Mom, Dad, and Em, plus Grac, Jackie, Amanda, Bruce, Dave, and Allison in attendance. The rabbi went around the room and asked each person for their wishes for Lucy's future. She sat on my lap the whole time, listening and looking intently with her big, blue, eternally surprised eyes. Ben kept saying he wanted to rename Lucy "Jack." We had a nosh after and a great schmooze.

Had a Zoom with someone making a compelling pitch for me to leave

Sirius. Mom, Dad, and Em all came to the Bob Weir show. (His butt-dial last month actually resulted in a booking! How about that?) He was on with Anderson, and Greg from Camp High was behind the bar. He gave me a great pants-and-hoodie set printed with bootleg Dead cassette covers, AND a candy bar with SIX HUNDRED MILLIGRAMS OF THC!!! I kept the groovy set and gave the super-charged THC candy bar to Dave Stanley. I wonder what Anderson did with his, now that I think of it?

Em was in the audience, and I found out after that Mom was sitting in the back row of the control room, heckling the show! She didn't like it! She was totally wrong. It was a GREAT, magical show. Natascha Weir brought me an insane amount of Bay Area (i.e., cool) gifts for the kids. Tonight was the rain date for the DiscOasis party at Wollman Rink in Central Park. I brought Em, thinking she would have a blast, and she wound up falling on her wrist during the fifteen seconds when she was rolling from the area where you put on your skates to the rink! I felt horribly, but not as bad as she did. Luckily, she could move her hand, so the medic said to keep it on ice and take Advil, basically. The rest of the party was swell, and my last skate was euphoria on wheels. That place is spectacular (wrist injury aside) and I hope they mount it again next summer. Walked to Rise with some of the *WWHL* boys (Danny V, JJ, Nick, Anthony) and it was a ball—a new back room and some cute guys. Interesting to be in a gay bar without a cocktail. The cheeba chew hit the spot, though. Met a very handsome former military guy who just moved here from the Midwest. This now sounds like the beginning of a *Penthouse* Forum entry.

## ⸭ FRIDAY, SEPTEMBER 30, 2022

Closed on the apartment and, while signing my life away, got the call that we'd come to a great agreement with Sirius for three more years. I was so relieved; I didn't want to leave a place I love where we've built two great channels. All day long I felt elated about that and the new apartment. Felt like a great one-two punch. Went to Via Carota with Ma, Pa, and Em. We toasted the apartment and new Sirius deal, and then I took them through the layout of the apartment and Mom laid out all her worries about it. I said the night of my closing was not the time, and she said that she is worrying so I don't have to. I said, but I'm NOT worried and don't NEED to! I assured her that there are things that I DO worry about, but the things on *her* list are not on mine, and I'm not looking to take hers on. It's how she's wired, she says. She's right. On the way home I met Molly Shannon and Anderson, who were (amazingly randomly) having dinner at Perry Street. It was a BALL being with Molly. Anderson and I walked home together, and it was great hitting the streets with him without the kids. We really don't hang without the kids anymore.

## SATURDAY, OCTOBER 1, 2022

Birthday party for Ben's friend Adrian. By the time I got home, the stomach bug I had on Tuesday returned in the most violent way. It turned into a really horrible day, spent in bed. Was supposed to go to SJ's for chili and sadly had to cancel.

## SUNDAY, OCTOBER 2, 2022

Woke up with Ben and turned on *Sesame Street*, and Theresa hung with him until Liza came to watch him and I went to that urgent-care emergency room. I entered with a fever of 102.5 and left seven hours later—after three bags of IV fluids—still miserable but with my temperature down to 99. They did a zillion tests on me. I went to bed at 8:00 p.m.

## MONDAY, OCTOBER 3, 2022

Another reminder that there's no sick day off for daddies and talk show hosts. I was up at seven with Ben, playing with stickers while my stomach made violent noises. It sounded like someone was in there trying to get out. Well, in theory that was the case, but the Imodium finally seemed to kick in. By the time I got him to school two hours later, I was exhausted. Did radio from home. Conference call about the new scripted show, and I cried (happy tears) when they got to the end. One question to come out was whether my family and friends want their real names used as the character names. I texted that query to the family text chain and got a quick "FAKE NAMES!" from Mom, with Em adding a thumbs-up to that and Dad abstaining. Turns out Em broke her wrist at DiscOasis! And she was walking around with it like that for the last few days. Grac sent me a bag of food from Citarella, and Ben kept saying, "You got a bag from *Cinderella?!*"

Teresa called and said she's not speaking to Melissa and never will again, so I should think twice about them appearing together at Bravo-Con, at which point we split the *RHONJ* panels into two couples panels so they'll be separated. Better to hash stuff out after the season airs. We want it to be fun and positive, not bloody. I had two shows tonight. I got through them okay but they absolutely exhausted me, which makes sense because I've essentially eaten nothing but one third of a sleeve of saltines in the last couple days. The first show was Iman and Sam Smith, whom I misgendered twice. Texted them after to apologize and they said it was absolutely not a problem whatsoever. I recorded voiceovers so we can fix it for the show—2022 is complicated. I was live at ten with Jerry O and Rebecca Romijn, who of course made me feel like I had the night off, with Rabbi Kleinbaum at the bar.

## ⠿ TUESDAY, OCTOBER 4, 2022

Ellen Barkin is moving into the building soon, and I saw her new place today. It's outstanding. Then I ran into Sally Field, whom I helped with her garbage. I'm always paranoid Ben's been making noise she can hear because they share a wall. Danielle Staub emailed saying she'd love to connect. I didn't respond. A couple summers ago she did an hour-long podcast in which she was meant to "expose" me and wound up trashing me all over the place. So that's that. Good thing I got some time in with the rabbi last night, because for the first time in many years I missed Kol Nidre. Ben now has an ear infection, and I'm still sick, so we watched *Alice in Wonderland*. The last time I saw it I believe I was shrooming at Jackie's, in our senior year of high school. It played differently with Ben, who turned to me twenty minutes in, scared out of his mind and wanting something else. We did *Winnie the Pooh* instead. I wound up crying at the end when Christopher Robin went off to school. Ben thought I was crazy.

## WEDNESDAY, OCTOBER 5, 2022

Incredibly cozy day at home with the kids, Ben with a hacking cough that he is intent on passing on to me and his sister. I at least got to rest. I'm still shaky. Lucy and I are deep into the Grateful Dead catalogue of lullabies.

## THURSDAY, OCTOBER 6, 2022

I was telling Margot that Liza died when Ben turned to her the other day and said, "Excuse me, I need to take a little break," and Ben yelled from the other room, "*LIZA DIED??????*" Ruh-roh. Then he came in and said, "Can we talk more about the old queen who died? *Why* did she die?" We told him she lived a very long, amazing life. He wants to be a "fierce lion" for Halloween. When I write "fierce" I think of it the way a gay guy does, but when he says it he roars. He means FIERCE!

People were posting clips of me calling Austen a "pussy" at the *Southern Charm* reunion, something I have zero memory of. I DMed him and told him he could punch me next time he sees me, and he said we'll sort it out on *WWHL* at BravoCon. I need to add that to the list of nonsense to wade through at BravoCon!

## ⠿ FRIDAY, OCTOBER 7, 2022

Did the most low-impact workout with Stanny today, the equivalent of two eight-year-olds throwing a balloon back and forth. Watched the Cardinals wild-card game with Ben, which was a total joy. Not sure he understood much of it, but I tried. It was my first time seeing A-Rod call a game, and I liked him. Tonight was a date with an old pal that had been on the books for like three months. He's in town for a couple days, and unfortunately I'm not exactly feeling in my prime. He picked me up at my place, looking like a Jewish Rhett Butler, and I think seeing that my kids are actually *real* freaked him out. As we walked out of the apartment, he turned to me and said, "Wow, you're really doing it. That's no joke." This was in response to Ben being pretty cheerful but Lucy screaming her head off. We wound up having a lovely time at the Waverly Inn. Kept thinking Ralph was gonna call for a nightcap but realized he's not getting in from London until tomorrow, which is all well and good because I'm still not drinking.

## ⠿ SATURDAY, OCTOBER 8, 2022

Today was a day to be irritated by selfies. Woke up to a text from last night's date asking if I would post the selfie he took of us on my Instagram, which was deflating. I pushed him about why it was important to him for me to do this, then I relented and posted on my story. He was pretty sincere on the phone, saying he gets a kick out of being on my Instagram. That's honest!

There was a chill in the air, and I spent several hours at the playground with Ben. Had an early dinner with SJ at Sant Ambroeus. People at the next table were pretending to take selfies all night but clearly taking pictures of her, which became more and more irritating as the night went on. I walked her to Gourmet Garage, and on the way we walked by Carrie Bradshaw's town house, where two families stood in front, looking down at their phones, completely missing the ultimate cameo right under their nose. She said she walks by with her head down on her way to that place she loves, and no one ever sees her.

Ralph called *as Robert Moses*, whom he is in town to portray on Broadway. So we did some Robert Moses role-play ("I'm gonna build roads through your parks") and agreed to meet tomorrow. I watched the Cardinals' season go down the drain until 11:45 p.m. and went to bed sad.

## ⸬ SUNDAY, OCTOBER 9, 2022

I wore a jumpsuit today—more like a corduroy work suit—from Alex Mill. Ralph met us at the playground, and after he left a bird shat *on my face*! Jackie and Jeanne came over for sushi. They voted to keep their characters in the scripted show named after them.

## ⸬ MONDAY, OCTOBER 10, 2022

What's the appropriate response when your baby nurse walks into the room asking, "What's a top?" I asked her three times if she really wanted to know, and *why* she wanted to know. Turns out she's reading *The Andy Cohen Diaries*, and in it I mention that Anderson announced on *WWHL* that I'm a top, which activated my mom ("Does THE WORLD need to know YOU'RE A TOP?!?!"). I told her it's someone who is active in bed. She thought it was someone who spins around like a top, which begged more questions that I didn't ask. She turned to Neicy, who has been cleaning this apartment for at least twenty years without ever a mention of tops and bottoms, and asked if that's what she thought the definition was, to which Neicy drolly replied, "I'm not thinking about it." Neicy for the win.

Emailing with Alex McCord, who is not a no but not a yes. She has a lot of questions. Was chatting with Jerry O'Connell today, and apparently the comment I made last week on *WWHL* about him "carrying *The Talk* on his back" didn't go over too well with some of his cohosts. I'm a truth cannon, like Lisa Rinna! I'm obsessed with that show because they talk about everything except what anybody is actually talking about. I'm obsessed with the lengths they go to avoid being topical! And it's a live show! Why? But I digress. It'll be great to see Jerry at BravoCon this weekend. I feel like I'm in training for it. I do nothing at night. NOTHING!

## ⠿ TUESDAY, OCTOBER 11, 2022

Great show with Maddow and Etheridge. We played Do! Lesbians! Give a Damn?! I'd forgotten I asked John to record some stuff for my five *WWHL* episodes for BravoCon this weekend, like an F-boy trivia game. He reminded me today to send him a script. What a guy! Honestly. This was after I'd already asked him to come up with something for New Year's Eve. Another night at home—watched Johnny Carson and *Designing Women* before bed. My mouth was on the floor at some racist jokes (in both shows!) that were "okay" then but wouldn't pass today.

## ⠿ WEDNESDAY, OCTOBER 12, 2022

Had a really fulfilling workday, interviewing amazing folks. The radio was Kandi and Geena Davis, followed by *WWHL* with Victoria Beckham (her first time in the Clubhouse, and it was glorious) and Anne Hathaway, followed by a special town hall interview back at Sirius with the B-52s, which was thrilling for me personally as a lifelong fan. It all felt really good. Through it all were lots of BravoCon issues: Kathy wants to be on the *RHOBH* panel, but we feel like it'll get too divisive and the reunion should speak for itself; will there be an after-party after the Legends Ball Friday night? (looks like the answer is now YES); also, what do Lindsay and Carl want to speak with me about tomorrow?

Ben's "fierce lion" costume arrived, and it is the pansy-est thing I've ever seen. There is no way in hell he's gonna wear it. Watched an hour of *Fireman Sam* with Ben tonight and, since I have become a complete homebody, was soon in bed watching Carson and *Designing Women* again.

Carson had Keenen Ivory Wayans's stand-up debut, and there was some racial humor that I wonder if he could get away with today. Watching these old shows is fascinating, but I feel like I'm rushing old-ladyhood.

## THURSDAY, OCTOBER 13, 2022

A rare day off to get ready for the weekend. Rinna is posting that she can't wait to be on a live stage where people can't manipulate her story, which makes me think she's going to quit onstage or try to spin something. This after we stopped Kathy from being on the panel because we don't want it to be too negative. Meanwhile, we're doing a medley at the Legends Ball tomorrow, and Luann decided *today* that she DOES want to be included after initially passing. We can't make it happen! Emailed Danny Vee asking him for roasty jokes for tomorrow night's Ball, and I thought he was going to be annoyed at the last-minute work, but he sent back a big list in an hour. Jokes! I never tell them, but I'm gonna try. They're funny. Jeff is trying to get me to meet him and a big group including the Tres Amigos, Margaret and Dolo from Jersey, and a bunch of others. Ben refuses to try on the lion costume and says he wants to be a skeleton now. A SCARY skeleton. I'm so glad he's going to St. Louis tomorrow, because it'll quell some of my guilt about working for seventy-two hours.

It's fun they're all in town—every Bravo person. You can feel it in the air. And they're all staying at the same hotel, very close to me. Erika texted looking for CBD gummies. Texted Tamra, thinking she's in the business and she might have some. She said she didn't and added that she was with Teddi. I asked her if Teddi crashed, and she said she didn't. Took the subway to Seventy-Second Street to see the B-52s at the Beacon. I can't believe after all the shows I've seen—and this may have been the last one—that it was one of the best. They were, weirdly, the loosest they've been onstage since I started seeing them in college. Went with Grac, Neal, and Bruce Cohen. We really had a ball. Texted Jeff Lewis at eleven thirty that I wasn't gonna be able to make it to the Gansevoort for drinks, and he said it's a good thing because it was (inevitably) turning into a shit show. That story wrote itself.

## ⠿ FRIDAY, OCTOBER 14, 2022

A beautiful day for BravoCon! The day started early, with a hit on *Today*—Caroline was doing my makeup at 7:00 a.m. I said "ferkakte" during the segment, and Hodes and Savannah looked like they'd seen a ghost. I think they thought I said "fuck-cock-tah," which *would* be scandalous, but this was Yiddish! On the way home I was texting with the Bs' manager, trying to figure out how to get them into the Rock and Roll Hall of Fame. This needs to happen.

Walked into the apartment, and there was Ben, watching a recording of me on *Today*, going absolutely nuts with excitement over seeing me. I thought he'd seen me on TV before, but it sure seemed like the first time. He was gleeful, then on cloud nine when they showed Lucy. "That's my *sister*!!"

BravoCon was a real trip. The entire experience felt like, "If you build it, they will come." Drove by lines of people in front of the Javits to a side entrance where all the talent was hustled onto golf carts to ride around the huge backstage. Ran into countless Bravolebs—on and off golf carts—all over the place. I (patiently!) did an hour of press in the large press room. I walked in feeling super snatched, looking good in a denim-ish suit I haven't been able to button for a few years, then got several people asking me if I was *retiring*. Like, what? Is this a narrative? And what do you say to that without looking defensive or scared they're gonna fire you? I said I'd stay as long as they wanted me, or something like that. Then someone said the rumor was that Craig was going to replace me, and I said now we know who started the rumor! Craig?! It all got better then. Saw Teddi in the press room. Tamra told her I asked if she was crashing. That Tamra!

My panel had great energy and was fun; Hoda and Savannah interviewed me. A woman stood up who had lost her daughter in a drunk driving accident and she said Bravo had helped her through sleepless nights. We brought her onstage, and I hugged her. It was really moving and connective and really the whole point of us all being there.

Someone asked during the panel when Rinna is getting fired, and I walked backstage only to run right into her. Haven't seen her since the reunion and haven't mentioned anything about her quitting in any of the back-and-forths we've had. There was something of a stampede before the *RHOBH* panel, and someone tweeted that this is the Fyre Festival, and that's getting pickup. Rinna wound up getting booed at the Beverly Hills panel. I hated that. She turned it around though. Bruce has a Mujen booth in the bazaar, and I wanted to see the Bravo Museum thing, so I did a walk-through with four security guards. To say it was chaotic is a bit of an understatement—really exciting and crazy energy. People are so happy to be there. It was so fun seeing Bruce, whom everybody knows. Running into Martina Navratilova (carrying Julia's shoes, no less) was one of the Felliniesque moments.

We're doing five *WWHL*s this weekend at the Hammerstein Ballroom, which is about two thousand seats, and tonight's Legends Ball is the big one. I got to rehearsal feeling a little edgy. The show has 140 guests onstage, starting with a runway show; going into me doing "jokes," which I'm increasingly worried about; and ending with a musical medley. You might've thought rehearsal would be incredibly stressful, but it was actually fun. My staff is so put together it's incredible. They don't break a sweat, and Deirdre and Rocco are unflappable. So all this makes me super easy breezy too. Tamra texted as I was chilling in my dressing room before the show, listening to the Dead, saying Jen Shah is here and wants to crash the stage tonight. Anderson interrupted that nonsense when he arrived way early for his gay shark cameo. He seemed tickled that he was doing it, and I got him some red wine to make sure that feeling persisted through what could be a long night. Indeed, the show started late and was plagued by some audio issues in the house (we had like fifty people onstage, miked, and none of them were projecting for the balconies, who couldn't hear and were irate). So it was me running around with a hand mic, like Phil Donahue, and a lot of time-killing during commercial breaks. The jokes went well, with the exception of one I made at the expense of Gizelle's fashions, which I considered low-hanging fruit. She was *not amused*. I felt terrible and told her during a break we'd cut it out for the show. (We did.) We'd already cut a mean joke about Rinna, since she'd been booed earlier. (The joke was something about Kyle bringing the villain from *Halloween* with her.)

The rest of the jokes were fine. Squash! That! Beef! was wild—it'll all be great edited down, but it was taking so long we were losing the house *and* the Bravolebs on stage. The Anderson gag went SO WELL. Everyone was kind of dead and wondering what this shark was doing humping me and who it was going to be. When he lifted the head off to reveal his translucent hair, the audience and all my guests went wild. The Housewives were woken up by it. (They also couldn't hear from the stage, so a lot was going on.) Between Anderson and the musical medley at the end, the show ended on a real high. I also started drinking toward the end of it (today was my official green-light date) and continued backstage with my very buzzed crew of Jeanne, Jackie, Fred, Bill, Chris, and, of course, Bruce. It was a ball. They were in the second balcony, and seeing them there all night, having fun, was giving me great energy, and had I lowered my eyes from them one time I would've seen Chrissy Teigen losing her mind in the balcony under theirs. Duh! I never saw her!

Went to the after-party on the Gansevoort roof and had sweet talks with so many people. It was an incredibly festive vibe, with every variation of Bravolebrity in conversation. I brought some friends from the UK, whose minds were blown. I was bopping around from Marlo to Shep to Kandi to Whitney Rose to Sandoval and Schwartz when, lo and behold, Jen Shah showed up. I talked to her about wanting to do an interview with her before sentencing, which we'll hold until after she's sentenced. Our fear is that she'll be sentenced and have to surrender immediately. She seems like she wants to get her point of view out. After many tequilas, I got to bed around four. Am I back in my old life?

## SATURDAY, OCTOBER 15, 2022

My pickup wasn't until 3:00 p.m. today. Even bigger, with Ben in St. Louis and Lucy with Theresa, I had no kids demanding anything of my time. So I could've slept SO late. And what did I do with my free morning in the middle of a marathon weekend? Woke up at 8:00 A.M.!! I got four hours of sleep when I could've had ten! This was a *very* frustrating way to start the day. Had a photo shoot at the Gansevoort Hotel, which is incidentally where every single Bravolebrity is staying. It's like a dorm over there, and there are fans waiting in front at all hours of the day.

We're supposed to announce the new *RHONY* cast tomorrow night at the doorbell show, but Jenna's deal isn't done. We gotta close it! I had two *WWHL* shows, and Lucy came to rehearsal. She was wonderful to have around, and I posted the cutest pic of us. Someone said she had dry skin and here is what product to use. I restrained myself from responding. The first show was "Charm House Rules," combining those shows. It was delightful and dramatic, and those guys are all such great sports. We played "Should They Apologize," and I asked the audience whether I should apologize to Austen for calling him a pussy. Predictably, they said I shouldn't. The energy at the Hammerstein is ELECTRIC. I feel like Madonna, and the crowd is intensely responsive to everything. They're so invested and ready for fun. It all felt so great and beyond positive.

The second show was dynamic duos. An audio lady tripped during commercial break and really hit the floor. A lady in the audience said she was a doctor but Dr. Jackie and Dr. Simone were already on the case. I loved seeing them in action. We finished by ten, and I was so happy with how fast it all went, and then I turned to Garcelle, who clearly was sharing my excitement. Joe doubled down on Teresa, saying his comedy career would last longer than her marriage. They hate each other at this point. It's so sad to see.

After the show, the team wandered over to the other theater in the same complex as the Hammerstein, where Sandoval's band was performing after hours. The balcony was a VIP area, with basically everyone from *Southern Charm*, *Vanderpump Rules*, and *Summer House* mixed with some Housewives and *Below Deck* people. It was fun flitting around, talking to everyone, figuring out who was going to have sex when the night wound up. Ashley and Luke were certainly contenders, based on their canoodling. And this made me proud! Long talk with Carl. DJ James Kennedy was very sweet and emo and full of gratitude. I told the mom of his new girlfriend I think it's a good idea for her to watch the show. (She hasn't!) Austen said, oh wow, I thought you were gonna apologize; you apologized on DM but not at the show. I said, well, I asked the audience, and he said, how'd you think that was gonna go, and he was right! So then I felt bad, like I'd played him. Players playing players. (Did I just write that?) Sandoval was fantastic—in full rock-star mode. He gave me an extra-sweet shout-out from the stage and then called us all down to the front of the stage to ring in Schwartz's fortieth birthday. It was all very positive vibes, and Schwartz's mom was there cheering him on too, which was lovely. I hit the road, stopped by a party in Chelsea, then met the *WWHL* guys at Barracuda for late-night drinks. We really rang the bell. It's fun being back on the party train.

## SUNDAY, OCTOBER 16, 2022

No sleep again. I'm functioning on pure adrenaline at this point, and I love it. Woke up to a text from Dolo saying Jen Aydin and the Gorgas had a late-night fight in the hotel lobby. Walked in that backstage entrance of BravoCon and rode on a golf cart with Kyle Richards, then ran smack into Shep and the *Southern Charm* guys coming from a panel. Got some quick intel on the hookups from last night. I had another "Ask Andy" panel, and Dorinda showed up, asking when I was taking her off pause. It was live theater! Loved it. Also, someone asked where Jen Shah was, and I guess my answer pissed her off.

Went back through the crowd to serve shots at Bruce's Mujen booth, and they gave me a lot of security. I feel like (thin) Elvis walking around BravoCon, and it feels good! Saw the Miami Housewives and saw Larsa, who was with Michael Jordan's son, who must be her boyfriend? I'll never get over it! We had two shows again tonight, and both were awesome. The doorbell show consisted of the audience going absolutely apeshit every time a new surprise guest walked in. We did a Squash! That! Beef! with Teresa and Caroline, and just seeing their faces together made everyone nuts. They, of course, opted not to squash their beef. (I'd told them both in advance that we were putting their faces up there and they didn't have to do it.)

The final doorbell was the new cast of *RHONY*, and they looked wonderful. The beginning of a new chapter! Though we're just beginning shooting, the announcement was the culmination of a lot of work and planning. Immediate fan reaction gave no one any grace. ("They look boring!" "No sir!" "Where are the other ladies?! I need Ramona!") I read like three comments and then said, I'm not doing this. During a commercial break, an audience member asked who I'm sleeping with, and I said the night was very young and it's anyone's ballgame.

The last show of BravoCon was "Queens of Shade," taped at 10:00 p.m. in front of a rapturous crowd, and it was spectacular. Heather Dubrow was traumatized for the entire show, wondering why she was with this crowd of shade assassins. My favorite moment of the night, and maybe the weekend, was when a question came up about "who onstage is the worst dressed" and Ayan chose to go after the absolute wrong person: Phaedra. Before any words were spoken, I was speechless. Then Phaedra, with very few words, just decimated her. The crowd went wild. When we were all walking backstage after the show, Ayan told Phaedra, "We should talk," and Phaedra said, "We really *shouldn't*." We had a *WWHL* wrap party at an Irish bar around the corner. Everyone was running on fumes but *so* excited. We wondered if we all were going to get Covid this week and just fall together, or what. I have not interacted with this many people in *years*. The Legends Ball was airing and trending and people were loving it. Went to bed at three thirty, trying to take in the rarity of so much positive energy coming at me in the form of a feed full of happy tweets.

## ⁞⁞⁞ MONDAY, OCTOBER 17, 2022

Today I was simultaneously exhausted and walking on air. I've gotten used to walking around with two bodyguards, so I was lonely today! Also, I'm really patting myself on the back for setting a goal at the end of the summer to get my shit together, put a pause on the drinking, and lose some weight before BravoCon. It actually worked—I'm not looking unhappily at the zillions of pictures I'm in from the weekend. And I feel a lot better about myself and where I am as a parent after really localizing my social life too. My current plan regarding alcohol is to be more deliberate about when and how much I drink. It'd be nice if I could wind up only drinking twice a week. Took an Ambien at nine forty-five and passed out.

## ⠿ TUESDAY, OCTOBER 18, 2022

Feel like I got hit by a truck—a BravoCon truck. Took a two-hour nap in the middle of the day. Had Ben try on his "fierce" lion costume, and I was in a fit of giggles because it was so awful. Truly "fierce" in the gay way and not the scary way. He refused to put it on. I put on the hat (more like a bonnet) and was growling at him, and Lucy was terrified, screaming. I made it FIERCE! We wound up ordering a scary skeleton costume on Amazon, but it doesn't look scary enough to me, so I'm expecting more disappointment from Ben. The whole family is coming for Thanksgiving in a month, for the first time ever. I'm so excited to host. Got a caterer, via Bruce, and it's insanely expensive. I won't even say here how much it is. I've always told Abby that if we were ever in NYC for Thanksgiving, we could ride on a float in the parade, and now I find out the Peacock float has the cast of *Pitch Perfect* performing on it. She may not be going on a float. (We would have to wake up super early, anyway, so that's a reason not to do it.) Melissa sent what felt like a two-thousand-word text responding to me saying on *ET* that the drink-toss hotel lobby fight at BravoCon the other night was "gross," and I texted back, "I'm disengaging from your lobby fight," took an Ambien, and went to bed. Daddy is Bravo-done.

## ⠿ WEDNESDAY, OCTOBER 19, 2022

Jen Shah is pissed at me for implying she's fired. She ripped off the poor and elderly and is going to jail for who knows how long, but is upset to be considered "fired"? I'm trying to interview her at some point, so I'm just biting my tongue. I have gone from the glory of feeling like Elvis, with screaming fans and bodyguards, to feeling like the most hated man on earth on Twitter. I had a tremendous wave of discord coming at me all day: for tweeting about antisemitism (!), for not "doing anything" about the *RHONJ* hotel lobby fight, and for my double standard in how I treated Teresa versus Jen Shah. (Well, the crimes were inordinately different and Teresa plead while Jen was convicted.) Then tonight I got home after taping two shows, and Garcelle and I were texting as the *BH* reunion aired, she saying she was disappointed in how it went. I said I agreed, I felt like I shit the bed on several levels and have thought of things I wish I'd said as I watched the cuts. Then I went on Twitter and saw how disappointed the fans were in me. I tossed and turned all night thinking about that.

## ⸬ THURSDAY, OCTOBER 20, 2022

Abby taught Ben to use the word "slay." A few people from BravoCon got Covid, but I feel fine. Chrissy Teigen texted about the *BH* reunion, saying she's worried people don't realize they're watching a show. I said I have to stay off Twitter, and she said, don't forget, sane people don't tweet. That made me feel better. I had a long, positive talk with Garcelle. We got on the same page. I'm so glad we spoke. Then I heard from Rinna, who said I was really hard on her and she let me be, but that she would appreciate it if I never do it again. I told her I actually think I went light on her. So she and I are on totally different pages. We're going to see if she's still in quitting mode after the last part airs and figure out where we are. Personally, I think she should go on pause but absolutely come back. Feels like she has a toxic relationship with the show at this point, and taking a breath away could do everyone good.

Got the first outline for the scripted *Most Talkative* show, and it was cute. I hosted a melanoma fundraiser tonight, then had a drinks date with a finance guy I reconnected with last week in the midst of all the chaos. We had a really nice time, but the kiss on the street was kind of awkward. Not sure where that leaves us.

# FRIDAY, OCTOBER 21, 2022, TO SUNDAY, OCTOBER 23, 2022

Full weekend of kid stuff, kicking off with a pizza party for Ben's nursery school class and their parents, who are all super low-key and friendly. Dinner on the Upper West Side with Amanda and Liza, then to the Dublin House, where I caved and had a tequila. Was in bed by eleven. Saturday I had a great morning, doing low-impact baby stuff with Lucy (my favorite thing to do with her), who is sending me love bombs with her eyes and smile. Took Ben to Brooklyn to hang with Jason and Lauren Blum and the kids. Being in Brooklyn continued to make me question my real estate choices. It's so quaint and West Village-y. Then I started thinking how long it takes me to get to *WWHL* (five minutes) and the radio (ten minutes on the subway) and I got over it.

I thought about the *Most Talkative* outline all weekend and I couldn't get my head around how to give notes on it. I'm so good with unscripted, but scripted comedy is entirely new to me. I sent it to B. J. Novak to see what he thinks. Had another date with the other gay dad. He's a darty kisser. Sunday was a birthday party at a carousel in the mist, and my head wasn't in it, and neither was Ben's. He refused to get on the carousel until the very last ride, which was perfectly fine with me. I hate a carousel.

Put Ben down for a nap and shot the *Below Deck Mediterranean* reunion. Natasha didn't come, and I said she took the coward's way out by not showing up. I said it just to make everyone in the control room laugh. I know they're going to want to use it in the show, but I look like an asshole. I could say it to one of the Vanderpump people I have a history with, but I feel funny saying it about someone I barely know unless they're objectively horrible, and she's not. Sometimes I love a remote reunion because I just have to stare straight ahead and look at the camera the whole time. I don't have to make actual eye contact. How lazy is that?!

Aunt Kay and Uncle Dick came to see the kids, and we went for dinner. I won't say where, because I love the restaurant but our waiter had absolutely terrible body odor. What do you do? By the way, I have the most beautiful bar at home, and I'm just walking by it left and right without

219

stopping for a cocktail. Feels criminal, but also great. Spoke to B.J. about the outline on Sunday night. He was so thoughtful with his questions and wound up inspiring me about the project and giving me great stuff to think about. He also made it really fun to think about, which is what it should be.

## ▦ MONDAY, OCTOBER 24, 2022

In bed, drowsily scrolling through Twitter, and I saw that Howard was going off about something relating to me. Turns out the CEO of Sirius did a company-wide meeting, and she had a photo of me behind her desk. Howard was SO ANNOYED that it wasn't *his* photo and kept saying, "No offense to Andy *Cohn*; I like the guy a lot . . ." (He mispronounces my name, and I think it's purposeful.) I have to say, I was completely flattered to have been included in the conversation, which by the way went on for the first forty-five minutes of his show. On mine, I apologized on the radio for brushing off Garcelle's feelings at the reunion, which was met predominantly by more trolling. An apology, in this day and age, is either too late, not enough, or just discounted. I'm glad I did it, though.

Came home and got a text of a Jonah Hill movie trailer from who I thought was *John* Hill. I watched it and texted back, "and . . . ?" I realized a half hour later that it was in fact Jonah Hill who'd texted me the trailer, not John. DUH. So I texted him to say that I thought it was someone else texting me and it looks amazing. (FOURTH WALL BREAK: Let's take a poll to see how many of you readers think I got a text back after that king-sized blunder. If you guessed "none," you're right!) Had a meeting scheduled with a new nanny today, who didn't show up. So I need to start looking again.

Ralph came over, and my phone started blowing up with news that Leslie Jordan died. With all the assholes we have to deal with, we have to lose *him*? A human joy-bomb? I can't wrap my head around it. Ben is being extra cute, and Lucy is trying to sit up down and all around. Sent a bunch of notes on the scripted show, which made me excited. Had a long talk with Mom and Dad while DJ Sammy Jo spun in the *Kiki Lounge*. Dad's ninetieth is coming up, and I'm going home for the night for a dinner. Put Ben to bed, took a steam, and crashed. Clicked thru 225 people on Tinder who had swiped right on me. I chose two to match with and four that I hit the X on too soon and couldn't get back.

## ⠿ TUESDAY, OCTOBER 25, 2022

Bummer to wake up and find out your hero finds you annoying, but it took five minutes of listening to Howard this morning for that to click in. He was carrying on about the photo again today and let it slip that if it had been someone *other* than me, he might not have cared as much. The fact that it was *me* annoyed him. This activated me, and I texted Gary Dell'Abate telling him Howard sounds like Trump. He said to call in, but I had to take Ben to school. By the time I got home I was really activated. I took a breath, called the hotline number, and got right on the air with Howard. He was very gracious but wouldn't cop to my point, which is that clearly I annoy him, but I got my points across, and it was probably good radio.

Worked my anger into a good session with Stanny, then ran up to Sirius to interview Chaka Khan, who said I remind her of Soupy Sales. I'm inviting a bunch of orphans to join my family for Thanksgiving. The Blums are joining, Ralph is in, Tom Hollander is in town, and now John Mayer is joining. It's feeling like a party! I hope this caterer is good. Ben's "scary" skeleton costume arrived, and there's a yellow bow tie on it! We're coming off the "fierce" lion costume with the bonnet for a headpiece into a chorus-boy skeleton outfit?!?! This poor boy just wants to be scary on Halloween. *I'm* scared to show it to him.

We taped *WWHL* on a cruise ship parked in Bayonne, New Jersey. I was in a real mood when I got there, but the whole thing turned out really fun. We had all five *Below Deck* captains on for the first time, and they're all lovely. Went to the Buffetts' for dinner after, which felt cozy, up there in the sky with fog everywhere outside. Thought about getting a nightcap going, but I'm not on drinking lockdown and no one was around, so neither was conducive. Ralph called as I was pulling up to home, I thought for a nightcap, but actually he was looking for a pizza place that was open. I sent him to Arthur and Sons and crashed.

## ▦ WEDNESDAY, OCTOBER 26, 2022

I figured Ralph was with someone last night, but it turned out he was alone! So I could've caved and had the nightcap at Arthur and Sons with him after all. It was curriculum night at nursery school, but I had three shows tonight. Is it bad that I feel like curriculum night at a nursery school is an automatic "skip" anyway? If I'm gonna skip a curriculum night, I better make it nursery school and not when it counts. Talked for a long time about the Howard thing on my radio show, and then SJ texted asking what was going on, and I realized I kind of sounded like a crazy person myself. His neurosis wore off on me! Got a message on Grindr from a stranger who wanted to let me know that I'm responsible for the downfall of democracy and the rise of Donald Trump. So . . . I guess he *wasn't* into a hookup? Worked out with Stan—I'm really starting to get in shape—and went to do three shows.

Heather Gay was teetering before the show, I think overwhelmed following BravoCon but also realizing the precarious, fickle nature of the idea of being beloved and then questioned/hazed by the fans. There is no guidebook for this shit. I gave her my best pep talk, then handed her my number in case she needs some more love. In the meantime, I was having Rizzo monitor Twitter to see if people thought I'd done something horrible on Part Three of the *RHOBH* reunion, but I seem to have gotten through it unscathed. Didn't drink all night, but as I was leaving Bruce texted that he was hungry, so I met him at Corner Bistro and had a tequila and a half while he ate a cheeseburger. Asleep by eleven forty-five.

## THURSDAY, OCTOBER 27, 2022

This was my moment of pure bliss today: while I was walking Ben to school, he asked me to put on the song "Lollipop" (by those hitmakers the Chordettes). As the fall leaves fell, the air full of the promise and excitement of Halloween and pumpkins everywhere, we both danced our way to school. It was the best three minutes of my week.

## FRIDAY, OCTOBER 28, 2022

This morning I was the nursery-school room parent, which really consisted of camp counselor–type energy. It was adorable to see Ben running around with the other boys. They are such . . . *boys*. Bruce came over to see Lucy. This girl is going to rule my life. Went with Jackie to Ralph's play about Robert Moses—*Straight Line Crazy*—which was phenomenal and, for a New Yorker, fascinating. It was odd seeing a play about Moses in such an *un*-NYC venue as the Shed, which is beautiful, by the way. A beautiful fire hazard. Went to the Waverly Inn around eleven for a late bite, and the place was cleared out by eleven thirty, which made us feel like there was something wrong.

## SATURDAY, OCTOBER 29, 2022

Ben got bored with *Sesame Street* this morning after an hour, and I caved and let him watch *Fireman Sam* for a few hours in my bed before we went to his nursery school fall/Halloween party. Ben didn't seem to notice the bow tie, and the joy he got out of being in his (NOT) scary skeleton outfit was enough to fuel me for weeks. People on the street were noticing his yellow bow tie and calling him cute, and I had to correct them and say he was actually terrifying, which cued him to roar like the lion he was supposed to be before the Pansy Lion costume fiasco. We stayed at the party for three hours (!), him running around with friends and me kibitzing with the other (very nice) parents.

Tonight was Horse Meat Disco, which Anderson and I committed to going to on Monday, but by this morning I texted him saying I assumed we were both blowing it off. The reality of me going to one of those huge parties and returning in questionable shape at 4:00 a.m. doesn't fit with my current lifestyle. And as tempted as I was to go, I can't say I was shattered.

On the way to dinner at Via Carota with Amy Sedaris, Anderson called and said he'd been writing all day but was totally up for going to Horse Meat, which made my head spin with possibility and the effort of trying to redirect my mind, which had permanently closed to the idea. You'd think I was deciding where I was sending my kids to school, that's how wrapped up in the conversation I got. I said I doubted I was going to go but I thought he should. (I knew he wouldn't but hoped he would.) At dinner, Amy reminded me of our night out exactly one year ago tonight. I've never tried ketamine, which is a fairly common gay party drug as well as a current treatment for depression, but a friend of mine had given me some nasal ketamine spray (who knew this even existed?!) with the assurance that it wears off after an hour or so. I somehow convinced Amy we should have some before having dinner at the Polo Bar. Well . . . we were absolute lunatics, and nasal ketamine and the Polo Bar made for very unlikely bedfellows! We lived to tell, and I never did ketamine again. And I certainly wasn't going to do it tonight at Horse Meat Disco.

## ⠿ SUNDAY, OCTOBER 30, 2022

If I'm speaking like an optimist, Ben's level of commitment to being an asshole today was almost admirable. He doesn't want to go trick-or-treating tomorrow, refused to acknowledge his friend who was dressed as Kristoff from *Frozen* at the playground (this would normally be huge, I swear), refused to say hi to Ricky's new baby, and wouldn't put his coat on in the elevator, which somehow triggered me having a breakdown that I didn't try to rein in when the doors opened in the lobby. "LIFE IS GREAT!"

I bellowed as we burst into the Sunday-morning comers and goers, Ben wailing in tears behind me. Met Anderson, his Ben, Wyatt, and Sebastian at the park and had lunch. (Anderson didn't go out last night.) By the time he had dinner, Ben was back to his lovely self. I couldn't get enough of him. By eight forty-five I'd put Ben to bed, shut down the great lighting downstairs, and was on my bed when Hickey texted for a nightcap. Immediately refired the mood lighting and music, and we had a kiki. He split, and I watched *The White Lotus*—which I felt like I didn't know why I was watching because it's kind of boring, but it's also kind of hypnotic.

## ▦ MONDAY, OCTOBER 31, 2022

This morning Ben not only said he wasn't going trick-or-treating, he said there's no use because today is Christmas. Before school I showed him his costume, and he said, "You gotta cut off the yellow thing, Daddy. With scizzors!" So the kid KNEW the bow tie was all wrong. That made me proud of him. It was still a whole dance about whether he'd consent to going trick-or-treating, an issue I decided I absolutely was not going to force. In prep for interviewing Matthew Perry tomorrow, I watched Diane Sawyer's hour on him, which felt like it was forty-five minutes too long.

Liza and Jackie came over to trick-or-treat with the kids, and I played it *so* cool with Ben when he got home from soccer. I was all, "Okay, it's great if you don't want to come trick-or-treat, but if you change your mind, there's your costume, and you and Frafraca [what he calls Francesca] can come meet us out. But it will be very dark if you come later." He said, "Okay, well, maybe it's a good idea if I come now." Perfect. I cut the bow tie off, and Lucy was adorable in a princess outfit Ben had picked out for her on Amazon.

The West Village was like a mobbed version of a Nancy Meyers movie. In a Nancy Meyers scene, there would be the exact right amount of people, and they all would be hot. This *was* a hot crowd, though, all in costume, with some knockout dads. I made a huge discovery tonight: Reese's

THiNS. Incredible! And now I find out they have them in dark chocolate! Lucy was a dream on the streets, looking at everything. We showed Ben *It's the Great Pumpkin, Charlie Brown.* Last year we only made it through eleven minutes before he got bored (it's a li'l slow), but tonight he was all in. We ordered Sugarfish, and the night was over early.

## ⌗ TUESDAY, NOVEMBER 1, 2022

John talked on the radio yesterday about a news story that said picking your nose can give you Alzheimer's—something about the lining of your nose being connected to your brain—and I've thought about it every time I've reached to clean out my nose, which it turns out I do *constantly. I'm a nose picker!* And now my brain is in jeopardy as a result. The silver lining is not only the lining of boogers that will now forever remain in my nasal passages but also that I'm not touching my nose. Okay, enough of this talk!

Ben hasn't even mentioned his Halloween candy today. It's like the whole night never happened. Maybe our endless loop of Fireman Sam cosplay today made him forget. Interviewed Matthew Perry for radio about his book. I feel for the guy. Had a call about *Most Talkative,* the TV show. I like the direction it's going. Then a *UGT* call. Alex McCord is in. We have one more slot and were toying around with some interesting names. Off the nostalgia of BravoCon, I suggested Caroline Manzo, then called her, and she said she's in. I'm excited to get her back in the mix! The live show tonight was Meredith Marks and Arden Myrin. Meredith's daughter, Chloe, was bartending, and I mistook her in the hallway for Arden, telling her what a great job she did in the Radio Andy Theater at BravoCon. I knew I had missed my mark (pun intended) by the look on her face.

Had a date tonight with a model who asked me out on Instagram. I was powerless to a tequila (okay, I had two), and we actually had a really nice time. He walked me home, and we had a kiss on the street, but I was really conscious of the fact that Jose was at the front desk, probably watching on his sidewalk cam (the doormen see *everything*). I walked into the lobby, and we nodded, he pretending he hadn't just been watching me have an awkward first-date kiss. Spent the elevator ride trying to figure out whether he watched the kiss or not, which led me to wonder whether he was watching me on the elevator cam too. In other words, I started going a little nuts. Anyway, I'll never know because Jose has a real poker face.

## ⬛ WEDNESDAY, NOVEMBER 2, 2022

Ben got in bed with me at seven fifteen asking to watch Madonna videos. *Could I be prouder?* (I do realize this is his way of getting screen time he knows I'll give him, but if I can teach him young, so be it.) Big Housewives day: first all-cast event for the new *RHONY*. I'm so excited! Called Gretchen and Camille to offer them *Ultimate Girls Trip* (both quickly accepted). It feels so good to be calling to *offer* a job. Taped Daniel Radcliffe (charming!) and Evan Rachel Wood (perfect talk show guest!), then was supposed to have Wendy from *The Real Housewives of Potomac* and Vishal from *Family Karma*, but one of them tested positive for Covid, so we had to tape them remotely.

Jane Buffett took me to the Beacon to see Bono's first night performing stories from his book and songs from his life—his *Springsteen on Broadway* moment. It was wonderful. His musical performance was purposefully and beautifully subdued, but the songs are all such anthems that the crowd is hanging there, ready to lose their minds. It was exhilarating hearing the music performed this way, though—I was gripping the sides of the seat and rocking from side to side (which sounds nuts). It was a whole swanky NYC crowd: Bill and Hillary Clinton, the Edge, Tom Hanks, Gayle King with her cohosts, and the whole music industry, from Irving Azoff to everyone else. I loved it so much I didn't even really care or notice that I spilled a drink all over my lap and up my ass. On a related note, I was white-knuckling for the last forty-five minutes, holding in a massive pee. After the show, I lost myself in the basement of the Beacon, going to an almost otherworldly place while taking what I think was the longest pee of my life. It felt so good—and I was just high enough—that

I wondered if I emitted any moans or loud breaths during it. Then it occurred to me that I think I've peed in every bathroom in that joint, front of house and backstage.

On the way home I took the subway, which is still the fastest ride in town. When I walked into the building, Jose asked me what I said about him on the radio (I think his mother-in-law listens), and I told him I'd been speculating about whether he watched my awkward first-date kiss. He promised that he doesn't look at what's happening on the cameras—he claims he tunes it out—and I said I didn't believe him. I don't know what to think.

## ▦ THURSDAY, NOVEMBER 3, 2022

We parted ways with Ramona today, and her energy about it was very zen. She's into a guy who wants nothing to do with the show, and she thinks she sabotaged herself purposefully by running her mouth on that podcast about *Legacy* being lame. Lots of Sturm und Drang surrounding beach house construction. I swear this is going to do me in.

After the kids' bedtime, I judged a virtual costume contest for *Bitch Sesh*, but my Wi-Fi sucked. After all the shitty Zoom meetings I'm in with perfect connections all the time, here's the one thing I actually *want* to do, and my Wi-Fi craps out! I spent the rest of the night nervous about my Wi-Fi connection, because I'm on Meghan Markle's podcast tomorrow virtually. My Wi-Fi better get its *act together*. She usually only features women as guests, but for her "finale" she's conversing (separately) with me, Trevor Noah, and Judd Apatow about stereotypes of women. I'm going into this expecting to have to defend my beloved troop of Housewives, something I've grown accustomed to and enjoy doing. Also, I plan to beg her to come on *WWHL* and the New Year's Eve show. We shall see . . .

Here is the status of my dating: WhatsApping a bunch with the Superman-y Tinder guy from the UK; FaceTimed and flirted with Atlanta guy; the young ad guy from two weeks ago told me today he ran into an ex and it's complicated, which is clearly a lie to extricate himself; and the date from Tuesday is texting, and we will go out again. So this is far more than I had going on for the entire summer of monkeypox, but actually these little flirts have all been chaste, so it wouldn't make a difference if we all had monkeypox anyway. Thank the Lord *that's* out of the equation, though.

## ⠿ FRIDAY, NOVEMBER 4, 2022

Today was quite a journey with Meghan Markle. And it (thankfully) didn't involve shitty Wi-Fi. My server was SERVING, girl! At the beginning of the recording, I said it was nice to meet her, and she responded with exactly what you *don't* want the Duchess of Sussex to say back to you: "We've met before. *Twice.*" Oh G-d. I covered my face. "*Was I mean?!*" I needed to know what happened, and she seemed equally anxious to tell me!

The first time we met, she peppily recounted, was at an upfront party before *Suits* premiered, at the SLS Hotel in LA. I remembered the party but not her coming over to introduce herself and say what a Housewives fan she *was*. (She then said, or I inferred, "was *at the time.*") She said I raised my eyebrows ("but in a nice way") and said thanks. The second time she met me was when she came with her *Suits* costar to *WWHL*. She was a fan and wanted to get booked on the show and couldn't. I said not booking her will go down as the biggest mistake in the thirteen years of the show. If there was footage of a pre-Harry Meghan Markle dissecting Vicki Gunvalson, wouldn't we all love it? I told her I always had a "thing" about *Suits*, which is why we only booked one person from the whole run of the show. She didn't ask what my thing was, and I'm glad, because how could I explain that it always looked like some simulation of a TV show to me, like it was shot on tape and broadcast in a vacuum?

She was lovely, and we had a great time together, in which I found an opportunity to throw in the question "*Were you silent . . . or silenced?*" I was so proud of myself, but she sat there, not understanding the reference at first, until it dawned on her. How did she not immediately get what I was talking about? I took the opportunity to start drilling her with questions about the Oprah interview (general things, like, "Were there things you regretted saying, or things you wish you had?"). All she would really tell me is that she and Haz (she didn't call him that; I am) didn't watch the East Coast broadcast of the show; they only have ever seen it once, and that was when it aired live on the West Coast (they had to put Archie to bed while it was airing in the east). Not exactly headline news, but I thought it was interesting. At the end of the interview, I did *not* take the opportunity to pitch coming on *WWHL*. Our rejecting her when she was on *Suits* seems like it ended that conversation. We talked for over an hour, and I'm so curious what she's going to leave in the show. I hope she keeps "Were you silent, or were you silenced?"

While I was chatting with the duchess, my phone was blowing up, with paragraphs-long texts coming in. It was a seemingly *activated* Lindsay from *Summer House*, who was outed on last night's *WWHL* for being rude to people on my staff. I called her back and she was in the car with Luke and Carl, on their way to see Ashley in DC. So it was all very Bravo. We worked it out. Called Deirdre after to tell her the Duchess of Sussex has been to *WWHL* and that we passed on her. She said, "Wow, you just really never know who's going to become a princess these days." And she's right. Watched *Minions* with Ben. We loved it!

## ⊞ SATURDAY, NOVEMBER 5, 2022

Today was a birthday party at this candy-making place in Tribeca. Ben was really shy for the first twenty minutes but then engaged in the activities, which were making things like edible candy slime and candy tacos. They were painting, and the party hype girl informed them that the paint and paper were edible, so they should go ahead and EAT AWAY! Go to town! Thankfully, Ben seemed uninterested in eating the paint or paper, which relieved me. Is he going to go to school Monday expecting to *eat the paint*? What are we teaching these kids? How will they know what to eat and what not at this point?! Pizza seems to be the typical thing served at kids' birthday parties, and after all the candy I was gratified to see Shake Shack at this one. A big W for the parents in the room.

During naptime, the Arkins came over for a visit—they're in town for the marathon—and we gossiped about St. Louis stuff for a couple hours, a conversation that could only happen between two families who grew up across the street from each other. Late in the afternoon, I was on my way to introduce Kathy Hochul at her Stonewall appearance and stopped at Tea and Sympathy, where I ran into lovely Sean, who gave me edible paint that his friend had just launched. Again with the edible paint? Twice in one day! Maybe *I'm* the one who's out of it. Edible paint is where it's AT. Lukas Thimm came with me to Stonewall, and we hung out on that little stage upstairs, chatting with the governor before going outside for the event. She seems very salt of the earth, very *Buffalo*. She kept making this (bad?) joke that if she wins she's going to call it the "Cohen Bounce" from appearing with me. The first time she told it, I kind of mustered up a laugh, but when she repeated it to her crew, I looked away, and then when she said it onstage in front of the crowd and press, I was wondering what she was thinking. Anti-vaxxers showed up while she was speaking, and the crowd started to feel combative, so we kind of slipped out onto Christopher Street and met Shady Bill outside Duplex for drinks. It was HOPPING in the Village, like a parade of hot straight men. Had my first bad experience at the Perry Club, which was absolutely packed and seemingly down a bunch of chefs and waiters. Was with Martin and John, who I hadn't seen since the summer, so it was in theory okay that it took thirty-five minutes to get our tequilas, but I was kind of activated by it. From there we went to a birthday party at Simon Huck's house that was all very handsome men who seemed to all be in couples. I did an Irish goodbye and was fast asleep by ten forty-five!

## ⸬ SUNDAY, NOVEMBER 6, 2022

Coming off Daylight Savings wasn't too terrible. As a matter of fact, Ben was the most fun all weekend, and Lucy was looking perpetually and adorably surprised with her big eyes. Ben woke up cheerful as ever, and we had a blast at the playground for three hours. There was an avalanche of hot dads there, and I wound up talking to two of them who were so femme-y I swore they were gay until both brought up their wives. So either my gay-dar is busted or else *These Kids Today?!?!* One or the other, or both. Cousin Kevin met me, and I tried to give him life advice. The amount Ben loves Fireman Sam is incredible. Put Lucy's hair in a Pebbles bow.

Twitter has been an extreme—even for Twitter—cauldron of bile and hate since I appeared with the governor yesterday. To change the subject from politics, I tweeted something innocuous this morning about Daylight Savings Time not being fun as a parent, and the gays, of all people, came after me. "You have nannies! You're on Grindr all day!" It was all gay men critiquing my parenting and life choices in general. Thanks for the support, fellas! I tell myself the same thing I tell everyone else, which is not to pay attention to online shit, but sometimes your mind goes back to that *one* tweet you wish you'd responded to, like a piece of dreck that's hanging in the very back of your brain, and it's just sitting there *festering*.

Met Ralph, Hickey, and Tom Hollander at Anfora for cocktails, then Hickey and I tried Arthur and Sons for the first time. It was excellent. New neighborhood spot!

## ⠿ MONDAY, NOVEMBER 7, 2022

I can talk about anything on TV, but when it comes to politics, I'm gun-shy— I think pre-bruised by the idea of getting beaten up for saying something stupid or incorrect. Which is not to say that I'm an idiot about politics, I just don't want to *look* like one. So that was the merry-go-round in the back of my mind in the dressing room of *Morning Joe*, bright and early this morning. I haven't been on that show in forever. Tomorrow is going to be a bloodbath at the polls, and I sat in the greenroom wondering what to say. Came up with a brilliant plan: to take the offensive and try to keep the conversation *off* politics for as long as I could. This was actually easier than you'd think: I started the segment saying Mika had offended me during the commercial break (she told me I looked pale), then asked them what they fight about and if Mika gets mad because Joe talks too much. That took at least three minutes, and then I got very patriotic about the vote and said even though everything looks terrible for the Democrats, the power is in all our hands as Americans, and that's what's great about the country. Then Joe wanted to talk about crime in New York City and the governor's race, and I got through it.

Did radio, then went back to the Bravo floor at 30 Rock, which was totally empty. I think they only come in on Mondays and Fridays, which—and I'm going to sound a hundred years old here—is ridiculous to me. Everyone should get their ass into the office. (Okay, maybe people should work from home on Fridays.) Then went to Dr. K to use her ear machine to deliver what I'm sure is a new fetus growing in my ear, just like she did in April. Turned out my little wax baby would have to wait; the doctor was in Cabo! Went to Ralph Lauren and picked out a coat for New Year's Eve. It's the same as the camel hair from last year but charcoal gray. Interviewed two nanny candidates. Great night at home with Ben and Lucy. Ben got bit on the playground today. Poor guy.

## ▦ TUESDAY, NOVEMBER 8, 2022

I was all prepared to spend an hour in line at the polls after dropping Ben off at school, but I breezed in and out in ten minutes. I was wearing my Camp High sweats and hoodie that have Dead cassettes on them, and the lady who lives on the fifth floor told me I looked like an escaped convict. *Thanks.*

Dinnertime with Ben and Lucy has become such a joy. We feel like a real interactive family, with her propped up in the booster seat and him eating his alphabet soup. Started to turn on the election returns, but I was too nervous about watching the red wave live, so turned it off and instead took a Cheeba Chew and put on the Dead. Which reminds me—I want to take an edible on the air on New Year's Eve but I want to see what our *WWHL* lawyer says about where New York State is in terms of that, before even knowing it's okay or checking with CNN or Anderson or anyone. *It's legal, after all.* (Or, I think it is.)

It's Dad's ninetieth birthday on Saturday, and I realized today I have nothing for him. Contemplated getting him the coat I got myself for New Year's Eve (not regifting the coat, getting him his own coat—lest you think I'm a monster), but it just didn't feel right. Like, does my dad care about a new winter coat? Googled "what to get a 90 year old for his birthday." The first thing that came up was a T-shirt with a pic of an old car that says, *Vintage Built 1932.* I bought it, but that didn't solve the problem of what to actually get him. Then I wandered onto some site where you can buy a newspaper from the day you were born. I was stoned enough to think it was a fun idea, but then I think they tried to bill me twice (or else I was paranoid, which as I type this I realize I totally was) and I didn't wind up buying it. Wound up on the *New York Times* page, where they have a book with the *NYT* front page for every day since someone was born, bound really nicely and engraved. I got that. I'm still feeling like that's not enough, though.

Mike Goldman texted that Nardie Stein died. He was the perfect camp director for his time, like a Jewish Fred MacMurray (I might've aged myself with that reference). Looked around online for more presents. Left Mayer a voice note asking about the ninetieth-birthday gift. He'll have a good idea.

## ⬛ WEDNESDAY, NOVEMBER 9, 2022

I'm elated! Walking on air! The election was NOT the red wave everyone thought. The democracy seems to be saved! Hilariously, I was talking on the radio this morning about the *New York Times* book for Dad, and I got a text from Em saying that not only had *she* bought him that book but she texted me about it in mid-September, telling me that was going to be her gift. Uh-oh. People had a lot of opinions, though, about what I should get him, and the phone lines were jammed with what I thought were predominantly depressing ideas (like a blanket with his grandchildren's pictures on it). Called Mom from the taxi home—she was listening to the radio and thought it hilarious that we both got him the same book—and pitched her the idea of getting him my Ralph Lauren New Year's Eve coat. She thought it was a great idea. So that's done. (Just want to clarify one more time that I am getting him the coat *and* I will have one too; I'm not regifting or giving him my hand-me-down!)

Had meetings all afternoon about the *Most Talkative* outline (which is back and much improved), *RHONY: Legacy* (a call with Luann to discuss some of her very valid concerns that I won't go into here because they will have been addressed), *WWHL* bookings, and my thoughts about improving Radio Andy's Instagram account. Got a voice note from John, who said that ninety-year-olds don't expect much, and they're not doing that much, so because of contained expectations, anything will be appreciated: a good book, a cashmere blanket, cozy things. The *$25,000 Pyramid* category would be "Things You Can Enjoy in a Chair"!

## ⠿ THURSDAY, NOVEMBER 10, 2022

Highlight of the day was a major dance around the kitchen with Lucy to "Philadelphia Freedom." Euphoric! Parent-teacher conference for Ben. All is good! Ben and I had a planned movie night tonight, and he said he was in the mood for a movie with a panda in it. Thus, we watched *Kung Fu Panda*. Cute! I marveled that his category was "Movies with Pandas" and that that very movie existed! After he went to bed, Adam texted asking when I was going to book him for a massage, because it's been forever. I said, "How about half an hour?" and lo and behold, there he was a half hour later, giving me a brilliant massage! I dissolved into bed.

## ⠿ FRIDAY, NOVEMBER 11, 2022

Dad is ninety! I posted celebrating him on Instagram, and he got thousands of comments from well-wishers, ranging from every Housewife to Khloé Kardashian to Susan Lucci. I think he was tickled. (I was!) He opened his gift on the phone, and listening to him and Mom pretend to give the coat a shot when I could tell they were not on board from the get-go was . . . frustrating. They kept saying they think it's too *heavy* and they don't know *where* he would wear it because it's so *heavy*. I said it's a WINTER COAT, but that wasn't enough to convince them. Still haven't found a new nanny, and Theresa leaves in a week. I kept her for what might be considered a longer-than-normal time to protect my sleep, and that could (will) all go out the window now as Lucy is teething. I keep interviewing new people.

Hosted the Humane Society gala at Cipriani 42nd Street, and Amy was my date. Justin Theroux was there with his adorable dog. I was onstage interviewing the head of the organization and thinking that if I raised the mic to my mouth and said a racially insensitive word, I would lose everything. *That's* what was on my mind. Am I sick? Amy and I had a ball after at Bar Centrale. We laughed so hard.

## ⚏ SATURDAY, NOVEMBER 12, 2022, TO SUNDAY, NOVEMBER 13, 2022—NEW YORK CITY TO ST. LOUIS

Sat next to Ozzie Smith on the plane home! Dad picked me up from the airport, and it was thirty degrees out, a perfect day to wear *his new winter coat*! There was no reasoning with him and Mom on the topic, though, because it's just *too heavy*. What was too heavy for *me* was them complaining that the coat was too heavy for him. He put the coat on to demonstrate the heaviness and he was really leaning into the idea, so the coat was just wearing him. He didn't have ownership over it, nor did he *want* ownership over it.

Dinner was in a private room at Café Napoli with my dad's three brothers; their wives; Mom's brother, Stanley, and Judy; and Em's whole family. I was in charge of the toasts, and the best came from the grandchildren—I found Abby and Jeremy to be so on the money. Jeremy recounted six years having dinner at my parents', every Tuesday night, from junior high on. His details were superb: about Dad "cleaning up his sideburns" with a razor and the way Mom and Dad fought about the flank steak. I was very happy with my toast ("Five Traits I Inherited from Dad") but I didn't think it really landed in the room. I felt a little like Rodney Dangerfield. We'll all be together in Manhattan next week, and I think the family is far less excited about my Thanksgiving party than I am. (Jeremy referred to the other guests—I'm up to about twenty-eight people—as a "bunch of randoms," and I said, they're not random *to me*.) Met Jackie, Jeanne, Fred, Kari, and Karen P at a restaurant called the Benevolent King, then we went to a gay bar called Rehab, where we danced to bad music. Wound up at an arcade where Balaban's used to be in the Central West End playing Galaga and Ms. Pac-Man. We could've stayed all night, but they shut it down at one thirty.

Flew home Sunday. On the way to the airport, I brought up my family's lack of enthusiasm about Thanksgiving at my place. (Em is *very* enthusiastic because she doesn't need to host it this year.) Mom said that they were hoping it would be the family around a table for Thanksgiving, whereas mine will be a buffet and more of a Thanksgiving *party*. So I need to figure out a way to make her feel like it's Thanksgiving. "Will we even play Balderdash?" she pleaded. That's our family's post-dinner tradition. I told her I'd grab all the best people for the game, and we'd go in the den area and play. She wasn't sold about the choreography of that. Got home, and Ben quickly suggested we turn on the disco ball for a dance party. Highlights were Johnny Cash's "I've Been Everywhere" and the Gap Band's "You Dropped a Bomb on Me."

## ⸬ MONDAY, NOVEMBER 14, 2022

Today was all radio. We announced the new deal with Sirius and the new schedule for Radio Andy. John and I will be daily for an hour, Monday through Thursday, and the Smith Sisters will be daily starting in January.

We were live in the clubhouse with *Below Deck* people tonight, and I couldn't stop yawning. It was a *me* problem, and nothing to do with *them*.

I met someone today with anxiety, and his dog has it too. Turns out they're both on lorazepam! It was that kind of day—fun! Worked out with Stanny. I've been bitching and moaning for so long about how boring it is at that gym, so I'm going back to Equinox on Friday to work out with a trainer there. I'm going there once a week, which feels like I'm returning to gay civilization.

Got home to silence: Lucy was at music class, and Ben at school. I had ninety minutes alone in the apartment and I felt like running around naked or freebasing or doing something absolutely insane. (I realize there is a big spectrum between running around naked and *freebasing*.) Instead I played Word Chums, took a shower, and went to *WWHL*, where we taped Ralph, in a triumphant solo appearance, highlighted by a Shakespearean performance of Lisa Barlow's hot-mic moment. He had worked on it and marked up his text (which he signed, and we kept). During the show, I missed a call from Cher, looking for Anderson, wondering if a French lady had answered his phone. I texted her his number. Did I ever think Cher would call my phone looking for someone?

Was looking at (poor) ratings for Sunday night's show, and Deirdre and I were wondering aloud how long the show is going to go. Beyond it going on forever, which isn't going to happen, my hope is that Bravo would pick it up through '24, which would give us fifteen years. *Fifteen years?!* We marveled at the idea of having been together for that long. After we taped Ralph, John Mellencamp was on with Teddi, and his people kept telling us he doesn't like games and doesn't like doing TV, but that he loves cigarettes, so if I brought up cigarettes that should make him happy. The truth is that there aren't many ways to bring up cigarettes, but I did try, and I attempted to let him smoke on the air, but Mayor Bloomberg sealed that verdict years ago. (Sidenote: taking edibles on CNN sounds too complicated, based on what the lawyer said.) He does indeed seem like he hates being on talk shows, but I really liked him, and the two of them together were sweet. She's as co-dependent as anyone would be with their famous dad who hates going on talk shows but is clearly there to support and love them. At the end, he perked up and said he loves watching me and Anderson, which made *me* perk up.

Fun dinnertime with Ben and Lucy tonight. I lit a fire, and we got hair-cuts from Tonee (not Lucy—I can't wait for her hair to get long!). Lucy can't take her eyes off Ben. After bedtime and all that, I met B. J. Novak at Arthur and Sons for a 9:00 p.m. dinner. I felt like a REBEL going out at nine and told Jose so. He glossed over it, wanting to talk about Dionne Warwick saying she was gonna date Pete Davidson next. I hadn't heard! B.J. was late, having gotten in the wrong Uber, but it was pouring, and the booth was so cozy, and the tequila so nice, that I didn't mind the wait. Was bustling in there despite the monsoon, and we had a great hang. I love New York.

## ▦ WEDNESDAY, NOVEMBER 16, 2022

Radio in the morning. Lunch at Fresco with the agents, Matt and Alan. Went to Gucci. I'm not sure who is buying their absolute garbage with the exception of Harry Styles. Meeting at Gordon's to look at plans for the new apartment and pick out finishes for the beach house. The Ferris wheel of construction turns and turns. I quoted Countess Lu to Ben today: "Be cool. Don't be all uncool." It worked. (He'd thrown a fit about putting his diaper on before bed.)

CNN has decided it's a bad look for all their correspondents on New Year's Eve to be drinking, but that AC and I can. Based on the headlines, people on Twitter were flipping out, thinking Anderson and I were going to be sober all night, and they were PISSED. I corrected the confusion on the live show with a declaration that we would party harder than we ever have before.

## ▦ THURSDAY, NOVEMBER 17, 2022

With all my bluster about how wasted we're going to get on New Year's Eve, I completely forgot that last night was our last taping before Thanks-giving and ran out of work like Fireman Sam going to save a kid dangling from a tree over a body of water (that is *always* the emergency on Fire-man Sam, literally in every episode). Maybe it *is* time to hang it up if I'm not going to party hard after the show anymore. *Who am I?!* I texted JJ, Melissa, and Deirdre this morning saying that we should be waking up with massive hangovers today. They agreed. We were sheepish!

Showed Ben a live version of Madonna singing "Vogue," and he lasted about two minutes before rejecting it. I suppose it does have a slow start if you're a toddler. I subsequently put on the live "Holiday" from the Blond Ambition tour, which starts like a bullet. Seconds into the first chords, he was UP and DANCING. I was as proud as I could be. SENSATIONAL. The kid gets it. He literally couldn't stop himself.

I've been thinking about Mom's concerns about Thanksgiving, and in order to preserve the spirit of the holiday and make sure we play Balderdash, I'm organizing a game for the afternoon, pre-dinner. Ricky said he'd come, and he's the most fun to play with. At my press tour this afternoon for Fresca Mixed, everyone was asking about whether we could drink or not on CNN. I said we could. I left the event and spoke to Anderson, who said CNN actually *doesn't* want us to drink after all. Whoops. We were not pleased—and the viewers won't be either. Very annoying.

"Excuse me, will you light a fire, Daddy?" That's the question every night from Ben. And I do, and he "helps" me. By the way, him starting every sentence with "Excuse me . . ." never gets old. Had a delightful dinner with Hickey at Jack and Charlie's. I'm sure I yammered on about not drinking on New Year's for far too long, but he was a sport. As I went to bed, the vibe on Twitter seemed to be that the platform was over. Elon laid off thousands of people, and I guess people think it won't be able to function, or everyone's leaving, or it was just a general doomsday mentality that created a really melancholy and kind timeline. How poetic—it takes the ship sinking for the humanity to come out. By tomorrow it'll be "back," and everyone will become assholes again.

## ⸬ FRIDAY, NOVEMBER 18, 2022

Fighting with Ben's gloves in the morning is a fate worse than death. Just horrible. Anderson and I can't drink; it's official. People want this for us *so badly*.

We're not giving up trying. Worked out at Equinox, and it's mainly the same guys I've been seeing for years, but so fun to be there. Justin and George had a dinner to thank their friends for their support of George during his health journey. It was so warm. George says getting cancer has been a blessing in his life, and that even after years as a very successful marketing exec in the fashion industry, this has given him a purpose he never had. He is spreading awareness and raising money for glioblastoma research. I was sitting across from Bevy Smith, and we had the best kiki. Later ran into Don Lemon, and we discussed how activated we are about the booze ban.

## ▦ SATURDAY, NOVEMBER 19, 2022

Freezing day. Lots of indoor playtime with Ben, then we went to Zazzy's for pizza. Mayer really helped me think of funny bits for New Year's Eve in case we can't change this drinking rule, like having AC lookalikes do shots at the top of every hour, and Mystery Shot!, where I feed AC a different shot every hour, and he has to guess what it was. He also said he would join our afternoon Balderdash game. It was a tradition in his family too, at Christmas. Told Mom about the concrete plan for a game, and she was thrilled. I heard relief in her voice. Thanksgiving is saved.

Ben and I watched the fire together for a long time tonight. Dinner with Amy Sedaris and SJ at Don Angie. Hickey, Jeff, Gary Janetti, and Brad Goreski were at the next table, which felt like a tease because both tables were watching the other have a great time.

## ▦ SUNDAY, NOVEMBER 20, 2022

Ben had a new babysitter who plays guitar and sang to us playing the guitar that Mayer gave Ben. He played "Queen of California," to which Ben responded: "The *other* queen is dead." Thank you, Ben. He is fixated. Anderson and I had a Zoom with the head of CNN who said we cannot drink. We vented. Had a dance party, and Ben was doing a silly dance for

Lucy, which had her in absolute hysterics, over and over and over. Nightcap with Theresa, whose last night it was. The new world starts tomorrow! (And so does a new nanny, who will be here five days a week.) And just when I thought the night was over, I got a text from B.J. saying that he was at Bond Street asking if I wanted to nightcap. He came over with his college pal, and we had a rollicking time.

## MONDAY, NOVEMBER 21, 2022

Almost lost my fucking mind fighting with buttons on the elastic waistband of Ben's jeans this morning at 8:20 a.m. Then his pants were falling down on the way to school in the subzero weather. I was at the end of my tether trying to do the pants vertically on the sidewalk, and he was upset. I felt triumphant after I fixed it.

Great radio show today, then I volunteered for Feeding America uptown. Handed out probably a few hundred frozen turkeys, which felt great. The captain from the catering company came by to survey the place for Thanksgiving. He turned out to be someone I flirted with on Facebook (!) about twelve years ago and would see on Fire Island. He is still very cute and will be running the show on Turkey Day, which as of today has turned into a day of *possibility*! If we *did* fall in love, it would be the ultimate meet-cute. Got invited to do press for *WWHL* in Australia next February. Apparently it, and the Housewives, are big there. I think I have to go; when else will I? Spent all day figuring out if I should feel guilty about leaving the kids for a week to do this before deciding I'll see how Mom reacts and make my decision then.

Worked out at Equinox, where there are a lot more straight guys than I remember. But it's hard figuring out who's who because there are a lot of guys in tights, which is a look that always confuses me. Are they gay guys in tights or straight guys in tights? It could go either way. Lit a fire at home and had symphony music going for a change of pace. Lay in bed with Ben for a long, silly convo before he fell asleep, then watched *The White Lotus*. Took me four episodes, but I'm so hooked.

## ⬚ TUESDAY, NOVEMBER 22, 2022

Lucy had me up half the night. Took her to the doctor and learned some things about vaginas. Every day is a new adventure! Lunch with the Alters was so fun. We got right into the swing of things. Picked the final cover for this book that you're reading right now! (I like it; do you?) FaceTimed with Anderson from Brazil. He had an even better idea, which is to totally downplay the not drinking and say New Year's Eve is often a night that doesn't go the way you planned, and this is a great example of that. Smart! But we're still gonna do mystery shots at some point.

Mom and Dad arrived for Thanksgiving (the rest come tomorrow), and the kids sat on my lap in front of the fire for a cuddly twenty minutes waiting for them to show up, but they were waiting forever for an Uber at the hotel. Took them to Jack and Charlie's, which was really nice. Mom thinks I should go to Australia, so that's done. I went into annoyed-son mode a few times (yelling at my mom for waving her flashlight during what was an excruciating seven-minute process of ordering) and then regretted it when I got home.

## ⬚ WEDNESDAY, NOVEMBER 23, 2022

Showed Ben a slideshow of past Thanksgiving parade balloons that I think got him pumped for tomorrow's parade. Given his threats not to trick or treat, I've been worried he'll wake up on Thanksgiving and not want to go. Today was going through last-minute loose ends for tomorrow. Daryn found J&B scotch for Mom and Dad, so I can cross that off the list. Ricky is bringing Balderdash—I can't find mine. I decided the afternoon game wasn't going to work after all for a variety of reasons, and we'll do it after dinner. Mom is skeptical it'll happen. I have enough forks and napkins and, man, this is a boring list to share. Mom and Em laid out Thanksgiving "options" for Lucy to wear tomorrow night. I love her little dresses! I booked a restaurant based on where I thought would be the quietest for my parents, and we wound up at RH, the Restoration

Hardware restaurant. I never need to go back, though it was perfectly lovely. The first strike was when we sat down and discovered they only serve beer and wine. Dad and I kind of grimaced. I was visualizing a tequila. But at least it was quiet! And beautiful. I don't understand the economics of that massive showroom space. Do they generate sales that make it worth it?

Mom announced at the table, "I wonder if we're ever going to have a NORMAL Thanksgiving again?" *Normal?!* I know this event feels more to them like it will be a party because we're not all sitting around a table, and because these are *my* friends joining us, but I'm hoping they wind up feeling some ownership of the evening and not like guests at a random mixer. I then gave the table a soliloquy about who the "randoms" in attendance actually are and why they're not random *to me*. We then spent twenty minutes explicating "cis" and gender to my mom, which makes a total of probably twenty hours spent on this topic with her. She ain't gonna get it. Realized during dinner that the parade starts uptown at nine, which made me wonder what was going to be happening in front of Macy's, where we're sitting. Toward the end of the night, Dad pulled out Mom's engagement picture, which he's kept in his wallet for sixty-four years. Is that the sweetest or what?

## THURSDAY, NOVEMBER 24, 2022

The parade EXCEEDED the hype!!!!! We were right in front of Macy's, with wall-to-wall entertainment right in front of us for three hours. (It did take about an hour to get to us, but somehow it went fast, and we got to see a few numbers from Broadway shows while we waited.) The whole thing is one big lip sync, from Dionne Warwick to Paula Abdul to Mariah—not a live mic to be found. Ben was in fantastic spirits, and it was an absolute THRILL seeing Big Bird, Cookie Monster, and Oscar the Grouch while lifting him for a better view. In terms of balloons, the Paw Patrol and Snoopy were big draws, and the biggest star of all was Santa Claus, naturally. Abby had the time of her life too. I did a hit with Hoda and Savannah on NBC's coverage of the parade. Hodes asked me who was cooking tonight, and it sounded so cold to say, "I hired Bruce's caterer," so I said, a friend runs a catering company so she's cooking for us. That somehow sounded homier to me. More personal. But—I lied to Hodes!

Afternoon was a nice family hang, with everyone doing their own thing and symphony music throughout the apartment. Mom and Dad fell asleep on my bed, and it was an adorable sight. The Thanksgiving team showed up at 3:00 for a 5:00 p.m. party. I had three waiters, a bartender, and two cooks here—which felt wildly excessive to me, but I just went for it.

The evening was a wild success. Jason and Lauren Blum were here with their kids, and Ben and Booker immediately started playing like wild animals. Lucy, incidentally, was the perfect party guest—completely unfussy and didn't care that I changed her out of the Burberry dress because she looked a little too butch in it. Mayer made a wonderful playlist for the dinner. Ralph was here with Francesca Annis, and he bonded with my family in a very sweet way. (I still can't figure out what they were talking about, but that doesn't matter.) Tom Hollander is here shooting the Truman Capote thing for Ryan Murphy, and *The White Lotus* is so big right now, so Em was excited to meet him. John Mayer and Ricky wound up doing a hard-core rally for Balderdash after dinner, and I grabbed (*forced*, actually) Hickey to join us, and he was furious that I pulled him away from his cozy chat with Sedaris. The game was fantastic. Barkin showed up for nightcaps, and so did SJ and Matthew. I wound up kicking out the last four people (Mayer, Sedaris, and Shady Bill and Chris) at twelve thirty. Did I mention that dinner was *delicious*?! I'd like to host every year if I can get the family to come back.

## FRIDAY, NOVEMBER 25, 2022

Coziest day ever. With steady rain outside, I had a fire going all day, with Miles Davis on a loop. The kids and I stayed in our PJs and had visits and recaps from Ma, Pa, Em, and the whole family, who all were back in St. Louis by nightfall. They had a ball at the party, and they weren't alone. It got rave reviews! Amy called to say it was perfect—lighting, music, food, guests—and that I yelled at her for filling up on crackers before the food came out, which she found hysterical. She thinks I look for things to yell at her about. Had dinner with Mayer at Don Angie. He has so many great ideas for New Year's Eve. I got really pumped for the show.

## SATURDAY, NOVEMBER 26, 2022

I have no clue what gut instinct made me pick up for an unknown caller three hours into the day. I never pick up numbers I don't recognize. Maybe I was just bored at 10:15 a.m., but that ceased when I heard the voice on the other end. "Are you up?!" Howard Stern bellowed into the phone, with Beth in the background. "Am I *up*?? Yeah, I'm *up*!" (Sidenote: How do these people think I'm raising my kids?) The Sterns were on speaker and wished me a happy Thanksgiving, to which Ben replied, "It's NOT THANKS-GIVING!" It sounded like they were on a walk, and they got to their point quickly, which was to find out why Beverly Hills Housewives was "on pause." I said my comments in the press had been greatly overblown, that it was just standard down time between seasons and there was nothing to worry about. We did a round of complimenting each other—me on his Springsteen interview, and him on the last *RHOBH* reunion—and that was that. As quick as it was, I was energized from the call, much like I am when I call into Howard's show. He has that effect on me!

My jolt of energy turned into annoyance when I discovered a tray of shrimp in the fridge that I'd forgotten to serve on Thursday night. Called down to the front desk and asked Jose if he had any use for thirty-five shrimp. He said he didn't but that there was a party in 4L, and they might want it. He said to stand by, then texted, "4L would love your shrimp!" Wearing our PJs, Ben and I grabbed the shrimp and delivered it to a neighbor I'd never seen before. He was thrilled. I love being a neighbor.

That night was a party for Mayer's sister-in-law Shera. I was seated across from the guy behind the @DrunkDrawn account on Instagram. He does amazing work. I've gone wayyyy off my booze and food regimen the last few days. I gotta rein it in.

Another rainy day that felt like *ten* rainy days. We had high highs and low lows. Sitting in my refrigerator, like a time bomb waiting to go off, is cookie dough from that place, Dō, that Abby is obsessed with. I cannot keep it out of my mouth. When Em pulled it out on Thanksgiving, I said, "*Oh no!*" And now is the actual "Oh no!" period of me fending off eating it.

Put up the fake Christmas trees. Now how do I convince Ben that Hanukkah is really the jam? That's my goal. Jackie came, and we had a journey, all in three hours—attended a virtual shiva for Amanda's dad, Mickey, which was beautiful and made me think more about both Mickey and virtual shivas. Decorated the fake silver tree (as opposed to the gold tree that's upstairs) with candy canes and the vintage ceramic Snoopy ornaments Mike Robley gave me from his aunt on Long Island last year. I treasure these Snoopy ornaments; they're amazing. That being said, there are several culturally inappropriate ones that I put in a clump on the back of the tree. Lots of the candy canes from last year's tree were broken, so I ran to CVS to get more (and some light bulbs and milk). I'm in that CVS on Eighth Avenue twice a week, but tonight when I went in I was super famous in there. You would've thought I was some big star, the way people were coming up to me. I wanted to say, "You guys, I was in here yesterday, and none of you cared—remember?" Ben was eating the broken candy canes when I got home, and I turned into my mother on him. "You do NOT EAT THE BROKEN CANES. WHAT DID I TELL YOU?! WHAT DID I TELL YOU?!?" How fun for everyone in my path that I'm now turning into my mother. Happy holidays!

Noticed that I've had a bottle of hand sanitizer on my front table for like two years and immediately trashed it and stuffed that big bowl of masks in the closet. So that's that. Andy Fauci says it's done in this house. Put Ben down and then put Lucy to bed, and Jackie and I ate Sugarfish and toasted Mickey Baten over a delicious Chardonnay. Tried to get Hickey or Mayer for a nightcap, but no one bit, so I watched *The White Lotus*.

## ::::: MONDAY, NOVEMBER 28, 2022

When I lock eyes with Lucy, I get sucked into a fully collaborative love cyclone unlike anything I've experienced. I think I'm starting to get the father-daughter connection.

## ::::: TUESDAY, NOVEMBER 29, 2022

I was the room parent at Ben's nursery school today. It was so sweet playing with the kids and seeing them do their chores around the classroom. Also, there was snot everywhere. The gauze is gone from outside my bedroom windows, which is a good sign from the workmen. I wistfully waved at one of them while I was walking through the kitchen today. I never wave at them anymore. The thrill is LONG GONE on that.

Meghan Markle's podcast came out, and it was interesting to see how they produced it. She narrates it, which is an effective device, especially if you're cutting an hour down to twenty minutes, which she did. *However*, in that narration, she talks about what a tough conversation this was for her, mentioning that she has conflicting feelings about the Housewives. I thought it was interesting that she said it in narration but didn't discuss it with me head-on. Wouldn't that have made for a more dynamic conversation? She cut out the Oprah conversation (and me saying, "Were you silent, or *silenced*?") and left in the part where she busted me for having forgotten meeting her in her pre-duchess days.

Taped a show with Hoda and Jenna Bush today. I love that Hoda! Every time I see her, it's like seeing an old friend who you never quite get enough time with. While we were rehearsing in the control room before the show, it came up that Jenna recently revealed she doesn't wear panties, and that it became a thing in the press. I announced that I had no *intention* of bringing it up and of course wound up mentioning it twice, which did lead her to say she wasn't wearing them at dinner with Prince Charles, which will become clickbait on top of clickbait. I was on a real undergarment kick and transitioned the convo to panty liners, which during the commercial break I copped to having no understanding of, and Hoda was kind of nodding back and forth. The gals in the control room later told me they're to cover your period or something, and I still don't want to know what they are. Panty liners won't be a thing when Lucy is of age, right? (I'm not sure they're a thing now.)

There is a sentiment on Twitter that I shouldn't host the Potomac reunion because we have to discuss colorism as it relates to how the women treat each other, and the perception is that as a white male I can't have that conversation. I called the head of diversity at NBCUniversal for his advice, and decided to reach out to Ziwe and another expert on the topic so I can be as informed as I can in whatever case. Worked out with Stanny, then went to a party for Imani's farewell at 30 Rock. She tweeted when she was in college that she wanted to work for me one day, and here we are after eight years of her being my publicist! Who's gonna clean up my messes now? Took the subway there and back, and it was such a breeze except that there was a little hot dog rolling around the floor on the way uptown. I was transfixed. It didn't look too bad! It was a little one, which made it seem cuter than a full-sized wiener. Spent an hour with Ben and Lucy on my lap, watching the fire and listening to Miles Davis. Cozy.

## ⁝⁝⁝ WEDNESDAY, NOVEMBER 30, 2022

I've been thinking about the hot dog on the subway and the fact that someone probably stepped on it during rush hour, which makes it disgusting. I have seven episodes of Housewives with notes due today and tomorrow, and there's no way. I'm so behind. Crazy day. Lucy was up "singing" (if you want to call it that—the important thing is it's not crying) at all hours, which meant I was too. Ben and I had five fights about nothing. It feels horrible to fight with your kid. I hate it. Is this going to be my life? (Don't answer.)

Talked about Meghan Markle on the radio, and Page Six ran, "Andy Cohen Didn't Remember Meeting Meghan Markle: She Threw It 'in My Face.'" Of course that was a clickbaity thing. On that topic, I remember a horrible woman I'd run across for years when I covered premieres for CBS. She treated me like shit in every interaction. A couple years into

*WWHL*, she came up to me at a party and said she *had* to meet me. I said, you're kidding, right? Is that how Meghan Markle felt confronting me about raising my eyebrows at her and not getting booked on *WWHL*?

## ⸬ THURSDAY, DECEMBER 1, 2022

I was right—the men outside my window are starting to pack up. Ben has been waving to them a lot, and there's something *wistful* about the way they wave back. Maybe I'm reading into things.

## ⸬ FRIDAY, DECEMBER 2, 2022, TO SUNDAY, DECEMBER 4, 2022

I called Liz Rosenberg today to ask her how it's possible that Cher was on Kelly Clarkson today but won't come on NYE. She made a joke, wondering if CNN was gonna pay for her makeup. I said they will. Anyway, I don't think it's going to happen.

Spent the weekend working on this very book you're reading. Ate well. Didn't drink. Listened to a lot of *Andy's Kiki Lounge*, and *man* is it a wonderful thing having a channel where you only hear songs you love. I guess it's like having an old iPod with 630 songs on it and hitting "shuffle." But this is way more heavily curated than any shuffle I had. Okay, I'm arguing with myself now. Anyway, I was going back through diary entries since late summer, and it's incredible how my life has completely changed. Earlier this year, I was running out to dinners almost every night, and since Labor Day (and cutting back drinking), I'm in a complete zone with the kids for a long stretch every night. We watched *The Grinch*, and he references being fifty-three! *The Grinch is a year younger than me.* I don't know where to PUT that.

Ben was having meltdown after meltdown on Sunday, really putting me through my paces. Our big fight was a holdover from the summer. Sitting at Corner Bistro, he told me ketchup doesn't go on hamburgers. I've found it pretty effective not to dig in when we're fighting about something stupid, but I couldn't flip on this one. I could've made the fight go away, but I needed him to know that *ketchup absolutely does belong on hamburgers*! We were still going AT each other when we left, and I started shaking his stroller, asking him what he wanted to *do*—go home or to the playground. I saw a couple standing there who clearly recognized me, and perhaps thought they were seeing some real child endangerment in the flesh, courtesy of the Housewives guy. I turned on a dime and got REALLY SWEET. I bent down and turned into Mister fucking Rogers before his eyes. He was looking at me like I was a crazy person but he allowed me to negotiate a visit to the playground, where we saw one of his classmates having an even bigger meltdown than I was party to, which gave me the perspective I needed. I was quietly and momentarily elated. But it was a tough day, and at the end of it our big headliner for New Year's Eve dropped out. We have four weeks to figure it out.

## ▦ MONDAY, DECEMBER 5, 2022

"IT'S MORNING!" Being thrust into life first thing in the morning is both second nature to me at this point and still a complete trip. Two hours later, when I'd dropped Ben off at 9.05, I walked away from the school feeling like I'd accomplished something big, like building a log cabin. There's a holiday sing-along at the nursery school on the sixteenth, but I have the SLC reunion. I'm feeling bad that Ben won't have anyone there, so I'm gonna see if Jackie will take him. Told the story on the radio of the couple who saw me shaking the stroller in front of Corner Bistro. Then I second-guessed how much I'm sharing about my kids, which is also an eternal conversation ("TOO MANY LUCY PICS ONLINE," my mom warned me last night). I'd already been thinking about it all weekend, going through this book. I am conscious of them reading this one day, and I want them to feel all the respect and love I have for them. Again, I could have a B. D. Hyman situation on my hands. (I mentioned this many months ago. Maybe re-Google.)

Came home and hung with Lucy, who is teething so badly. I feel horrible. She has about four popping. Two great *WWHLs* today. Teresa and

Ego Nwodim were first. We played another round of Tre-Saurus, where we showed Tre words about comedy to see if she knew the definition, and she got none right. I felt bad. Then we played a game with her in front of the green screen with Ramona eyes, with her wedding hair dancing around in the back as Ego gave her clues about famous locations (the Eiffel Tower, the pyramids at Giza). She couldn't guess the White House, and when I said it's where the president lives, she said "Mar-a-Lago?" She was all freaked out after the show that people were going to hate her for that. I think it's fine.

Next show was Bethenny (with whom I'm in an overblown public feud) and Jeff Lewis. I got the feud out of the way at the top, saying she's been trashing the Housewives for three years, so I was surprised she's doing a podcast about the show. Jeff kind of took the ball while we were in the middle of it and started giving her crap about saying she'd come up with the idea of the rewatch podcast. He was relentlessly devilish, and it was a three-way jabfest among shit-talking pros who'd known each other for fifteen years. I was in heaven. After the show, she was texting about him. She's gonna have a lot to say once this airs.

## ⊞ TUESDAY, DECEMBER 6, 2022

I go to the supermarket on the way home from the gym every day, and I feel like I'm on a merry-go-round, buying the same assortment of stuff: yogurt, orange juice, milk, bread, sliced turkey, avocados, and spinach-and-mushroom quiche. I bring my reusable bag with me to the gym, fill it up on the way home, and do some variation the next day, to the point where I could do it in my sleep. Today I got home and realized I had forgotten the turkey at the checkout stand. *Fuck it*, I thought. I figured I'd buy more tomorrow. Then, out of curiosity, I checked the remnants of turkey we still had left to see how much a pound goes for: SIXTEEN DOLLARS. *Fuck THAT*, I thought, and put my shoes back on and walked in the damned rain to go get the turkey I paid for. That was *my turkey*, and I'm not throwing it, or sixteen dollars, down the drain. Does that make me cheap or someone who respects the value of a dollar? I say the latter.

More delays for the beach house and I GAVE IT to my builder today in my dressing room. SCREAMING. Pounding my fist on the counter. Everyone in the control room thought I was doing a bit at first, faking it. They were stunned. Apparently, my breakdown was the talk of the office. I wish I could say I felt better after I did it but I felt worse. Date with the Superman-looking guy I met on Tinder a couple months ago. We had a really nice time, although I was asking what he listens to, and he said he requests music from Alexa according to whatever mood he's in, not by artist, which seemed incredibly generic to me. But I kept telling myself, "Do not make this guy's music selection a roadblock in getting to know him better"—and I listened.

## WEDNESDAY, DECEMBER 7, 2022

It was in the fifties and foggy and rainy all day, which I had no problem with. Gayle King was on *WWHL* today. We're spotlighting small businesses behind the bar and had this guy from a pizzeria who ships thin-crust pizza. Noticed in the control room during read through that the bartender was setting up frozen pizzas at the bar. We all found out at the same time that that was the guy's display; he was propping up wrapped frozen pizzas on the bar. I went into the studio and said, "I need a slice of this PIZZA! MMM." He said, well, it's all frozen. I said, are you really thinking that's gonna sell your pizzas, to show a frozen pizza sitting there? He said that's what HE said too, but his boss didn't listen. I told him he had forty minutes to get hot pizza. He did, and was I happy! I noshed on it through the whole show. I *love* thin pizza.

Stanny came over and trained me at home, with Ben adorably joining in. Took the subway to the NBCUniversal holiday party at 30 Rock, with the *Kiki Lounge* blaring in my headphones. Forty-Ninth Street was blocked off from traffic. I walked down the middle of the street with a blur of Christmas lights and Radio City in my sights, thinking about the millions of New Yorkers who've walked down this very street, looking at this very same beautiful picture. I felt like I was walking in the footsteps of ghosts, and welled up with an incredible feeling of joy and gratitude. How fortunate to have lived my own life in this glorious city, to get to walk in their footprints but with my own imprint. What great perspective, to take in the majesty of the city around you with respect for those who came before you and wonderment at those who will come later. At the party, I traveled back to 2022, where all the reporters were asking off the record about not drinking on New Year's. I said nothing. Tried prying *Today* show gossip out of the press lady I love, to limited success. Everyone is very worried about Al; that's the main thing to report. Met a reporter from *Dateline* who is a big Housewives fan and wants to be on *WWHL*. Karamo and I had a sweet hang.

The Bethenny episode aired, and now she's wondering if she was ambushed. She seemed fine when we taped it but is now listening to her daughter, who says it was bad.

## ⦂ THURSDAY, DECEMBER 8, 2022

Was up at five with Lucy. She went back to sleep by six forty-five, but then Ben was up at seven. *Joke's on Daddy!* Bethenny was texting at six thirty to call her when I woke up, and that began several back-and-forths between us that were clearing the air about the show last night and also about some stuff she said about me in her podcast. We resolved everything, and at the end of the last call, she said we're at zero, meaning we're all clean. Had lunch with Jeff Lewis at Michael's and saw that I had a missed call from Bethenny. I was wondering if we weren't at zero anymore when she texted, asking if I'd called her. What a day for that Housewives Hack to return! We chuckled.

Had a conference call about New Year's Eve. Still trying to figure out how to play this not-drinking directive. SJ and I have been ferociously playing an online Scrabble game the last couple weeks, and I feel like the DM within our games is our new favored method of communication.

What a shit show of a weekend. I had a thousand pre-holiday plans (well, exactly four fun gay-boy Christmas parties, with a half commitment from Anderson to join me) that were all wiped away by the aftermath of my Covid booster, which completely knocked me on my ass. I was convinced I had Covid again (tested three times, and I don't) and was smacked in the face with the reality that people are getting it again like crazy and I cannot afford to be sick with the week I have coming up. I have commitments to Sirius, Colbert, finishing the *WWHL* year, and the *RHSLC* reunion on Friday. I just *have* to make it to then without getting Covid. I returned the fucking bowl of masks to my front hall and promised myself to wear one all week so I could do all I have to, and I began that promise at Sunday night's *Some Like It Hot* opening by masking all night.

I was so glad I felt well enough to attend; Amy and I had put those plans in our books months ago, but I totally botched the run-up to the show. Feeling loosey-goosey about our chances of whizzing up Eighth Avenue in a cab, I told Amy to get to me at five thirty. (The show started at six.) *Who's going to be on Eighth Avenue on a monsoon-y Sunday night,* I figured. It turns out I'm an idiot, and we should've taken the subway, because it was gridlock heading to the theater. Thankfully we were texting SJ, who was also stuck in traffic right around where we were, and we figured they'd hold the curtain for the Brodericks and we'd benefit from that. We all showed up at the same time—6:25—and indeed, we made curtain. The show was a triumph, a major tap-dance explosion with wonderful music and so many laughs. We were *guffawing* throughout. We didn't expect it to be so funny! The crowd was something: Bette Midler, Patti LuPone, Marty Short, and on and on came to celebrate Marc and Scott's amazing work. I kept my mask on the whole time and, feeling like it was March 2020, skipped the party.

Came home and lit a fire in my bedroom and watched *The White Lotus* finale, which was eminently satisfying. Was emailing DVF at the end of the night, and she asked how I am. I responded: "I'm a single father of two." I feel like there's nothing else to say that could describe my current state of being.

## ⠿ MONDAY, DECEMBER 12, 2022

It's a Christmas miracle—the men outside my window are gone! Meanwhile, everything is Christmas inside my apartment, and Hanukkah starts Sunday. I've been trying to build up some expectation about it for Ben. I want him to view it as the Main Event. It's tough, because I'm a sucker for Christmas propaganda—everything except the Jesus stuff (absolutely no offense meant toward Jesus. All respect!). Saw a homeless man on the corner of Twenty-Third and Fifth reading a book. I gave him money and asked him what he was reading. It was *Game Change*. Great book! "How about that Sarah Palin?" I asked. "Can't believe her!" He shook his head. I don't know what I expected him to be reading, but it wasn't that.

I realized today that emailing DVF that I'm a single father of two sounded kind of victim-y, and I need to call her. Watched *Frosty the Snowman* with Ben tonight, and it stunk. It felt . . . thin. Ben loved it, though. "Ramble On Rose" came on during dinner, and he said, "Isn't this the song we used to listen to in Sag Harbor?" Proud papa.

Had an incredible dinner with the Brit Witz at Via Carota—Liam, Ralph, Hickey and Jeff, Danny Neeson, and Tom Hollander, whom I ambushed with *White Lotus* questions. We came together all those years ago through Natasha, and it was so good to be together again. I got Ralph high on THC tincture, and he and I sat in a puddle of giggles in the corner of the table. On the walk home, I was animatedly telling Danny something and walked right into what I think was the wall of a deli—SMACK! We laughed SO HARD all the rest of the way home in the tundra. I really smacked into it! You would've thought it was fake!

# ⸭ TUESDAY, DECEMBER 13, 2022

Spent the entirety of the day with a pounding forehead from walking into that wall or post or whatever it was. Had a complete meltdown at the deli counter of the supermarket, waiting for the dude to make one hell of a sandwich for the guy in front of me. I don't know what the guy had on it, but it took at least eleven minutes to make, and the longer I stood there, the more I was stewing, to the point where I started exclaiming things *aloud*, to no one in particular. To the air. And of course that only made me look like an (insane) asshole. I just kept saying "WOW." And "Is this still happening??" Then I'd walk away and come back a minute later and get back in line. *I needed my turkey!* Oh, and I was masked for my entire fit, so I looked like a Karen. Or maybe a reverse Karen, because Karen wouldn't be masked? How about I just looked like an asshole. Yeah, that's it—an asshole. Finally the deli guy handed over his handcrafted masterpiece, and I announced (to the air), "That was all for A SANDWICH?!?!" The guy who got the sandwich said, "Oh, I'm sorry" to me, and then I made a big deal about it being ABSOLUTELY NO BIGGIE. Are you KIDDING? No problem. I swear there is at least one man with a sandwich out there who thinks I'm a deranged asshole. Three minutes later, I had my precious pound of sliced turkey, and don't you know karma bit me right in the ass, because I got home and realized I'd left the fucking turkey at the store! *AGAIN!* After all the time and energy spent, of course I marched right back there (in the rain, AGAIN!) and got it.

In better news, I'm still in awe of how transformed my apartment looks with the scaffolding gone. It is SO LIGHT! It's wonderful. Just in time for me to move! Taping Colbert on Thursday and wondering how we're going to address that we're not drinking on New Year's. We don't really have a plan. Spoke to DVF, who said that line in the email sounded a little *put-upon*, but once I explained what's going on over here and said I am building the life that I want, she understood and approved. At the end of the call, she reminded me that she is an oracle.

## ▦ WEDNESDAY, DECEMBER 14, 2022

Final day of *WWHL* for the year, and with everyone masked up and trying not to get sick, it felt somewhat anticlimactic. We even postponed the white elephant game until after the holidays. (I've been hoarding stuff for them since summer!) RuPaul was here, though, and we got to kiki about Diana Ross, which is what we *do*. On the live show, I had my first drink on-air since the summer. Stayed for one drink after the show but felt like the night should've been a whole blowout. One thing I've learned this fall, as I've curtailed my drinking, is that I'm loving the feeling of being in control. I never felt OUT of control, but I'm not coming home buzzed and starving, which is why I can coexist with a freezer full of nine (!) pints of ice cream and Janie's chocolate chip cookies. (I finally threw out the cookie dough Em brought for Thanksgiving.)

Ben seems like he's leaning into Hanukkah. He's inferring that the presents you get on Christmas aren't really the *thing*.

## ▦ THURSDAY, DECEMBER 15, 2022

Flurry of stuff today. Lunch with John Shea at Morandi. Apparently, I promised a guest at Shea's wedding (in *2014*!!) that he could bartend on my show when he finished a book. The book is done, and the chicken has come home to roost. This underscores not only how long it takes to finish a book but also that promises don't have an expiration date.

We're planning for tomorrow's reunion with the scenarios of Jen showing up or not showing up. Her lawyers have put a lot of restrictions on what she can and can't discuss, and I'm hoping to just talk to her after her sentencing so she can say anything she wants. Who wants an edited Jen Shah???

Met Anderson at Colbert, and the appearance actually went great. We just kind of laughed about not being able to drink and said we'd have fun anyway. Then Stephen brought out shots, Anderson grimaced and giggled a lot, and all was well with the world. He kept us out there for three segments, and I was increasingly getting more stressed about getting out of there because my live Holiday Hangout with Amy started at 7:00 on Radio Andy. We were still yukking it up with Stephen at 6:35. Made it out—in the pouring rain—by six-forty-something and wound up running half the way to Sixth and Forty-Eighth Street from the Ed Sullivan Theater with this MASSIVE golf umbrella the Colbert people gave me because they knew it was the only way I was getting where I was going in the rainy gridlock. The radio show with Amy—two hours live, taking calls and chitchatting while we're on an edible—was fun but muted. The studio audience was a little low energy, and so were the callers. We had fun, though, and it's a real tradition—our eighth year of the show! We had a late dinner at the Polo Bar and, as is our custom, laughed the entire time. If you go there, you're going to run into someone famous. Thus, at the table on the left was Monica Lewinsky, with Clive Davis on the other side. Had a great chat with Jermaine Dupri, who's here for Mariah at MSG.

## ⠿ FRIDAY, DECEMBER 16, 2022

Lucy was up screaming from four o'clock to five forty-five before putting herself back to sleep. The tone of her voice at that hour of the morning is . . . piercing. I fell back asleep at six only to have Ben come get me at seven, so I was bleary all day. I read *The Giving Tree* to Ben before school and was WEEPING by the end. Like, I was whispering the words to get them out, and I can't tell what he noticed or thought about that. He seemed a little unfazed. That book is a KILLER. The little boy grows up into something of a nebbishy, bossy man. Hmm.

Dropped Ben off at school, then headed straight to the SLC reunion. Heather was in an unhappy place, having had an adverse reaction to the last few episodes of the season. I had thought that without Jen Shah in the room, she and Meredith were going to be a little more free with their actual feelings about her crimes and behavior, but they stayed on message. At one point I kind of lost it with Meredith; I didn't understand where she was coming from in her inability to state an opinion about Jen's case. She did something disgusting and no one seems to be too outraged about it. We wrapped around seven thirty, which meant I could stop by Harry Smith and Andrea Joyce's very warm Christmas party. I feel triumphant that I got through this week without getting sick, having delivered every bit of content that was required of me. Let the holidays begin!

## SATURDAY, DECEMBER 17, 2022, TO SUNDAY, DECEMBER 18, 2022

Watched the World Cup finals, but in Spanish on Peacock, and couldn't understand the overtime rules. Ben turned to me at one point and said, "You know the queen is still dead." Then he wanted to know why she died. I said she lived the most full, brilliant life anyone ever could've led.

Hanukkah couldn't have been more successful. We met up with Jeanne, Fred, and Jackie in Abingdon Square, where I lit the neighborhood menorah (who knew there was such a thing?) and went home, lit *our* menorah, and gave Ben gifts. I went overboard for the first night, wanting Hanukkah to really pack a punch for him. It did! He was ECSTATIC at his loot: Fireman Sam PJs from me, a new galaxy projector for his ceiling from Ma and Pa, a Hess truck from the Consueloses, a dinosaur set from Jackie, a school bus from the Bozzis, an Elsa snow globe from Aunt Em, and a golf set from Uncle Rob. He was jumping around, saying, "I love Hanukkah! Hanukkah is the *BEST!*" I felt so victorious. And he's got seven more nights of presents (one a night), so this should work.

## MONDAY, DECEMBER 19, 2022, TO FRIDAY, DECEMBER 23, 2022

My FOMO levels were low as I watched all week on Instagram while the Fabulous migrated from the city. I'm firmly home, celebrating Hanukkah with the kids, cozily passing the time through the holidays until New Year's Eve. The idea of being anywhere with them but home for the next two weeks exhausts me. So the week was all family time—fires burning, working out, Ben in full DELIGHT mode and his sister charming everyone in her path, menorah lighting followed by the glee of a present—with some great holiday dinners thrown in: the Waverly with the Ansels, Polo Bar (Bob Iger at next table) with Ricky and Mayer, who sprung for massive amounts of caviar. Spent many sleepless nights listening to Lucy wail— she's teething and also flipping herself over in the crib without being able to flip herself back. So it's a late-night dance of wanting her to get back to sleep on her own before I go in there and help flip her over or calm her. Needless to say, I barely slept all week. Watched *Rudolph the Red-Nosed Reindeer* (multiple times), which is not only excellent but a robust fifty-two minutes long! Ben was terrified of the Abominable Snow Monster.

Having alerted the Cohens that their gift would be delayed, I spent all week putting off making my annual family photo album. People keep sending me TikToks of kids telling their parents that I died. It's part of some fucking TikTok trend, which reaffirms my desire to never engage deeply with TikTok. Besides not understanding the trend, I don't know why anyone thinks I'd want to watch one of these videos. I keep deleting them. Memo for next year: Do NOT wait till the day before Christmas Eve to navigate Eataly in search of lasagna and focaccia for Christmas dinner. It was an absolute nightmare in there. Never again!!

The week ended at the Waverly Inn with Mayer. He was looking around at the characters on the walls around us of people long gone, saying that being in New York City made him feel all of the ghosts of people who once lived here and that kind of made him sad. I said I've been having the exact same feelings about the ghosts around us in the city, but thinking about the joy of it all. We're all sharing this same glorious space, every one of us living completely unique experiences that will never be duplicated and that will continue long after we're gone. *We got to be part of the fabric of this magic*, is my point. We lived here too. Really went deep on it.

## ▦ SATURDAY, DECEMBER 24, 2022

It's ten degrees outside, which meant a cozy Christmas Eve inside in PJs with the kids. Barkin, my new Willona Woods, came with toys for Ben, and we had a lovely long hang. We watched *The Polar Express* before bed, and he was pretty scared (of the train!) and every minute or so asked if it was over. Every time, I repeated, "Do you *want* it to be over?" and never got a straight answer. I cried a little at the end. He was just glad it was through. Did an Instagram Live around 10:00 p.m. and it was too chaotic. I went to bed at 10:30.

## :::: SUNDAY, DECEMBER 25, 2022

I celebrated Christmas by listening to Lucy screaming in her crib from one o'clock to three-thirty in the morning. Merry Christmas to me! I went down once, at one forty-five, to flip her over. Then I sat Googling an old chestnut—"how long do you leave a baby to cry when sleep training"— and the answer is anywhere from thirty minutes to two hours. Two hours! Watched *A Charlie Brown Christmas* with Ben. Last year it bored him, but this year he was riveted. I have a feeling we'll be re-viewing all next week. During Ben's nap, I opened all my presents (I didn't want him to see that I held mine till Christmas) and made a big pile of stuff I had no use for. (Most of these gifts, by the way, came from production companies and business associates, not actual friends.) My agent sent me a Canada Goose down coat that I'm seriously considering giving to Dad.

My Christmas dinner turned out great. It was Jeanne and Fred with the boys, Amanda, Shady Bill, Barkin, Liza and Brian, with Jeremy and his pals coming later for drinks. I served the lasagna and eggplant parm, and Jeanne brought a big salad. Held a big white elephant for the twelve people here using all the gifts I opened but can't use. It was so rousing! People left happy!

## :::: MONDAY, DECEMBER 26, 2022

Margot came in wondering where her present from Theresa was—it had been under the tree. I texted Theresa and found out it was some TRUFF hot sauce that I'd inadvertently put in the white elephant (!) and wound up going home with Barkin, who thankfully lives three floors below and was completely fine with surrendering it. The White Elephant comes for everyone! I can feel the energy about New Year's Eve building, because everywhere I go people are being really sweet—saying they're going to be watching, they expect me to get Anderson drunk, and they want to see me rant again. I'm not correcting anybody about the drinking thing. It's a lot of positive energy, and I love that.

I'm *still* putting off making the family photo album. Dinner with Mayer at Jack and Charlie's and we played What! Band! Does John Hate!, an endless open mic of me throwing him band names and him reacting. We went back to my place and watched eighties episodes of *The Price Is Right* on my bed with a fire raging. It was delightful. If I could find a gay guy with John's personality, I'd be set for life.

## ⸬ TUESDAY, DECEMBER 27, 2022

Day trip with Hickey upstate to Liam's for a warm and delicious lunch and hang with the family, which happily included Vanessa Redgrave and Joely Richardson. I told Joely that walking around the house felt like I was on the set of a movie of my former life. Had dinner with Brazilian Andy Samberg, and Ben played with him before and asked him when Christmas is. I think I focused so much on Hanukkah that he totally missed Christmas. "Did it happen, Daddy? Did Christmas happen?" he asked. I told him it did, and he wondered if Santa came. I said, don't you remember you got presents that day? Watched old Carson before bed. Sherman Hemsley was on talking about *Amen*, which apparently Carson produced. My mind was kind of blown. Also I found out that Sherman Hemsley was painfully shy. And kind of a terrible talk show guest!

## ⸬ WEDNESDAY, DECEMBER 28, 2022

Up listening to Lucy cry and scream from one o'clock to two forty-five. She was on her stomach and kept almost falling back asleep, then would go into a panic, then calm herself down, and rinse and repeat. Today I finally did the family photo album so I feel like I accomplished something. Seacrest gave an interview to *People* saying he thinks it's a great idea that CNN is limiting our drinking. So now we know the one person who thinks it's a good idea. Ben and Wyatt had a great playdate, with lots of sharing. Speaking of sharing, Bruce got a DM from that woman in Philly who wants to share her husband with me in the form of a threesome. She messaged him saying she is having dinner around the corner from where I live and is available tonight! Unfortunately for her, and fortunately for her husband (!), I had a Tinder date with a guy who'd never heard of me and didn't know a thing about me. I loved it. We were on an even playing field. He lives in LA, and I'm not sure there was enough heat to take this thing any further.

I was so bored before bed that I started watching those TikTok videos of moms reacting to my "death." It was—no surprise—quite depressing. I should first say it was lovely to see complete strangers caring enough about my mortality that they burst into tears, but conversely, it was a lesson about life to see just how quickly people seemed to get over the "news." You die, people are upset, and then they keep living. (Sidenote: I am the person who pranked my mom by telling her Richard Nixon was dead, just to see what her reaction was, so I know I'm not one to judge. But when it's about *you, on tape*, it hits different. My prank was *quaint*. I swear it was.) I was in a cocoon of melancholia and watched more Johnny Carson. It was him talking to an old lady for an interminably long time. I started wondering what *her* death story was and went to bed at ten thirty.

## ⦂⦂⦂⦂ THURSDAY, DECEMBER 29, 2022

Ben's pissed that Santa didn't come to our house. I said he did, but where's the proof? People online are trolling Seacrest for being a stiff shoe about NYE. There's another wave of confusion in the press about whether I'm drinking or not because *Rolling Stone* published an interview yesterday that was conducted a month ago in which I said we ARE drinking. So I emailed Page Six directly and said we're not, but we're going to have fun. My first time leaking a story! Then there was another raft of articles saying we *aren't* drinking, which of course we said on Colbert two weeks ago but I guess you just have to keep repeating shit. Also, I offhandedly said on Bruce's podcast that James Corden ripped off my *WWHL* set, so that's everywhere. (This week is clearly the slowest news week of the year.) What I love is that they're running side-by-side pictures of both our sets, so I don't actually look like a crazy person.

Meeting about NYE. We have guest after guest and seem like we're in great shape. Anderson is concerned that it's just on us all night, and we don't really have a second to breathe (or pee). He has a point, but I still think it'll be fine. Dinner with Anderson and Benjamin at Indochine, which was absolutely packed full of fun people. I'm kicking myself for not taking Mayer there one of our nights out. (We were looking for fun people!) Went across the street for Sandra Bernhard at Joe's Pub. It was wonderful seeing her onstage again after all the Covid cancellations. Her wit, musings, and music were on point.

## ⊞ FRIDAY, DECEMBER 30, 2022

Weather forecast for tomorrow is rain all night! I had my coat Scotchgarded. Worked out hard at Equinox. Everyone everywhere is wishing me happy new year. I bought tequila for the crew (even if we can't drink, that shouldn't stop them at midnight) and juice boxes for us (seriously). I think this mystery shot thing is going to be really fun. I did something I haven't done since Covid, which is purposefully leave my phone in the other room and commit to spending a massive chunk of time with Ben without getting it. I'm ramping up for my no-phone resolution (which, as the reader knows damned well, lasts until the second week of January, or whenever I have my first flight to LA). It's easy to be apart from your phone when you aren't working. I feel like I'm always on call when I'm working because there's always shit coming up that has a deadline to answer. (Now I'm justifying my phone use to myself? As my mom would say, PATHETIC!) Lucy is kind of scooting on the floor while she's sitting up but doesn't seem interested in crawling even with hourly tummy time (she also hates that). Loic and Antoine came over for a nightcap, and when they were leaving I saw that Barbara Walters died. Cheri Oteri was supposed to "do" her tomorrow night. Need to rethink.

## ⬚ SATURDAY, DECEMBER 31, 2022

Woke up with the promise and weight of the long day to come. Watched *Rudolph* again in bed with Ben, which meant fifty more minutes that I could stay under the covers playing Wordle. Cheri is going to just chat about Barbara tonight and not do her impersonation. Katie Couric called out of nowhere. *Weird*, I thought as I picked up. "Andy?" she said. I said, "Katie? What's up?" "*You* called *me*," she retorted. The hack! The last day of the year, and the hack rears its head again! She said that Bethenny had been calling her but it wasn't actually her, and I had to explain the whole thing from the beginning. She was in Aspen, busy writing a piece for the *New York Times* about Barbara Walters. I guess the hacker got bored of our conversation, because they disconnected us. Then my phone rang again, and it was "Dina Manzo." Throughout the day, the phone was also nonstop with real people.

Everyone is wound up about us not drinking. Chrissy Teigen texted saying to fuck it, just get drunk. So did Erika Jayne. Tamra said to do mushrooms. If I didn't want this gig again next year, or knew definitively that they're not having me back, I'd go absolutely wild on the air tonight and go out with a bang. But I'd rather keep my job. Went to Corner Bistro for lunch with Ben and, after my trying all year, *finally* got him to put ketchup on his burger! It's the small victories. Chilled out all afternoon, feeling an impending sense of excitement mixed with dread. Anderson, conversely, was peppy and quippy via text. One can never predict where our moods will be! The cops showed up to take me into Times Square at six and, once there, we waited for AC to pull past the several barricades on Forty-Eighth Street so we could make our way through the throngs to the hotel holding area together. The crowds, herded into pens and wearing—to make matters worse—Planet Fitness top hats, seemed especially low energy and miserable. *Wouldn't you be?!?!* Jean Smart (a guest late in the show) arrived to the hotel very early (she's a huge fan of Anderson's), so we schmoozed with her for a bit. Chris Licht came by and encouraged me not to let the lack of alcohol make me any less opinionated. I said not to worry.

It rained for most of the night but was balmy. The constant umbrella work was a huge drag, but the show was very energetic. Our mystery shots were disgusting (pickle juice! Buttermilk! Apple cider vinegar!) but hopefully fun to watch. Patti LuPone dropped the F bomb. Amy wore a sparkly dress and said later that I told her she was yelling into the mic. (She was!) Toward the beginning of the show we were talking about our kids, and I knew Ben was watching so I waved at him. Margot said he sat there waving for a half hour!

The night became a lot about the fact that we weren't drinking, which seemed counterintuitive if the goal was to take the focus off the sauce. Stamos said we were funnier drunk. Kevin Hart went on three very funny tirades yelling at CNN about what a bullshit decision it was. The consensus on Twitter was we were more fun with drinks, but I'd argue we behaved exactly the same as when drinking. Anderson was in a puddle of giggles several times, and I was a sober truth cannon: I referred to the crowds as "edging out until midnight," kept calling Anderson a "nepo baby," said that we know our way around a chorus boy, had several hissy fits, asked Nick Cannon if he should get a vasectomy ("My body, my choice!" he said), and (playfully) slammed Seacrest. CNN perhaps wanted the show to be tamer but wound up with a ton of expletives and everyone complaining. So I'm not sure that paid off, but it sure was a great show.

Around 11:40—during the highest-rated half hour—we cut out of Jenifer Lewis early and found ourselves with six minutes of TV time to fill, with next to nothing to say. I felt like we were literally making conversation but having no choice but to push on. It was a funny feeling to be aware of. It's a hard show to host because it just keeps going on and on. I always say it's a telethon without a disease, and it is. Finally, midnight was that exciting mix of a big burst of energy, with Sinatra's "New York, New York" blaring, followed by the zen of Louis Armstrong singing "What a Wonderful World" as the confetti fully blankets the crowd. It's like a climax followed by postcoital bliss. Jean Smart and Cheri Oteri came back on the riser for midnight, looking mistily at the spectacle, while I poured tequila shots and passed them out to the crew and anyone else who wanted one. Brian Cox showed up for the last ten minutes with an open bottle of white wine that, throwing caution to the wind, I started guzzling. He was the perfect final guest of the night. I hope I'll be back. I love the gig, and being a duo with Anderson. It's easy, fun, and unique to be able to plan and execute something like this with a friend.

We took some pictures with the group, then wandered out of Times Square among the muck and stragglers around 12:40. On the car ride home, Anderson decided rather than getting a burger or going to the party on Fifteenth Street I'd prearranged, he'd rather just go home. He was done. Walking into my building, I flared into a momentary rage at him: How could my cohost leave me hanging on New Year's Eve? Shouldn't we be *out* somewhere—out *anywhere*?!?! It's *New Year's fucking Eve*! I came home, got out of my clothes, turned on the Grateful Dead, and made myself what I'd call a TRIPLE. I settled into the music and the couch, with a background chorus of screaming drunkards on the street below, and sipped my jug of tequila and Fresca. I let out a deep breath and realized home was exactly the only place I needed to be.

# EPILOGUE

I miss writing the diary, and every day as something noteworthy (my definition of noteworthy is clearly pretty loose) happens, I think about how I'd share it with you. So much happened in the immediate aftermath of writing this book: our ratings for New Year's were great (the only show to go up!), Seacrest inadvertently started a clickbaity, sad feud with me about not waving at him on New Year's, we mutually agreed with Rinna that she should take a break from the show (this is a real *pause*), Jen Shah was sentenced to six and a half years and continued acting like a victim, Megyn Kelly called me a "Boot Licker of Celebrity" on Twitter and I (miraculously) refrained from taking her bait, Mom went on a rampage, pleading for "no more DICK TALK" on *WWHL*, I successfully regifted to Dad the coat my agent got me for Christmas and it blissfully wasn't too *heavy* (!), and as February began Ben turned four.

It happened during the last two diaries and recurred this year: writing this book caused me to look at my life differently, or at least to think about what was happening in my life from outside of myself. It's kind of like the diary was my shrink for a year. After I'd finished writing, my publisher asked for a subtitle, something that might reflect the theme of this book. "The Year I Grew Up" immediately jumped out at me. I would've thought the year Ben was born was that year, but it took Lucy and all the personal angst, followed by self-improvement, that began in the month of August for me to feel the transformation in my life fully set in. I've always felt as light as a feather, and this year my feet feel firmly planted. I like how that feels.

# ACKNOWLEDGMENTS

I want to thank everyone in my life for trusting me with my account of our time together this year. I hope I didn't piss anyone off. Or I hope I only pissed off people I *meant* to piss off. And that especially goes for my children. I hope you read this many years from now and chuckle at how much fun we had when you were little.

At Holt, I'd like to thank James Melia for your enthusiasm and encouragement through the writing process. You made me feel like Hemingway when I was more akin to Cindy Adams. Maggie Richards and Pat Eisemann, you're incredible and have taught me so much about the book business. Also thank you Carolyn O'Keefe for the PR journey; Robert Risko for our fourth collaboration, along with Chris Sergio; marketers Laura Flavin and Caitlin O'Shaughnessy; Kenn Russell, Molly Bloom, and Janel Brown on the production side; Meryl Levavi, who has done the interior design for all three diaries and *Glitter Every Day*; Serena Jones, for being my "mother's eye"; Lori Kusatzky, for assisting on all; and of course Amy Einhorn for running the show!

# ABOUT THE AUTHOR

**Andy Cohen** is the author of four *New York Times* bestselling books. He is the host and executive producer of *Watch What Happens Live,* Bravo's late-night interactive talk show; he also serves as executive producer of the Real Housewives franchise and hosts the network's highly rated reunion specials. He's won an Emmy and two Peabody Awards for his work. He lives in New York City with his two children.